Locality and Belonging

The issue of belonging is crucial to the study of identity within social anthropology. *Locality and Belonging* explores how territory can become intertwined with belonging and shape a sense of community, often through bodily images, imagined pasts and experienced space.

Locality and Belonging provides an international overview of the relationship between locality and belonging, with the contributors presenting rigorous case studies from the Congo, Togo, Amazonia, Indonesia, Zanzibar, South Africa, Argentina and the United Kingdom.

Contexts range from the use of 'natural' features of the environment to those of nationhood and post-colonial identity-making. The examination of notions of space, memory, ethnicity, the mnemonic use of objects, mythologies of football and history, feature as some of the themes which reveal and express the relationship between locality and belonging.

This volume will be of interest to anthropologists and sociologists, as well as to all those who grapple with issues of cultural identity.

Nadia Lovell is Lecturer in Social Anthropology at the University of Kent.

D0229620

European Association of Social Anthropologists

Series facilitator: Jon P. Mitchell
University of Sussex

The European Association of Social Anthropologists (EASA) was inaugurated in January 1989, in response to a widely felt need for a professional association which would represent social anthropologists in Europe and foster cooperation and interchange in teaching and research. As Europe transforms itself in the 1990s, the EASA is dedicated to the renewal of the distinctive European tradition in social anthropology.

Other titles in the series:

Locality and Belonging

Edited by Nadia Lovell

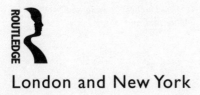

London and New York

BLACKBURN COLLEGE
LIBRARY
Acc. No. 83721
Class No. 304.23 LOU
Date May '99

First published 1998
by Routledge
11 New Fetter Lane, London EC4P 4EE

Simultaneously published in the USA and Canada
by Routledge
29 West 35th Street, New York, NY 10001

© 1998 selection and editorial matter, EASA;
individual chapters, the contributors

Typeset in Galliard by Routledge
Printed and bound in Great Britain by Clays Ltd, St. Ives
PLC

All rights reserved. No part of this book may be
reprinted or reproduced or utilised in any form or by
any electronic, mechanical, or other means, now known
or hereafter invented, including photocopying and
recording, or in any information storage or retrieval
system, without permission in writing from the
publishers.

British Library Cataloguing in Publication Data
A catalogue record for this book is available from the
British Library

Library of Congress Cataloging in Publication Data
Locality and belonging / edited by Nadia Lovell.
p. cm.
Includes bibliographical references and index.
1. Human territoriality. 2. Human beings – Effect of
environment on. 3. Geographical perception. 4.
Landscape assessment. 5. Place (Philosophy) I. Lovell,
Nadia
GN491.7.L63   1998
304.2'3–dc21   98–24886

ISBN 0–415–18281–6
ISBN 0–415–18282–4 (pbk)

Contents

Contributors

Eduardo P. Archetti is Professor of Social Anthropology at the University of Oslo. He has written extensively on society and culture in Ecuador and Argentina. His most recent book is *Guinea Pigs: Food, Symbol and Conflict of Knowledge in Ecuador* (1996), and he is editor of *Exploring the Written: Anthropology and the Multiplicity of Writing* (1994).

Kaj Århem is Professor of Social Anthropology at Göteborg University. He has conducted extensive field research among Tukanoan Indians in the Amazon, and among East African Masai pastoralists. He has published numerous articles in Scandinavian and international journals and books.

Anna Bohlin received her undergraduate degree at SOAS in 1994, and is currently completing a Ph.D. in social anthropology at the University of Göteborg. She has conducted fieldwork in Cape Town, and is writing her dissertation on ethnicity, collective memory and landscape in post-apartheid South Africa.

Filip De Boeck received his Ph.D. from the University of Leuven and is an assistant professor at the same university. He has conducted extensive fieldwork among the aLuund of southwest Congo. His research has produced numerous articles in various journals and books.

Jeanette Edwards is Lecturer of Social Anthropology at Keele University. Previous research has included fieldwork with health and social service workers in Greater Manchester, and a study of kinship and new reproductive technologies. She is co-author of *Technologies of Procreation: Kinship in the Age of Assisted Parenthood*, and she has published numerous articles on parenthood and English notions of kinship and community.

Kjersti Larsen is a lecturer at the Centre for International Environment and Development Studies, Agricultural University of Norway. Her fieldwork is conducted in Zanzibar, and her research focuses on Islam, ritual performance, spirit possession and the construction of memory. She is author of *Unyagi – Fra Jente Til Kvinne: Utformning av Kvinnelige Kjönsidentitet i Lys av Övergångritualer, Religiositet og Modernisering* (1988).

Nadia Lovell is Lecturer in Social Anthropology at the University of Kent. She obtained her Ph.D. from the School of Oriental and African Studies, and has conducted fieldwork in Togo, Ghana and Niger. In Ghana and Togo, her research has focused on gender and medicine in the context of *vodhun* religion. Her publications include *Unleashing Spirits and Unbounding Gender: Vocal Gods and Polyvalent Discourse in Watchi Possession* (1997) and *Pluralisme Thérapeutique et Stratégies de Santé chez les Evhé du sud Togo* (1995).

Arlette Ottino has conducted fieldwork in Indonesia (Bali) and Madagascar. She obtained her Ph.D. from the Australian National University in Canberra. Her major theoretical interests lie in the fields of ritual and the interface between knowledge and practice. She is Associate Fellow of the Research School of Pacific and Asian Studies, Australian National University, and is a member of the Unité de Recherches Interdisciplinaires sur l'Asie du sud-est et Madagascar, France. She is a lecturer at the Université de la Rochelle in France.

David Parkin is Professor of Anthropology at the University of Oxford. He has carried out research in east Africa for thirty years, and has published many books on subjects ranging from religious and economic diversity, medical anthropology and, especially, Islam among the Swahili speaking peoples. *The Politics of Cultural Performance* (edited with others, 1996) features among his latest publications.

Foreword

David Parkin

The juxtaposition of locality and belonging immediately raises the question of whether one can belong to a group which does not also have a territorial reference point. In fact, as this volume makes clear, it is a question which suggests that anthropologists can no longer assume that the people they study see themselves as attached to a particular, bounded locality. Diaspora, transnational community and dispersed network are typically some of the terms used to convey the image of movements of people who retain common socio-cultural consciousness in the face of constant displacement. This is not, however, really the problem of modern migratory globalism that it is often depicted as. Movement within one or two generations rather than fixed settlement has generally characterised human populations, and the earliest anthropologists built this fact into their analyses. What is really new is the awareness among many communities that there are innumerable other such populations linked globally by rapid transport, electronic communication systems and common access to the same consumer goods and styles, and that these often supplement rather than replace older ties forged through, say, trade and intermarriage.

Here we describe how groups, each identified by a sphere of overlapping activities, set up collective memories of themselves against a view of what is happening elsewhere in the world. These different local notions of global consciousness quickly change as new information comes in and so challenge the power and selectivity of collective memories. In her introduction, Nadia Lovell pithily notes that belonging is a way of remembering and of constructing a collective memory of place, but that, like genealogies, such constructions are always contestable.

'Belonging' under such conditions becomes problematic. Is it to 'imagined communities' whose members agree that they have a common origin, even if they cannot agree where it is? Or does one belong to a community whose members care less about origins, recognising that these may be diverse, and care more about the sentiments and habits they have in common? Or is belonging necessarily and absolutely rooted in a territory, sometimes confirmed by membership of a descent group?

The latter typifies the politically threatened group, which may or may not be dispersed. It is not a relevant question for communities which, while attaching themselves to a physical locality, nevertheless take cognisance at least in their ritual practices that the notion of territorial permanence is at best a long-term fiction. A corollary is the tenacity of central cultural assumptions to survive peoples' movement to new settlements. Territorial attachment is, then, the counterpart to transportable cultural ideas. As possible, though not necessary, counterparts, the two dimensions have to be taken into account.

According to Filip de Boeck in this volume, the rootedness of trees is a metaphor for the growth of masculine maturity and wisdom among the aLuund of southwestern Congo (former Zaïre). It provides fixity between the competing pulls of matriliny and viri-/patrilocality, and counters the influence of interconnecting pathways between the village-centred trees that take the person away, so to speak, from his or her homestead. The theme is echoed in Nadia Lovell's account of the Watchi of southeastern Togo, among whom the planted *hunde* palm tree gives an immobile centre to the male-headed household, provided a red clay pot is buried at its roots, which should then penetrate the pot as a man's penis fills a woman's womb. But it is gods, associated with women, who come from other places and who mark out not just the origins but the possible extent of society.

The focus on trees underlines the role of landscape in commemorating the origins of a people, a theme taken up especially in studies of Aboriginal Australia but relevant elsewhere. Anthropologists have for long studied the ways in which different spatial zones in a society may differentiate, or be differentiated by, rank, age and gender. A recent generation has turned to the more specific metaphor of landscape, first put forward for its rhetorical and epistemological interest by a few anthropologists in the early 1980s, but now with a focus on its notions of territoriality, habitat and background, and of foreground markers of persons, peoples and history.

Is to talk of landscape (and thence of flora and fauna, and earth and rock) inevitably to talk of what we may translate as nature in contrast to human society? Given many indigenous views of the inseparability of nature, society and even culture, we must be careful of such a contrast.

Thus, many of the contributors do make reference to the social world of humans being reflected in, say, the natural world of animals and plants, as among the Amazonian Pira-Pirana (Kaj Århem), or in the world of spirits and deities as among Watchi (Nadia Lovell), Balinese (Arlette Ottino) and Zanzibaris (Kjersti Larsen). The origins or territorial associations of such deities are, however, best taken as statements about where human society comes from or how it is has come into being. Thus, the Watchi gods are extensions of natural and environmental features, but their names are also place names associated with human origins, migrations and settlement. Although the Balinese are unaware of the names of many deities, unlike the Watchi, they nevertheless see them as manifesting the conditions under which, for example, a temple congregation originates. The people of Zanzibar, conscious of their cultural diversity, classify spirits or demons according to their human-like characteristics and ethnic and geographical origins. Such classes of spirits are like narratives, telling stories of the various peoples who have contributed to the making of the mixed Zanzibar population. Among the Amazonian peoples, the shamans' believed ability to travel 'mentally' in time and space and to turn into other animals points to a transformational world which seems always to transcend set boundaries.

It is clear from these examples that landscape may be a convenient metaphorical starting point but is soon made less relevant in the face of indigenous categories which merge, often imperceptibly, the so-called natural, social and cultural.

However, just as memories of the past as an index of current belonging are likely to be selective, so uses of the past can indicate ideal future choices, the two strategies sometimes combining to create communities which seem to aim for and then fall short of drawing boundaries round themselves. The effects of so-called cultural globalisation on localities can be viewed in this way. The people of the English town of Alltown, described by Jeanette Edwards, distinguish between those who are born and bred there and those who are incomers, echoing an earlier sociological distinction between locals and cosmopolitans. The originals or locals are of mixed, essentially rural background and habits, some favoured and some scorned, while the incomers, including the inevitable retirees and commuters, are depicted as of contrasting character, as from the metropolis (e.g. Manchester) and as indicating the way the community will develop.

Yet this recognition of the modern power of the external in reshaping local communities, including the sometimes overriding significance of gender and class, does not entirely eclipse the process by which even incomers in time become referred to as 'almost Alltownians'. The external, cosmopolitan or global may, paradoxically, be not just the contrastive measure by which locals define themselves but also the transformative means of their own further localisation: they may incorporate incomers' lifestyles and objects as an accepted and in due course indispensable badge of internal membership.

A variation on this process is presented by Eduardo Archetti in his account of Argentinean football. The early and best teams were British, who were revered for their machine-like power and triumphs. The game gradually became Argentina's own and its British origins less remembered or important. But a distinction between collectively disciplined football and undisciplined but creative individualism continues until the present. The successful Dutch and German teams of 1970s typify the former, in contrast to the flair of the Argentinean hero, Maradona, who in turn typifies an earlier stereotype of the flamboyant, free *gaucho* cowboy of the wild *pampa* terrain. To be Argentinean is to partake of this stereotype and its modern manifestations. The machine-like stereotype may be popularly rejected yet, again paradoxically, is an intrinsic, if imported, part of the nation's history, making the celebration of wild abandon and flair a contrastive possibility.

That landscape can be far removed from conventional definitions of nature is brought out in Anna Bohlin's description of a museum set up in District Six, a socio-culturally mixed or 'coloured' residential area in Cape Town demolished during South Africa's apartheid regime. The museum includes, for example, a mobile made up of street signs, and attracts former residents and other South Africans, of all ethnic backgrounds, who see in the recreated emblems of the lost town their own sense of belonging to the newly created 'rainbow nation'. In some respects this is a case of the local incorporating national and global perspectives and then re-presenting them to international public and media interest in the future of South Africa and its unique policies.

'Belonging' is not in this case a question of actually living any more in an area, which has since ceased to exist, but of living in the wider community of which the former District Six has become representative after the event. It is a belonging which supersedes the earlier apartheid separatism and claims instead membership of an egalitarian multiracial society. Yet, it is also unlikely that any of the museum visitors would wish to deny or forsake their sense of belonging to other more enclosed enclaves, whether ethnic, religious, class or occupational.

It is banal to remark that belonging exists on as many dimensions as people are prepared to delineate. It is less banal to ask how much these

dimensions are expressed as necessarily dependent on physical attachment to a particular locality. The line between a sense of belonging to
only one locality and belonging to a number is an important if sometimes fuzzy one. A distinction might be drawn between peoples for
whom one locality is all-inclusive of their remembered experiences, and
those for whom many places mark their histories and whose sense of
belonging is to that extent multilocal.

It might be argued that externally defined criteria are as significant as
subjective ones, or even more so: one may passionately seek repatriation
to a homeland, but if that is politically or legally denied, cultural solidarity or reinvention may not be enough. Is anthropology, then,
sometimes unrealistic in cross-culturally comparing practices and
concepts of belonging and locality among peoples but treating them as
unmenaced by outsiders?

Anthropology does not in fact ignore these modern issues of forced
population displacement but seeks to place them against the contrary,
namely a humanistic understanding of voluntary movement. In this
volume, all contributions except that on South Africa describe societies
which do not operate on the expectation that they will be expelled from
their home territory, although, as in the case of the Pira-Pirana of
Amazonia, that is regarded as a possibility. The resulting rich mixture of
eco-cosmological understandings of origins complements therefore the
increasing numbers of studies of refugees in which post-traumatic
disorder syndromes more typify the victims' experiences. It is important
to remember the former in the losses suffered by the latter.

The question raised at the beginning of this foreword, namely
whether one can belong to a group which does not also have a territorial
reference point, can now be rephrased. What is the concept of origin that
a self-defined group may have? To what extent is that origin a geographically known place rather than, say, a mythical account of creation? And
how is this concept of origin dependent on the nature of the locality in
which the group currently finds itself?

Such questions are treated best as a prolegomenon for research initiated by this volume rather than as answerable for the moment. I have
touched on a potentially useful broad distinction between a single origin
and multiple provenances, between a people who see themselves as
coming from one place to which they may wish to return and a people
coming from many places but who now recognise shared interests. But
there is also the possibility that peoples may in time alternate between
these different notions of origin, substituting the one for the other. Such
changes may test people's allegiance and cause some of them to break

away, or they may be the basis of an even more insistent sense of belonging. To belong either through descent or through incorporation in a group are thus major paradigmatic alternatives, sometimes combined but sometimes in conflict. The tension between them may be elaborated in ritual, myth, beliefs and collective memory, but is not always resolved, as the contributions to this volume admirably show.

Introduction*

Nadia Lovell

Belonging in need of emplacement?

Belonging to a particular locality evokes the notion of loyalty to a place, a loyalty that may be expressed through oral or written histories, narratives of origin as belonging, the focality of certain objects, myths, religious and ritual performances, or the setting up of shrines such as museums and exhibitions. Yet belonging is also fundamentally defined through a sense of experience, a phenomenology of locality which serves to create, mould and reflect perceived ideals surrounding place (Schama 1995; Tilley 1994). Accounts of how such loyalties are created, perpetuated and modified are of relevance to an understanding of identity at individual and, more importantly, collective levels, since belonging and locality as markers of identity often extend beyond individual experiences and nostalgic longing for a particular place. Belonging may thus be seen as a way of remembering (Connerton 1989; Fentress and Wickham 1994) instrumental in the construction of collective memory surrounding place (Hirsch 1995; Toren 1995). Yet belonging, with all its pragmatic connotations and potential for tying people to place and social relationships, also evokes emotions, sentiments of longing to be in a particular location, be it real or fictive. Rootedness and rootlessness evoke conditions of existence which tend to stress the emotional gravity of place. The exploration of how notions of belonging, localities and identities are constructed seems particularly relevant in current political contexts of 'globalisation', where the interface between localised understandings of belonging, locality and identity often seem to conflict with wider national and international political, economic and social interests. An examination of these concepts also appears especially topical since displacement, dislocation and dispossession have become such common themes in contemporary political experiences and debates. Locality and belonging may be moulded and defined as much by actual territorial emplacement as by memories of belonging to particular landscapes whose physical reality is enacted only through acts of collective remembering.

The notion of place, and one's positioning within it, remains highly topical in light of colonial deeds and post-colonial discourses. Recent newspaper articles strikingly reflect and illustrate the importance of emplacement and dislocation in postmodern popular contexts. On 19 June 1997, *The Times* in Britain published a full-page advertisement with the title 'First Their Children Were Stolen . . . Now Their Land Too? An Open Letter to Her Majesty Queen Elizabeth II Queen of Australia'. This plea, appearing at the initiative of various human rights organisations and urging for the restoration of land to Australian aboriginal populations, emphasised the obvious political and economic empowerment associated with rights of access to territory, but also underlined the 'exceptional spiritual and cultural importance' of land in sustaining Aboriginals' identity. Access to sacred sites and culturally significant landmarks were deemed essential preconditions to the establishment of an economically thriving community. In this sense, the centrality of cosmological origin precedes and conditions actual territoriality, spiritual well-being and material survival. Other recent media expressions of interest in the manifestation of sentiments of locality have included features on paganism in Britain, where more than 100,000 people are now estimated officially to belong to spiritual groups including druidry, shamanism, witch covens and other such groups where the sacredness of nature is emphasised. Importantly, nature appears explicitly to be used in this industrialised and postmodern context in order to 'give us a sense of belonging. It takes away our alienation[1] from our land and our community. It finds a sanctity with the natural world and a deep connection with the earth' (druidess quoted in the *Guardian*, Friday 20 June 1997).

Yet if belonging and territoriality can be thus linked in life, their power of attraction also extends beyond the boundaries of death. In the course of this year, Che Guevara has finally regained his original home, to be buried there after more than thirty years in mortuary exile, while the remains of Long Wolf – a prominent Sioux chief who died in London while on a Buffalo Bill Wild West tour – have recently been reburied close to Wounded Knee after their exhumation from Brompton Park cemetery. Relatives and friends spoke of Long Wolf's longing to return home. These two accounts featured in articles rather evocatively entitled 'Che comes Home as Cuba's King of Kitsch', a reference to his embodiment of contemporary political ideals in Castro's Cuba (*Observer*, Sunday 12 October 1997), and 'Chief Returns to his Beloved Black Hills' (*The Times*, Friday 26 September 1997). Home is emphasised as a place of return, an original settlement where peace can finally be found and experienced, even after death. By contrast, Mobutu was said to have unburied the ancestral dead before departing into exile from the then Zaïre (contemporary Congo), as their belonging to his ancestral line was deemed no longer predicated on burial in a particular locality, and could be better protected by their removal from the site, where their tombs would otherwise almost certainly have been desecrated and looted (*Jeune Afrique*, May/June 1997; this information also appeared on Togonet). Finally, internecine disputes over land, often reduced in some Western minds to simple skirmishes over usufructuary and material rights, can be – and regularly are – used to evoke the horrors of spiritual beliefs and religiosity among 'other' people, as was illustrated in the reporting of the recent territorial conflicts between local Dayaks and settlers in Sarawak (Borneo). The former group was described by a journalist from the *Independent* newspaper surprised by the intensity of animosity between these 'locals' and settlers as having receded into the ages of darkness and tribal tradition in their attempt to legitimise access to land (*Independent*, Monday 9 June 1997). The perceived 'resurgence' of ancient traditions such as cannibalism, witchcraft and head-hunting, believed by some to have died long ago as a positive consequence of colonialism's civilising mission, are held up as examples of amazingly tenacious and merciless savagery.

Traditions, in this view, can thus also return to haunt us. That such practices should experience a revival or, indeed, the possibility that they could have persisted all along – albeit sometimes underground – is rarely placed in a contemporaneous cultural and political context in popular discourse,[2] where the complexity of the interconnectedness of these issues remains, at best, a matter of ignorance or is, at worst, wilfully ignored precisely because its complexity challenges preconceived ideas about the order of the world. Nevertheless, it goes without saying that spirituality is indeed often used to lay claim to material and metaphysical landscapes, and it is precisely this spirituality which renders such claims more powerful and, sometimes, entrenched to the point of arousing seemingly unresolvable differences and humanitarian horrors. Contemporary history cradles many such examples. The recent altercations in Rwanda, the Bosnian or Israeli–Palestinian conflicts[3] all bear testimony to the complex issues of belonging and localisation, many of them couched and mirrored in idioms of religiosity and spiritual claim. In Algeria, killings and beheadings are perpetrated in a quest for spiritual territoriality and legitimate belonging in afterlife. Forced displacement features prominently in post-colonial, post-independence discourses where dislocation seems to occur as a state of *force majeure*. Yet this appears as highly ironic when other communities – such as gypsies or other travellers, for instance – are subjected to pressure to settle when their own understanding and sense of belonging are highly predicated on movement and the transcendence of territorial settlement and boundaries as defining features of communal identity.

This volume explores ways in which such notions of belonging and attachment to particular territories and localities emerge and are mobilised, maintained and modified through time. Primarily, the connections, dynamics and dialectics of the relationship between concepts of belonging and locality are explored in various ethnographic contexts and cultural frameworks. Locality often appears subsumed within the notion of belonging itself, which serves to provide collective identity and a sense of cohesion and cultural commensality (although conflict and differentiation can also emerge out of these processes). Yet belonging itself also appears at least partly predicated upon locality or a memory of locality. In addition, belonging to a place is viewed as instrumental in creating collective identities. But such identities may themselves be instrumental in forwarding particular political claims on territory, and may therefore be only temporarily mobilised to justify such claims. Even in displacement, the memory of a collective identity may crystallise around a notion of place. In such circumstances, the debate on hybridity and the location of culture in places in between (often associated with violence and diaspora) can be seen in a new light, as an emphasis on the transience of belonging to locality as identifiable place may coexist with highly localised memorised places. In the cases presented here (Bohlin, Larsen and, to some extent, Edwards) the focus is on how locality can be recreated as a particular place through the memory of its existence in the past. This memory is thus conducive to the forging of social bonds in the present, and for the future, among communities of displaced people but where belonging to a particular group provides one strategy or avenue of belonging among many others.

The concept of locality as a well-delineated and identifiable place is itself problematised in phenomenological, historical and political terms. 'Location', 'locality' and the 'local' are of course all problematic terms, as recent anthropological literature testifies. Fardon (1990) warned of the dangers of confining 'local' discourses into isolated and alienated hinterlands bearing little connection with the wider world through the methodological conditionings and theoretical insularity of the anthropological discipline itself. The 'local' is conditioned into being, and invoked into existence, through the necessity of creating an 'other' who

is as different from ourselves as possible, and is therefore often transformed into a highly artificial construct bounded both by pragmatic
constraints of fieldwork and by academic expectations (although these
are changing). What has now started to come to light is the anthropologists' long-standing quest for erroneously localising 'others' while
themselves remaining highly deterritorialised and sited in between
cultures and locations (Clifford (1997) saliently plays on the fluency and
malleability of concepts of roots and routes, of settlement and movement in paths of life). This in turn contributes to the construction of
sometimes equally misleading and bounded concepts of culture. As
Gupta and Ferguson point out, such localising discourses have played a
significant part in creating academic concepts of location as easily identifiable geographical areas, rather than as 'sites constructed in fields of
unequal power relations' (1997: 35). Unsiting and unsettling our
anthropological definition and understanding of locality is, consequently, closely tied to processes of unsiting knowledge. Similarly, Fog
Olwig and Hastrup (1997) question the usefulness of concepts of the
'local' and 'location' as viable entities for the understanding of culture.
Culture, they argue, is not necessarily tied to particular places, but is
rather created at the interstices between people in their interaction with
one another in everyday discourses which may be localised, but also in
the everyday experience of extraordinary events such as forced migration
or exile. Identity can thus also appear as deterritorialised (Appadurai
1991), located between places rather than being bound to particular
homelands (Bhabha 1994). Displacement and the experiential narratives
which derive from such a condition are not intermediary statements.
The lived experience of migration, exile or other forms of dislocation
may uproot settled locality, but it is not in itself a condition in between,
since meaning is derived *in situ* from dislocation itself. In addition,
memories of settlement, of particular belonging to a highly localised
place, may act to counterbalance the dislocation and displacement felt at
particular junctures in history. Locality in this sense becomes multivocal,
and belonging itself can be viewed as a multifaceted, multilayered
process which mobilises loyalty to different communities simultaneously.

The contributions to this volume avoid a focus on the question of
culture *per se*, whether localised or otherwise. Rather, they centre on
how notions and feelings of collective belonging are mobilised at particular times, and on the instrumentality of such feelings in making explicit
particular aspects of collective identities and claims on territory. The
meaning of locality comes to encompass tangible explicit localities (De
Boeck, Lovell, Århem, Ottino) and imagined places no longer in

existence, reconstructed in the present in mythical accounts and narratives that make use of collective and reconstructed memories to help mould communal identities of displacement centred around the loss of place, rather than its actual acquisition (Bohlin, Archetti). While all chapters tackle the issue of how a sense of belonging and identity are created and maintained around actual or fictitious, memorised (and sometimes memorialised) space, and on how these are transformed, the identities which emerge vary both in character and in terms of the social and political contexts which surround them. Identity can crystallise around a sense of belonging predicated on hierarchically defined rights of access to territory, which then serve to stratify social groups according to perceived origin. Alternatively, the memory of belonging may enhance a sense of unstratified, egalitarian commensality. Yet if looked upon primarily as experience and enactment, the emotional attachments produced and triggered by locality and a sense of social belonging provide the necessary elements for imprinting memories of place onto bodies and minds (Lyon and Barbalet 1994). As such, belonging and locality often come to transcend both local and national boundaries in order to encompass identity as it is temporally mobilised and crystallised at particular moments in history.

Landscape as locality

How, then, is this achieved? Recent anthropological interest has focused on the construction of landscape as a primary source of involvement for the establishment of human belonging and emplacement (Bender 1993; Tilley 1994; Hirsch 1995). Landscapes are turned into places by human action (Hirsch 1995), and specific places are notionally extracted out of undifferentiated space by becoming imbued with particular meaning by, and for, human sociality and identity. Bender (1993) emphasises how landscapes are inscribed onto bodies through the mutual positioning of humans within nature and nature within society, while stressing the political dimension of the appropriation of landscape (Lefèbvre takes a similar stance). Descola (1992, 1996) has recently contributed some of the most concerted and influential accounts of humans' relationship with nature, pointing to the many parallels which develop between human and natural worlds. In his joint introduction with Gisli Pálsson (Descola and Pálsson 1996), both authors point to the limitations of former anthropological models dissociating nature and culture. Structuralism of course encompassed the heyday for this fashion, with Lévi-Strauss spearheading theories concerning the ultimate domination of nature by culture (with all the ramifications which this dualism implied: the mind was confirmed as being superior to the body; the domination of women by men, the subjugation of animals to the will of humans, and the submission of the wild to the tame, were but 'logical' extensions of such theoretical experimentations).[4] Descola and Pálsson pointedly remark that these dichotomisations have remained unfruitful, primarily since they do not seem to be matched by ethnographic evidence. In some of his earlier work Descola (1994) remarks, for instance, that the Achuar Jivaro socialise the natural environment and the realm of animals in order to create parallel human and non-human worlds, thus stressing the fundamental similarities between the natural and social domains. Having thus rejected many of structuralism's assumptions about the dissociation of the human realm from the nature that surrounds it, and having argued for an approach based on social praxis à la Bourdieu, Descola then goes on to discuss the 'social objectification of nature' (1996: 85) in terms of general patterns which provide universal images for the construction of non-human, natural domains:[5]

> A common feature of all conceptualisations of non-humans is that they are always predicated by reference to the human domain. This leads either to sociocentric models, when social categories are used as a kind of mental template for the ordering of the cosmos, or to a dualistic universe, as in the case of western cosmologies where nature is defined negatively as that ordered part of reality which exists independently of human action. . . . Both processes imply establishing boundaries, ascribing identities and devising cultural mediations. . . . These . . . are not in my view universal structures of the mind which operate independently of cultural and historical contexts. These schemes or schemata of praxis, as I like to call them, are simply objectified properties of social practices, cognitive templates or intermediary representations which help subsume the diversity of real life under a basic set of categories of relation. . . . This is why I believe that the mental models which organise the social objectification of non-humans can be treated as a finite set of cultural invariants, although they are definitely not reducible to cognitive universals.
>
> (Descola 1996: 86–7)

Thus Descola sees the objectification of nature as one of the primary features of humans' involvement with their environment. If social praxis is emphasised, it is so inasmuch as it helps produce 'cognitive templates' which in turn help to organise the world. Although a certain dynamism is involved in shaping and altering humans' relationship to their environment through the social relationships they might entertain with one another, the mental processes involved are nevertheless emphasised. Descola's distancing from models of classification of the world as a universal structure of the mind may be useful, but it gives rise instead to a fundamentally social mode of thought which, although malleable and receptive to historical processes, nevertheless sets itself apart from the natural world which it produces through its mental mapping. The emphasis on social praxis, with its associated stress on the 'logic of relations' (Descola 1996: 92) and the positioning of classes and categories of beings in a relational organisational scheme thus provides the world with identities and meanings because of the relationships which various categories of beings entertain with one another. The categories themselves are thus socially constituted in the process. Nevertheless, the fact remains that in such a scheme, nature and the non-human remain fundamentally outside of the human realm, although they are seen as constituting parallel worlds. The ultimate paradox in Descola's argument is that it centres on social praxis as a mode of classification of that which lies outside the human world, thus still leaving humans out of nature. The meaning of nature may be derived from relational interaction, but the process serves primarily to socialise nature in human cognition. Jackson's critique of Bourdieu could easily be extended to include Descola's work: 'Bourdieu follows in the structuralist tradition of locating generative forces outside the immediate, lived reality of the lifeworld' (Jackson 1996: 21).

Thus, however theoretically useful in clarifying our understanding of the processual changes which take place in human interaction with our environment, the anthropological interest in the dichotomisation between nature as raw material and place as human construct is itself inherently ambiguous since it is premised, in the first instance, on a highly European conceptualisation of landscape and place as distinctive semantic categories. For instance Lefèbvre (1974), despite his firmly phenomenological emphasis, nevertheless differentiates architecture as human production from nature as raw material, framing such rapport in politico-social relations of knowledge and access to power. As such, this interest in the socialisation of the environment stems partly from a reflexive concern, where landscape remains defined as external to ourselves, a location we may visit, while place becomes highly internalised, an appropriation of landscape where we are no longer strangers. We enter a landscape and turn it into a place which we are no longer able to abstract from ourselves. The phenomenological debate was, to a high degree, triggered in the 1970s by the almost hegemonic dominance of structuralism in the previous two decades, itself a response to earlier scientific paradigms relating to the absolute 'reality' of the existence of space. Thus space, like so much else in post-Cartesian theory, had been subjected to objectifying tendencies, turning it into an entity whose existence could undeniably be positioned outside the human realm (for a positivistic stance, see Nerlich 1994). Thereafter it became a mental category, to be objectified by the human mind in order to organise human existence. Space (or scape) could be thought *about*, but did not represent an interactive field for the mutual definition of space and human life through phenomenological interaction and experience (for an early critique, see Lefèbvre 1974).

The dissociation of landscape and place should, at best, be viewed as a theoretical tool for the understanding of the processual changes enacted in human ecology. Appadurai (1988) has pointed to the danger of exoticising the Other by placing the anthropological object of study closer to nature in a continuum of hierarchically achieved appropriation of culture. Gupta and Ferguson make a similar point when discussing the 'naturalization of cultural differences as inhering in different geographical locales' (1997: 8), and also place this tendency in the context of early developments of fieldwork as field science, on a par with other naturalistic sciences in the nineteenth century (1997: 7). The study of landscape in ethnographic contexts thus runs the rather explicit risk of being made to represent a continuation of this trend, unless it is firmly positioned within a transformative and dynamic framework. This also raises the related question as to why nature so often continues to be perceived in Western anthropological discourses as being found and located elsewhere.

Nature – be it in the form of landscape, architecture or any other form of habitat[6] – may be understood differently if considered against the background of human experience. Of course, nature is also instrumental in shaping social relational discourses, and it is obvious that it is also part of social praxis. But nature is mutually reflexive in its own rapport to human beings. It serves to shape a human consciousness about emplacement, about the workings of the human body, and provides a reflection against which human imagery of the self, at individual and social levels, can be mapped and experienced. Nature and humans thereby become what they are because they constantly interpenetrate each other as realms of experience, and participate in a mutual transfer of understanding about the relationship in which they are engaged (see Jackson 1996).

This process in itself involves far more than cultural constructs about nature and its classification, since it primarily engages humans in a dialectical relationship where nature itself becomes inscribed onto bodies, and provides both the source and outcome of contextual interaction. Human bodies are thus intertwined with nature in order to create society in the first place, while also reflecting the human enculturation of nature. But these processes extend far beyond mental categories or ontological classifications; rather, they become mutually entangled and defined precisely through processual and continuous transformations.

Of emplacement and belonging

Landscape and the importance of nature in shaping local understandings of belonging to place feature as relevant themes of interest in some of the contributions to this volume (see in particular De Boeck, Lovell, Århem and Ottino), yet they do not constitute the final goal in these explorations. Landscape, as it is presented here, provides only one tool among others through which interrelationships between humans and nature, and between humans in social and situated communities, are produced and reproduced. Landscape, in this sense, does not stand as an absolute geographical site conquered once and for all, and the sitedness of belonging is therefore constantly re-enacted in order to transcend (and simultaneously allow) the vagaries of migration, of movement and of existential uncertainties. Rather than view the local as firmly situated through myth or ritual, the performative aspects of religious activities are considered essential in anchoring belonging and making it (temporarily) tangible through social practice (see Appadurai 1995). It is for this reason that the logic of the production of space *per se*, as it has been explored elsewhere, remains a tangent to the present enterprise. The production of locality therefore remains dubious in more than one way, since the local, it seems, is never quite what it seems. Landscape, as it is treated in this volume, is thus closely associated to myths (of creation, of origin) and ritual performance. However, rather than view these particular forms of attachment as highly localised and static forms of using the natural environment in order to establish spiritual and usufructuary rights over territory once and for all, the contributors convincingly demonstrate that there is nothing particularly local about the local, and that most ritual treatment allows for deterritorialisation, movement through space and time, and the transience of locality through the incorporation of dynamic, malleable and movable images of origin and conception.

The malleable nature of landscape provides the focal point for the exploration of notions of identity and attachment to territory in De Boeck's opening contribution. Features of the landscape are interwoven into aLuund (southwest Congo) conceptions of male identity and an understanding of belonging in terms of rootedness, stability and the anchoring of territorial ownership of the land. The landscape is thus used to provide images of ownership which overlap with an existential orientation of the human body as a direct product and reflection of this natural environment, expressed primarily through the image of the tree. The contributions by De Boeck and Lovell focus on the connectedness of landscape and (gendered) human bodies in their mutual constitution of each other, thus contributing to socialising nature without objectifying it, since humans themselves become constituted simultaneously as cultured and 'natured' beings through the performative actions of common and ritual praxis. In this sense, 'the human body and the body of the earth are metaphorically fused in terms of visceral, internal physiology and not just in terms of external anatomy' (Jackson 1996: 33). In addition, the constitution of highly localised place and belonging is paralleled in the cases of the aLuund and Watchi by an equally embedded imagery of movement through space, which is made possible precisely because the human body is itself fused in this way with its natural habitat. The transcendence of territory and settlement are thereby also tightly knit into mythologies of belonging which are only at times firmly grounded in territoriality.

Localities of memory, representations of belonging

Yet if landscape is interacted with, and created and defined through human experience, the perpetuation of the concepts surrounding its cultural construction also relies heavily on memory to perpetuate its existence. The inscription of nature onto bodies, and of bodies within nature, transforms the relationship which humans entertain with nature into a dialectical process embedded in memory. Its transformative properties thereby also become embedded in phenomenological terms, as the synchronicity of time and space allow for movement through history. The landscape itself becomes historicised. Rather than providing fixed features for the classification of human experience, nature becomes part of the dynamic processes which allow for movement through the very remembrance of settlement and belonging. Memory itself has been looked upon as a phenomenological process which uses both verbal and non-verbal forms of communication to inscribe societal meanings into past and future (Connerton 1989; Bond and Gilliam 1994; Fentress and Wickham 1994). Bahloul (1996), for instance, explores the commemorative processes surrounding particular architectural features which have helped define the present identity and relationship of Jewish-Algerian families now living in France, many of whom left Algeria more than thirty years ago. What Bahloul also emphasises is the diversified production of collective memory, and the multifaceted and overlapping dimensions of identity making. Memory recovers time and space in a synchronic gesture, streamlining and unifying some of its diversity and contradictions in order to create viable and cohesive collective images in the present. The (memory of the) house the family left behind remains, by and large, the focal point for defining and compounding this cohesive contemporary collective memory. Similarly, De Boeck also underlines the spatial and temporal dimensions of the embodiment of spatiality among a group of aLuund of southwest Congo (formerly Zaire) by highlighting the way in which bodies, and particularly those of male elders, serve to inscribe the textuality and contextuality of location by intertwining Luunda understandings of time and space through genealogies and ideals of masculinity. Landscape (both in its raw and unmediated form if ever its existence was conceivable, and in its 'culturally' mediated constructs) underpins these discourses by providing material for semantic exchanges – primarily expressed in the imagery of the tree – which synchronically transform nature and humans in a process of mutual definition. Most importantly, mythical place, embodied space and the processual interaction between humans and their environment are shown to be inherently transformative and mobile. The metaphor of the tree serves to locate the aLuund in their present territory, while simultaneously carrying with it the possibility for transience and movement across time and space, since trees can always be planted elsewhere. This reflects the aLuund's history of migration and conquest, but it also partly helps to bridge the underlying tensions which arise out of matrilineal ideals combined with virilocal settlement. The tree serves as the ultimate metaphor for Luunda malehood, and locality thereby comes to be defined and is, simultaneously, uprooted through the imagery of trees and masculinity.

This emphasis on the constitution of Luunda malehood, its location in and inscription into territory and landscape, parallels Lovell's exploration in Chapter 2 of Watchi (southeast Togo) gendered space and the primordially female essence of existence and locality. However, although landscape again provides fundamental experiential features and important food for thought, the mutual spatial codification of nature and humans (what Lefèbvre refers to as 'spatial practice' (1974: 48)) in which Watchi engage also allows for the expression of highly codified areas of gendered knowledge to be made socially intelligible and explicit. An understanding of belonging is thereby created through the dual appropriation of locality and a quest for cosmological knowledge. Through their close association with gods, women gain access to knowledge of a cosmological realm which is directly paralleled on earth, since new settlements can only be established with the prior agreement of the gods and the location of shrines where they can be properly worshipped. Women act as the primary agents in this process, since they provide the clay pots which help contain the gods. By analogy, they also procure the 'pots' of procreation, their own wombs, which supply the raw material for any new settlement to be established. The production of territory is itself embedded in the production and reproduction of knowledge, both processes being also simultaneously intertwined in the creation of highly localised modes of settlement and in the incorporation of migratory processes and transcendence of localised discourse.

By contrast, Århem (Chapter 3) describes the situation of the Amazonian Tukanoan Indians as one where the production of locality and exegetic understandings of the positioning of humans within landscape become increasingly localised and 'indigenised' due to particular political and economic constraints which threaten to undermine and dislodge entire populations from their perceived 'natural' habitat. Cosmological ideals of territory and locality have thereby become enhanced, serving as a means of identification in the mobilisation of political responses, and also helping to assert differentiated identities ('us' versus 'them') by internalising particular aspects of the landscape. Yet, if the highly localised dimension of belonging is emphasised at one level by the Tukanoan people, Århem also extends the concept of nature and landscape to include the transcendence of the fully localised modes of settlement expressed through cosmologies and the mapping of environment and territory, in order to include ever wider indigenous groups. Cosmologies are admittedly reflexive in defining and moulding collective ideals of belonging and identities, but they are also instrumental in shaping shared political responses and creating other overbridging loyalties which extend far beyond the local. For the Tukanoan Indians, the dislocations brought about by large-scale ore mining and the exploitation of gold dig at the very heart of spiritual location and sense of origin, and therefore threaten the environment and existence in more than a simply material way. They literally undermine the existence of the universe itself. Cosmological ideas are ultimately used – or, as Århem expresses it, are reborn – to express political discontent and mobilise this-worldly responses to perceived exploitation.

For Århem, landscape is socialised into place through practical and experiential interaction in order to allow its incorporation into society. The seemingly near universal *indigenous* propensity (my emphasis) to use features of the landscape in cross-culturally similar ways in order to achieve a sense of localised belonging 'would seem to generate a participatory ontological stance that manifests itself in a limited set of cultural representations of human-land relatedness' (Århem, this volume). This prompts a stress on the existence of a highly human characteristic to act upon the environment in particular ways, thereby leaving a human imprint on nature which extracts it from its own natural habitat and positions it within the human realm (some of this debate echoes aspects of Douglas' seminal theoretical insights on natural symbols and the body (Douglas 1966, 1975)).

That territory, locality and belonging should be produced through human interaction with nature, and through the interactions between humans in social practice as mediated through emplacement, is further evidenced by Ottino (Chapter 4), where the discussion is focused on how, in a Balinese temple, the intertwining relationships which arise between notions of origin, territorial emplacement, and the ritual exchange of spiritual and material substances between humans and real or mythical cosmological figures, help activate the materiality of emplacement and settlement. Belonging is thereby intricately linked to spatial and cosmological exchange, which serves to legitimate relations to the cosmos, and to one another in what is described as a highly stratified Balinese community. Ottino also convincingly demonstrates that communal belonging, activated through the ritual exchange of material and supernatural substances, supersedes territorial emplacement. The memory of origin, and the importance of remembering and forgetting, are also instrumental in forwarding contesting claims to socio-political positions.

Reference has already been made to the importance of memory and active remembering as markers of identity, and to the significance of memory as a potentially appropriative and amalgamating force where time and space become intertwined in a continuous process of unification. Fabian (1983) underlined the simultaneous and sometimes contradictory processes of the layering and 'flattening' of history, and problems of coevalness some years ago. Bahloul (1996) also points out that many younger members of the Algerian-Jewish community in France have never experienced either the landscape or the architecture which seem to mould their relationships with previous and contemporary (and possibly future) generations. The memory of landscape here serves as a memory of society, sociality and collective morality perpetuated through time,[7] and '[R]emembered time (becomes) a substitute for geography in migrants' memory' (Bahloul 1996: 9). This is similarly highlighted in Larsen's contribution (Chapter 5), where Zanzibari spirit possession evokes a memory of ethnic identity and territorial belonging inscribed in constructed historical pasts and processes of migration. Identities mobilised through spirit possession thereby crystallise particular ethnic affiliations in the present whose conjoined existence on the island are constantly reorganised, mirroring and helping to shape particular political junctures in contemporary Zanzibari history. Memories of origin thus encapsulate real and mythical places, whose imagery in the collective imagination evokes these past identities in the present, enabling them to be projected further into the future.

Bohlin's ethnography (Chapter 7) focuses almost entirely on memory. It argues that in the context of post-apartheid South Africa, the memory of place is recovered through the bodily re-enactment of locality and the use of material objects recovered from the past and displayed anew in an exhibition commemorating collective identities in a district razed to the ground at the height of apartheid. Members of the public who have had any association with the district are encouraged to bring back objects for these to be displayed, thus creating a 'virtual reality' of a past that no longer is. Here again, time serves as memory of collective belonging: it transports those who participate in the exhibition through time and space in a synchronic movement which recaptures both, while also transcending the boundaries of territory and heterogeneous racial identities. Collective memory of a place which no longer exists is used to further very contemporary ideals of national unification and homogeneity, subsuming previous apartheid narratives of social, cultural and racial disparity. One can easily surmise that although anthropologists are now busily (and finally) involved in dislocating their own assumptions about the sitedness and rootedness of the territories of 'others', 'many of the people we study are deeply involved in constructing cultural contexts which bear many resemblances to such cultural entities' (Fog Olwig and Hastrup 1997: 11), particularly when territorial and cultural identities may be perceived to be under threat.

Objects of mnemonic desire

An exhibition of objects, rescued by former residents of the district, acts as the primordial material for the containment of history, for remembering the past, and artefacts are thereby employed in the present as embodiments and representations of unified past and present identities that come to emphasise a sense of former cohesion, solidarity, egalitarianism and the homogeneity of identity and belonging among displaced residents of the district. These objects very much serve as mediating elements in the recreation of (the memory of) place, and act as surrogates for a memory–time–space which can never be fully recovered, yet which is also precisely recreated through the use and display of the objects themselves. A similar issue is raised by Edwards (Chapter 6) through the examination of recollected and reconstructed identities in Alltown, an unidentified town in northern England. Artefacts and their appropriation and positioning in the local museum serve as markers of a particular history, instrumental in the enhancement of specific local identities which are constantly (re-)enacted in present constellations between various groups living in the town today. Origins of, and in, place evoke particular histories, particular sets of relationships, and particular rights of access to legitimacy and belonging to the town. Verging on debates about ethnicity, both ethnographies evade the constraints of ethnic definitions and affiliations, since the identities which emerge through the strategic positionings of the actors and their experiences slide into the interstices left between ethnic identity markers, and penetrate into the realm of wider local and national political domains without being explicitly defined. However, whereas Edwards emphasises the heterogeneous nature of identities as they are brought forth in Alltown, Bohlin stresses the salient attempts made by former residents of District Six to demarcate the homogenous nature of their belonging to this locality.

Yet the meaning(s) ascribed to and inscribed onto objects are contestable, and rely again on memories of collective identification which are often codified in the present for political purposes. The meanings attributed to objects are often (as is evidenced in the cases presented here) publicly enacted and displayed alongside oral histories and narratives of remembrance of the past. What they come to symbolise, represent and contain in the present is, in some ways, highly eclectic, and it is precisely this 'non-dit', the untold and inarticulated embeddedness of objects and narratives which make them useful in the appropriation of the past and the projection of future political claims. Objects, in this sense, carry their own life histories, life-cycles and trajectories moving, as in the case presented by Bohlin, from personal belongings (books, hair clips, mirrors) to collective mnemonic devices used to conjure up a communal past and identities which emphasise a contemporary solidarity and shared identity, especially as it is set against the current context of South Africa's political agenda of forgiveness and reconciliation. Personal objects thus become alienable property, are turned from commodity for consumption to artefact for display in order to fulfil collective ideals and weave ties of communal commensality to a particular place (see also Appadurai 1986; Thomas 1991). However, whether these objects should be read as text is open to debate (Vansina 1985, 1994),[8] as the memories which inscribe themselves on objects or, indeed, narratives themselves, are never 'objectively' synchronic in the way that a text can be (Fentress and Wickham 1994: 6–8), in spite of the fact that they aim to synchronise past and present, and time and space, by positioning past in present and time in space in overlapping motions. Perhaps it is best to view objects, alongside nature and memory, as the epitome of in-betweenness, as the ultimate repositories of meanings which are never clearly there but are nevertheless always present, and therefore always on the move. As Edwards and Bohlin demonstrate, however, the power of objects to evoke such particular images of the past, and make use of them in politicised contexts, also derives from the highly emotive attributes with which objects can be imbued (see also Thomas (1991: 30) for a discussion on the nature of the value attributed to objects). Emotional ties may carry strategic significance in these respective political and ethnic settings, but the power of the emotions attributed to, and conjured up by, these objects leaves few people unmoved.

The use of objects naturally raises the question of representation. As we have already seen, the quest for an 'absolute' representation of local modes of relating to nature is in itself highly problematic, and raises the spectres of misconceived Otherness and the potential danger of naturalising local knowledge of nature while objectifying anthropological locations as laboratories of natural science. Equally, objects on display in museums or purposefully collected and reconstituted in exhibitions can testify to the same disconnectedness, to the same potential dissociation between object and represented (group of) persons (Stocking 1985; Ames 1992). Yet, the right to represent – oneself, others, third parties or 'simply' objects – has a disconcerting tendency to subvert the intentions of both displayer and observer, revealing in its stead the circularity of the relationships in which the objects are mere material entanglements. Thus representations (of nature, of objects, of Otherness) are also ever present in local and not so local discourse, wherever one chooses to position oneself. Representation in this sense becomes highly articulate, highly malleable and also exclusively instrumental in the constitution of political responses to oppression and the emphasis of homogenising egalitarian ideals (Bohlin) or alternatively, in the articulation of stratifying identities which can be hierarchically organised (Edwards). Relationships, rather than objects, are mobilised in these exchanges and often become translucent through the materiality of their expression. However, beyond the obvious manifestations of such relationships through the mobilisation of objects or concepts of origin, what also emerges here in the context of apartheid and northern English communities is the very malleability of such an enterprise, and its direct positioning in the constitution of present history and territorial memory.

The dead, mythical landscapes and territories of state

The issue of representation takes on new relevance in the context of the workings of the nation-state, with its often globalising attempts at creating hegemoric national identities and cohesive political discourses which seldom coincide with more localised, fragmented and, sometimes, subversive forms of 'being in the state'.

Archetti's exploration of territorial imagery, and its reflective play of hide-and-seek with national politics of identity in Argentinean football, is illustrative of these dynamics and of the mutual interplay between local and national discourses which, while reflecting one another, also remain highly contested and elusive. Territories of the Argentinean landscape are opposed to one another as representations of various political institutions that inscribe a national memory of historical events. State and 'raw' nature thereby continually confront and mirror one another, and testify to the various phases of Argentinean history. The *pampa* comes to represent a pre-colonial past, associated with freedom, resourcefulness and the original Indian populations. Yet the positive attributes of 'savagery' – creativity, fertility, imagination – are offset by the tragic reality of the Indians' perceived inability to adapt to new political circumstances, dooming them to extinction in popular national imagery, in what Taussig succinctly describes as 'the magical harnessing of the dead for stately purposes' (1997: 3), adding that: 'In the making of modern nations, the dead do double duty. Out of nowhere, it seems, people conjure up a slice of deadness and borrow from it their names, battle cries, and costumes, in order to present the new scene of world history in dazzling form' (Taussig 1997: 10). In the case described by Archetti, the latent memory of the dead, their displacement and replacement by a more 'home grown' national product, the *gaucho* cowboy, also help inspire the national imagery of football as being very much alive and kicking.

The significance of various locations of the Argentinean landscape is directly imprinted onto the bodies of individual football players and their physical attributes. Yet the relationship between national political arenas and the local imagery applied around the bodies of the most successful players, in both past and present, is ambiguous and fraught with contradictions. The best players are made to embody ideals of freedom, of resistance and rebellion, ideally suited to carry forth post-colonial representations of contestation against outside domination, and come to portray, at individual levels, ideas of containment, independence and self-sufficiency. In the larger societal context, they embody images of neo-colonial liberation from white Western masters. However, if the imagery of the '*pibe*' or young boy is fruitful in contexts of external international politics, it also carries within it the potential for representing a liminal condition subversive to the internal workings of the contemporary Argentinean state and political context. In spite of this liminality, the imagery of rebellion becomes an iconographic representation of Argentinean national identity, as presented and re-presented to the public and to the outside world. The nation-state is therefore ever present in the imagery of football, while simultaneously remaining highly marginal to its mythical origins and bodily imagery. As an extension, the players themselves affirm their belonging and attachment to the nation by acting as physical reminders of the very diversity of its landscape and, thereby, its history, while containing also the very subversion and unruliness of this history.

Finally, and on a more personal note, I view the diverse contributions to this volume as bringing together several strands of theoretical anthropological interest, and as bridging between discourses of knowledge in anthropology which have gained increasing relevance over the past few decades. The study of cosmologies, myths and symbolism, for instance, has been with us for a long time, but what has been particularly enlightening in the organisation of the two EASA workshops, and later in the editing of this volume, are the various ways in which these areas of interest and study have been transmuted into discussions which come alive because of their topicality and contemporaneous relevance in current political and historical contexts. I am grateful to EASA for the opportunity to organise these workshops, and to David Parkin and Dick Werbner, who chaired them.

There is therefore an obvious continuity with our own disciplinary past, as myths and symbols retain their importance and continue to be recognised, but are also used to make new statements and gain relevance in the understanding of new theoretical and ethnographic contexts. Other anthropological areas of interest have included debates about ethnicity, boundaries and identity (there are classics, naturally, such as the works of Cohen, Barth and Leach, and more contemporary ventures by Banks, McDonald, MacDonald and Strathern). Some of these themes reappear in this volume, yet take on new forms and modes of expression as they become couched in idioms of revival of history without necessarily crystallising around ethnic identity *per se*. Ethnicity, as we know, has always remained elusive as a marker of identity, yet what some of the contributors attempt to show here is that the definition of ethnicity and belonging in the present may not be the ultimate goal sought in the transformative actions of, for instance, possession or the setting up of exhibitions or museums commemorating past identities which may indeed, at some point in the past, have been defined in terms of ethnic affiliation. While ethnicity is therefore defined 'backwards' as legitimating past notions of origin, present concerns may be motivated by factors far removed from marking ethnic affiliation. Finally, the politics of landscape – which sometimes include material objects – and mythology also serve to shape, define and embody particular national discourses. Again, anthropology has shown an extensive and prolonged interest in questions of nationalism and identity, of late focusing on the hybrid relationships between local integration and global politics, places in between, and on what has come to be rather fancily termed 'modernity'. Several chapters in this volume explore highly contemporaneous ideas and dilemmas of belonging, while looking at the mutual processes of definition and appropriation which take place between what could be termed local and global settings. Yet, what is apparent here is that these concepts are highly malleable and cross over boundaries of mere territorial definition. Ultimately, the phenomenology of belonging, and of experiencing territorial affiliation – whether couched within an actual, material landscape or the memory of a place that never was or disappeared – may hopefully transport us beyond the bounded territories of both localities and theoretical analysis.

Acknowledgement

* I am grateful to David Parkin and Kent Maynard for their comments on this introduction.

Notes

1   Was this druidess fully aware of the dual connotations ascribed to the term? It obviously connotes a spiritual alienation, but the Marxist undertones cannot easily be ignored.

2   The Archbishop of Canterbury made an official visit to Rwanda a few years ago, when the conflict between Hutu and Tutsi was at its peak. Having visited a church where several hundred people had been massacred a few days earlier, he commented to the British press that such atrocities were attributable to the merely 'skin-deep' penetration of Christianity in Africa.

3   The original panel on 'Locality and Belonging' at the European Association of Social Anthropologists' conference in Barcelona in July 1996 included a contribution by Dan Rabinowitz from the Hebrew University of Jerusalem entitled 'Belonging to the Place that Disappeared: Zionist Settlers and Dispossessed Bedouins re-imagining the Hula Lake in Galilee'. This contribution could unfortunately not be included in the present volume, but would have added another excellent focus to this particular topic.

4   These ideas did not, of course, originate with Lévi-Strauss. They all feature strongly in seventeenth-century imagery of the taming of nature and in Descartes' discourse on body and mind.

5   Descola's text here shifts between using terms such as nature, environment and non-human domains as interchangeable idioms.

6   These distinctions become obsolete since no 'raw' state of nature is conceivable outside of the human mind.

7   The same theme reappears in the unfolding of events in Bordeaux in 1997, in the wake of Papon's trial for crimes against humanity during the Vichy collaborationist regime. Meriadeck, an 'open ghetto' in the centre of Bordeaux, is today described by survivors of the war as the epitome of cross-cultural solidarity, and the memory of belonging to this 'quartier', long ago razed to the ground, still evokes and echoes the diversity of cultural traditions (from displaced and deprived north Africans to persecuted Jews and working-class French people) and overbridging collective loyalties (*Le Monde*, Sunday 3 November 1997).

8   The reading of history into oral tradition lies outside the scope of this volume. Suffice it to say that the significance of narratives and other forms of oral tradition and their 'translation' into an understanding of historical processes in non-literate contexts (rather than societies) is highly controversial. Since an absolute chronology of events can never be established, other ways of codifying and decoding 'other' histories have been employed. The structuralist preference for viewing oral traditions simply as myths, reflecting the human mind's capacity for the classification of time and space, tends towards a unification of other people's histories, thereby circumventing the question of objectivity or truth of other peoples' past and history. While attempting to provide a more composite interpretation of oral tradition which extends beyond mythification – and mystification – the reading of oral traditions as texts equivalent to those of literate traditions presents other difficulties, as the textuality and contextuality of memory of the past fundamentally differs from that of historical written texts (for a critique, see Fentress and Wickham 1994). To juxtapose memory and text presents some

obvious difficulties, since text tends to presuppose (or at least rearrange events according to) an ordered chronology, whereas memory provides a synchronic and more jumbled recollection of events in time and space.

References

Ames, M.M. (1992) *Cannibal Tours and Glass Boxes: The Anthropology of Museums*, Vancouver: UBC Press.

Appadurai, A. (1986) 'Commodities and the Politics of Value', in A. Appadurai (ed.), *The Social Life of Things: Commodities in Cultural Perspective*, Cambridge and New York: Cambridge University Press.

—— (1988) 'Theory in Anthropology: Center and Periphery', *Comparative Studies in Society and History* 28, 1: 356–61.

—— (1991) 'Global Ethnoscapes: Notes and Queries for a Transnational Anthropology', in R.G. Fox (ed.), *Recapturing Anthropology: Working in the Present*, Santa Fe, NM: School of American Research Press.

—— (1995) 'The Production of Locality', in R. Fardon (ed.), *Counterworks: Managing the Diversity of Knowledge*, London and New York: Routledge.

Bahloul, J. (1996) *The Architecture of Memory: A Jewish-Muslim Household in Colonial Algeria 1937–1962*, Cambridge and New York: Cambridge University Press.

Bender, B. (ed.) (1993) *Landscape: Politics and Perspectives*, Oxford: Berg.

Bhabha, H.K. (1994) *The Location of Culture*, London and New York: Routledge.

Bond, G.C. and Gilliam, A. (1994) 'Introduction', in G.C. Bond and A. Gilliam (eds), *Social Construction of the Past: Representation as Power*, London and New York: Routledge.

Clifford, J. (1997) *Routes: Travel and Translation in the Late Twentieth Century*, Cambridge, MA and London: Harvard University Press.

Connerton, P. (1989) *How Societies Remember*, Cambridge and New York: Cambridge University Press.

Descola, P. (1992) 'Societies of Nature and the Nature of Society', in A. Kuper (ed.), *Conceptualizing Society*, London and New York: Routledge.

—— (1994) *In the Society of Nature: A Native Ecology in Amazonia*, Cambridge: Cambridge University Press.

—— (1996) 'Constructing Natures: Symbolic Ecology and Social Practice', in P. Descola and G. Pálsson (eds), *Nature and Society: Anthropological Perspectives*, London and New York: Routledge.

Descola, P. and Pálsson, G. (1996) 'Introduction', in P. Descola and G. Pálsson (eds), *Nature and Society: Anthropological Constructions*, London and New York: Routledge.

Douglas, M. (1966) *Purity and Danger: An Analysis of Concepts of Pollution and Taboo*, London: Routledge & Kegan Paul.

—— (1975) *Implicit Meanings: Essays in Anthropology*, London: Routledge & Kegan Paul.

Fabian, J. (1983) *Time and the Other: How Anthropology Makes its Object*, New York: Columbia University Press.

Fardon, R. (ed.), (1990) *Localising Strategies: The Regionalisation of Ethnographic Accounts*, Washington, DC: Smithsonian Institution Press.

Fentress, J. and Wickham, C. (1994 [1992]) *Social Memory: New Perspectives on the Past*, Oxford: Blackwell.

Fog Olwig, K. and Hastrup, K. (1997) 'Introduction', in *Siting Culture: The Shifting Anthropological Object*, London and New York: Routledge.

Guardian, 'Pagans Gather for the Solstice', Friday 20 June 1997.

Gupta, A. and Ferguson, J. (1997) 'Introduction', in *Anthropological Locations: Boundaries and Grounds for a Field Science*, Berkeley, CA: University of California Press.

Hirsch, E. (1995) 'Introduction', in E. Hirsch and M. O'Hanlon (eds) *The Anthropology of Landscape: Between Place and Space*, Oxford: Oxford University Press.

Independent, 'Head-Hunting Returns to the Jungles of Borneo', Monday 9 June 1997.

Jackson, M. (1996) 'Introduction', in M. Jackson (ed.) *Things as They Are: New Directions in Phenomenological Anthropology*, Bloomington, IN: Indiana University Press.

Jeune Afrique, issue 1899, 28 May–3 June 1997.

Lefèbvre, H. (1974) *La Production de l'Espace*, Paris: Editions Anthropos.

Lyon, M.L. and Barbalet, J.M. (1994) 'Society's Body: Emotion and the Somatisation of Social Theory', in T. Csordas (ed.), *Embodiment and Experience: The Existential Ground of Culture and Self*, Cambridge: Cambridge University Press.

Nerlich, G. (1994) *The Shape of Space*, Cambridge and New York: Cambridge University Press.

Observer, 'Che Comes Home as King of Kitsch', Sunday October 12 1997.

Schama, S. (1995) *Landscape and Memory*, London: HarperCollins Publishers.

Stocking, G.W. (1985) 'Introduction', in G.W. Stocking (ed.), *Objects and Others: Essays on Museums and Material Culture*, Madison, WI: The University of Wisconsin Press.

Taussig, M. (1997) *The Magic of the State*, New York and London: Routledge.

The Times, 'First Their Children were Stolen . . . Now their Land Too? An Open Letter to her Majesty Queen Elizabeth II Queen of Australia', Thursday 19 June 1997.

—— 'Chief Returns to His beloved Black Hills', Friday 26 September 1997.

Thomas, N. (1991) *Entangled Objects: Exchange, Material Culture and Colonialism in the Pacific*, Cambridge, MA and London: Harvard University Press.

Tilley, C. (ed.) (1994) *A Phenomenology of Landscape: Places, Paths and Monuments*, Oxford and Providence, RI: Berg.

Toren, C. (1995) 'Seeing the Ancestral Sites: Transformations in Fijian Notions of the Land', in E. Hirsch and M. O'Hanlon (eds), *The Anthropology of Landscape: Between Space and Place*, Oxford: Oxford University Press.

Vansina, J. (1985) *Oral Tradition as History*, London: James Currey.

—— (1994) *Living with Africa*, Madison, WI: The University of Wisconsin Press.

Chapter 1

The rootedness of trees

Place as cultural and natural texture in rural southwest Congo[*]

Filip De Boeck

Introduction

This chapter analyses notions of place (as localised space), ancestral space-time, history and remembrance as revealed in, and through, the tree symbolism of the ancestral *miyoomb* shrines among the aLuund of southwestern Congo (ex-Zaire). Victor Turner, in a brief sentence in *The Forest of Symbols*, describes how, among the Luunda-related Ndembu of former Northern Rhodesia, the *miyoomb* trees (singular *muyoomb*) are 'planted as *living shrines* in the centre of villages' (Turner 1967: 10; my emphasis). I will elaborate on this intriguing and enigmatic notion of 'living shrine' to investigate the Luunda sense of place. More generally, I will look at the relation between trees, notions of rootedness and (male) personhood, and the way in which these give rise to a sense of place, in which both history and ancestrality are spatialised and incorporated. As such, the concern here is not with locality, and its loss of ontological moorings, in the context of processes of globalisation or destabilisation of the nation-state (Appadurai 1995; De Boeck 1996), but rather with a more traditional anthropological preoccupation, namely the 'production' of social space and, through it, the (re)production of society and its history.

What turns a space into a place for the aLuund of southwestern Congo is, literally, its rootedness in the past and its capacity to constitute, and conjure up, a *living* spatialised memory and link between past and present. Among the aLuund, the (image of the) tree and, by extension, the land, becomes the means by which one's place in the social landscape is 'rooted' in a material historicity and in an ancestral space-time. The tree and, in particular, the *muyoomb* tree, seems to be one of the aLuund's preferred means for the production of historically situated locality. Trees convey a meaning of rootedness, of immobility. The tree simultaneously conveys the idea of a central nexus, combining notions of immobility with images of interconnection, knotting and hence mobility (as spatialised in the pathways leading into and away from each village). Therefore, in a seeming paradox, the Luunda notion of 'place' (*pool*), although drawing on a pool of meaning related to rootedness, fixity, tying and knotting, allows for movement through space, as the centuries-long Luunda history of migration and conquest exemplifies. Although place, and a sense of locality and belonging, are strongly situated in socially and spatially defined communities, they are also in a sense transportable and repetitive. As such, locality can be moved through space, recreated or repeated in different spaces, by planting new trees and thus creating or 'growing' memory, history and belonging. Physical and metaphorical roots can thus emerge out of any social and material landscape, thereby allowing the transformation of forest into village, turning the subjects of newly conquered, dominated space into localised (i.e. Luunda) subjects, and rooting the present place into the ancestral past while tying it to Luunda history. However, the image of the tree also suggests that the production of culture and history are underpinned by a history of natural rhythm and processes of gestation, germination and growth. The interpretation of the production of Luunda locality as a practice of birth-giving, or 'world-making', informed by the cyclical rhythms of the natural world, has certain implications for our understanding of the relationship between nature and societal production.

Situating the Luunda world

The village of Nzofu forms the traditional political centre of the Mabeet, the land of the western aLuund, situated in the southwestern corner of Congo's Bandundu province (Kwaango sub-region). Luunda-land forms a major part of the administrative zone of Kahemba, an area of some 20,000 square kilometres. The village of Nzofu – which with its two hundred inhabitants is one of the largest villages in the Mabeet – is considered the 'royal' village (*musuumb*) where the Kwaango's paramount Luunda title-holder holds his court. The royal court is called the 'knot' (*mpuund*), the central nodal point of a wide-ranging network that connects the numerous small villages and hamlets that lie dispersed in a glowing landscape of endless hills and valleys, an ecologically varied habitat characterised by a mixed vegetation of savannah, bush, flood plains and large stretches of gallery forest.

The Luunda social system is characterised by matrilineal descent and viri- or patrilocal residence. As aLuund say: 'the husband builds the house, the woman gives birth to the children'. The father and his brothers play an important role in daily life. In the residential household unit, 'one leans towards one's father'. The agnatic household, referred to as 'fireplace' (*jiikw*), is thus headed by an 'elder of the fireplace' who may be either a male ego's (classificatory) father or older brother. It is he who represents the social unity of the residential unit, which also consists of his wife or, in the case of a polygamous household, co-wives (usually two to three) and their children. They may also be joined on a more temporary basis by some of the family head's unmarried sisters, sisters' children, (unmarried) younger brothers, some of his wives' younger sisters and some of his grandchildren.

Lineage membership, however, is predominantly reckoned in the mother's matriline through a common female ancestor, who is seen as a source of female regenerative powers. A number of related residential 'fireplaces', which are scattered over several villages, constitute a lineage or 'womb' (*vumw*), headed by an 'elder of the womb' who is normally one of ego's mother's brothers.

Both the father and the maternal uncle thus play a constitutive role in ego's life. Both are referred to as 'guardians of the herds'. Both intervene on one's behalf as representatives in disputes, ritual practices, therapeutic interventions, divinatory consultations and in the most important moments of one's life-cycle: birth, ritual initiation, marriage, pregnancy and death. To be a *naantany*, someone without an elder to take care of you, is to have 'no *place* to go to'. Such a person is compared to a goat, for goats do not have a herdsman, nor a place to which to belong.

The poetics of Luunda politics

The role of the Kwaango's Luunda paramount title-holder is marked by the dual (masculine and feminine) entities of opposing complementarity that are at play in Luunda society at large. The paramount title-holder of the Nzav lineage is believed to be a direct descendant of the *mwaant yaav*'s royal dynasty of the Ruund homeland (*kool*) in the east (in Kapanga, Shaba province). Some three centuries ago Nzav and his followers started to migrate 'downstream', westward towards the Kwaango. Other Luunda groups migrated to the east and the south.

The paramount stands at the apex of a pyramidal political structure. In his capacity of sovereign lord (*mwaant mwiin mangaand*), he rules over a large geographical and political unit (*ngaand*). Although Nzav is identified with the land of the *ngaand*, he does not own it. In his capacity of political overlord, the paramount title-holder allocates large parts of the *ngaand* to the sub-regional title-holders (*ayilool*), who represent him one level downwards. All these major titles (as well as those of the numerous minor local title-holders) are distributed according to a system of perpetual kinship and positional succession (Cunnison 1956). In this way, the use of land and political administration are linked to perpetual titles that are defined in terms of real, putative or fictive consanguinity, and that strengthen the typical Luunda tributary network (Bustin 1975). This serves to incorporate the various layers of the smaller segmentary authority structures into one integrated whole.

The politico-cosmological imagery which metaphorically associates the paramount title-holder to the sun, the rainbow, the flash of lightning or the rain pouring down, illustrates how the social and political organisation of the *ngaand* is converted into more vertical and hierarchical relations on the level of the *mwaant mwiin mangaand*.[1] As a sovereign ruler, Nzav represents these hierarchical structures of social organisation, vertical and linear public order and social control. He embodies the mythical ancestral order (*wiinshaankulw*) which precedes the origin of society, but he is also the source of this social order and of cultural, ritual, and political Luunda institutions.

Yet, the nature of the paramount title-holder's rule is twofold. No distinction is made between *dominium* and *imperium* (Crine 1964), that is, between chiefs and landowners. Instead, Nzav unites the function of sovereign ruler and paramount political territorial chief (*mwiin mangaand*) with that of *mwiin mavw*, a title that refers to his personal identification with, rather than his ownership of, the land.

In his capacity of 'lord of the soil' Nzav assumes the responsibility for fertility and fecundity, social and biological reproduction, and the material welfare of the community as a whole. In this capacity, the office and function of the paramount title-holder is marked by a regenerative and mediating characteristic. The paramount thus combines typically agnatic and vertical/linear, political, principles with uterine and more cyclical ones. The royal body politic embodies a continuous attempt to integrate these convergent and divergent forces.

The *muyoomb* tree

As father and mother (or mother's brother, 'mother without breasts') to the subjects of his territory, Nzav will invoke the royal ancestors, represented by his *miyoomb* trees (*Amnacardiaceae*, *Lennea antiscorbutica* or *L. welwichii*) at the royal courtyard's entrance, for matters that regard his own lineage. He will also address the ancestral trees in matters that transcend the interests of the royal lineage proper to ensure, for example, the well-being of all the commoners in the *ngaand*, to welcome newcomers and bestow an ancestral blessing upon them, and to enhance social and natural reproduction and fertility (such as, for instance, before the start of a new agricultural cycle and the preparation of new fields in the *ngaand*, before the caterpillar harvest or a major collective hunt, on the occasion of a sub-regional title-holder's enthronement or death, or in times of hunger). On each of these occasions, the title-holder, assisted by senior court members, will recite a royal charter or genealogy, relating the migration from the Luunda homeland (*kool*), and the battles and events that marked each title-holder's rule. This discourse is rooted in a memory characterised by a linear, diachronic and historical conception of time.

All major or minor political title-holders possess their *miyoomb* trees too, planted in front of their houses after the construction of a new village or following their own enthronement. The health and life of the tree(s) as 'living shrines' is indicative of the elder's authority and wisdom, and thus of the health of the village (or the *ngaand*) as a whole.

In the paramount title-holder's case, two groups of trees are planted in two separate enclosures, one to the right of the courtyard's entrance, representing deceased patrilateral male kin of the title-holder, and a second to the left representing his matrilateral male kin. While planting the trees immediately after his enthronement, the title-holder invokes the ancestors and asks for the protection and the prosperity of the village or the *ngaand*.[2]

Representational space: emplacement between the boundaries of body and landscape

For aLuund, place is the space where agnatic and uterine qualities – verticality and cyclicity – conjoin, and where the natural and cultural orders of things (*nshiku*) converge. In order to promote our understanding of local concepts of 'place' and identity, and of the tree symbolism which is used in *miyoomb* shrines to express these, it is necessary to present an ethnography of Luunda representational space. How does Luunda society generate its social space and time, referred to here as its representational space (body, house, village, land, graveyard and so on)? How does emplacement occur between the boundaries of body and landscape, and how does this representational space tie in with a representation of space, time and a notion of place?

This section reviews the structuration of the various spaces that constitute the environmental horizon of experience and the daily life-scene for the aLuund, by focusing on the quotidian activities that take place in each of these spaces. It highlights the spatial and temporal relations of contrast and complementarity, and shows how they underpin the social organisation of the Luunda community, and its relation to the natural world. Basic to these sets of complementary oppositions is the masculine/feminine polarity. The physical facts of the human body, and the corporeal praxis of the male and female body-self, signify and convey their own structuring logic onto the aLuund's social and natural worlds, the architecture of which, in turn, produces living bodies.

The dual sets of spatio-temporal relationships are combined into social relationships, for example through related series of complementary oppositions between public and private, or individual and collective. As such, the aLuund's experience of their daily environment is rendered by means of metaphorical–metonymical processes that combine and shift between the complementary attributes of sense (visual, tactile, olfactory), gender and orientation (east, west; right, left). These inform the perception and structuration of the different spaces that constitute the village and its surroundings, and link these to cosmological time-space and historical narrative. They also pattern the various social activities and the gendered labour divisions in each of these spatial units.

Space, as it is lived, experienced and organised by aLuund, is a topological space, combining what Lefèbvre (1991: 164) has called isotopias, heterotopias and utopias (analogous places, contrasting places, and places for what has no place which, in the Luunda case, refer above all to the omnipresent rhythms of life-force) into one projective space in which different social spaces interpenetrate and superimpose themselves onto one another. Taken as a whole, this topological space forms the expression of the way in which the aLuund perceive and live their own body, their social relations, their history and their relation to the surrounding environment and cosmos.

It is in, and through, the body that space is perceived, lived and produced. On the day of the coming out ritual which ends a long period of seclusion in the boys' circumcision camp (*mukaand*), the novices sing: 'Oh mother, Foot gets lost in the surrounding world. Foot rejoices. It looks at the world and how it wakes up. Foot looks at the world awakening. Oh foot!'. According to the aLuund, your feet provide you with the joy of discovering the world which, as we shall see, in itself constitutes an image and a living reflection of one's corporeality. The joy of discovery is above all of a practical, rather than aesthetic, nature. The Luunda sense of the natural environment is firmly anchored in the necessities of daily life. In this sense, people stand in a very pragmatic relation to their natural environment. Yet, the characteristics of this environment simultaneously provide a constant reminder of one's own place in the world. They are a tangible comment on one's own insertion into the natural flow of time, of one's own life-cycle, one's relationship with past and future generations, and one's place in the village community. Relationships with the surrounding world are basically characterised by a doxic, taken-for-granted sense of oneness, 'at homeness', and rootedness in the here and now, constituted by complex links which connect the here and now to a historical, ancestral and mythical space-time.

The cradle of Luunda culture (*kool*) in Shaba, is situated in the east and is considered by the aLuund to be a geographically higher point. It is there, in an eastern or upstream direction, that the source of the (male) cultural order springs. It is in the east that the sun comes up (-*vuumbuk*: 'to grow', 'to come out of the ground', 'to resurrect') and 'the world awakens'. Therefore, enthronement rituals will always spatially unfold from east to west, in a cosmogonic enactment of the migration movement from *kool*, situated at the headwaters, downstream to the west, to the land the aLuund of the Mabeet presently occupy. The waterflow from east to west also represents the course of masculine life-flow, which springs in the east.

When the sun disappears, in the evening, in the west, it goes to the underworld, *kaluung*, the site of death. Significantly, the west is also referred to as *kuchitookil*, the place where one is 'made white' (-*took*), that is, where one meets the dead. Within the context of circumcision, for example, the western end of the circumcision lodge is called *kwifiil*, 'towards the place of death'. When the setting sun slowly sinks into the underworld, its last red glow against the sky is spoken of as the 'fire of the dead', at which the latter warm themselves. As in other savannah cultures, it is said that in the underworld at night, the sun follows a subterranean river which carries it back to the east, to appear again at the source of the river in the morning.

The life-giving connotations attributed to the upstream direction are reversed for the downstream orientation. In Luunda mourning songs, downstream is invariably associated with sterility, barrenness and death. At ritual purifications, water pacifies and purifies because it carries pollution, illness, misfortune, conflicts and death downstream.

The waterflow from east to west, from upstream to downstream and from day to night is a powerful image of the flow of life, and of the life-cycle, situated between birth and death. To dream of quickly fleeting water is considered a bad omen, for it indicates a short life-span. The crossing of the river is as the crossing of the life-stream. The river forms the frontier, or limit, between this world and the afterlife, and the notion of the underworld is often linked to that of the river (*nzadi ni kaluung*).

The vertical spatial axis is linked to a second, horizontal pole that connects the east/west, and upstream/downstream, directional points (with their associations with beginning/end, or life/death), to other oppositions informed by the human body, such as the contrast between *right* and *left*. I have mentioned that the ancestral *miyoomb* trees to the right of the entrance represent the paternal side, those at the left the maternal side. The right hand is referred to as the 'hand of the father', and denotes masculinity, authority and fatherhood. As such, the right is also associated with the east/high, with a life-giving principle, with the sun and the day. The left hand is called the 'hand of the mother', and denotes femininity, docility and motherhood. Left is also associated with the west/low, with death, the moon and the night. The microcosm of the human body is expanded to structure the space of the macrocosm: aLuund will always point towards the east with their right hand, and to the west with their left hand. In daily life, the right hand is the predominant one: it is the 'hand for eating', for giving things to others, and connotes positive actions. The left, female or maternal side has much more ambivalent connotations.[3] This ambivalence of the female polarity is further strengthened by its characteristic cyclicity. Given the female connotations of the west/downstream, the water-flow (through its association with the 'underworld') is also equated with the womb, with birth-giving and female fecundity through its cyclical movement, which includes a return into the night, and the association with the lunar. The river links life to death, and the place of the underworld in which the river disappears is, like the womb, the hidden and unknown place where life is processed anew. In more than one instance, birth and death are inextricably linked to one another as two opposing poles, nevertheless united through a cyclical movement symbolised by the maternal womb. The river as linear metaphor of (male) beginning contrasts with the more cyclical metaphor of the river/underworld as womb, which mediates between life and death, like the sun which 'dies' in the west only to be reborn again in the east. It is important to note, however, that the river's water-flow expresses the spatio-temporal notion that the vital life-flow (*mooy*) and cosmic rhythm, constituted of male/eastern/upstream beginning, and female/western/downstream recycling, is neither male nor female, but both.

The spatial lay-out of the royal village, and the male and female activities that take place in it, conform with this basic east–west axis. The western edge is referred to as the downstream part, whereas the eastern part is called *kwimpat*, 'up there' or 'in front'. *Mpat* (or *ngoong*) also denotes the bush or the savannah. As such, the bush, which includes the wooded savannah (*matuumb*), differs from the *mihat*, the stretches of land (fields and hunting grounds) that fall under the authority of a lineage, a village or a title-holder.

The bush is thus conceived of as 'the place where the sun rises', a space that is located higher than the village (*ul*) or communal space, denoted by the crucial notion of *pool*, which I would translate as 'yard'. *Pool aap* is the space around a habitation, the village, a courtyard; *-y pool* means 'to go home'. *Aap* is a locative 'here', as opposed to the 'there' of the bush, whereas the word *pool* is etymologically related to *kool*, the primal beginning of Luunda culture in the east. Yet the 'higher' location of the bush also means that the space of the bush stands closer to the origin of societal life. The bush is, indeed, a space that has been there from the beginning. In a way, the bush points back to a mythical ancestral time prior to the origin of society. It is also the source of this social order, of cultural, ritual and political Luunda institutions. 'High' and 'east' point to this ancestral space-time. The 'high' space-time of the bush refers to a spatial and temporal continuity with society's founding ancestors. Therefore the bush will also be the place of burial. The village burial place itself is usually situated to the west of the village (i.e. in the downstream direction of the underworld). Graves are always oriented along an east–west axis. The body is invariably buried with the crown of the head facing west so that the deceased can look at the rising sun in the east.

The 'high space-time' of the bush thus takes one back to a primal order which in a sense exists prior to, and yet is the source of, Luunda culture. As such, the bush as 'high' space also points to a historical continuum, to Luunda origin, to processes of migration, to earlier dwelling places and to the now deserted sites where the ancestors built their villages, recognisable by the remaining palm trees. As such the traces of previous generations are grafted, or rather, planted and rooted into the bush space.

Most importantly, this complex spatio-temporal continuity is also conveyed by the notion of *ku mashin*, 'to the base or trunks of the trees', which refers to the bush but also to the 'origin' or the 'source of things'

(-*chishin*). This tree metaphor will be discussed in more detail later; suffice it to mention that the roots and the trunk are a tree's male parts, representing male fecundity, rooted in and springing from the ancestral past. As such, the bush is a predominantly male space, where most of the men's hunting also takes place. A culturally highly valued occupation, hunting continues to define the main mode of existence for many Luunda men.

Whereas the bush is a 'higher' space with many masculine connotations, the forest (*tikit*) is a feminine, 'lower' place, both geographically and symbolically. In the Mabeet, the forest only grows in the valleys, in relatively small stretches alongside the rivers. The river as life-flow mediates between, and unites, the high/male space of the bush and the low/female space of the gallery forest (see Turner 1969: 58ff on similar male and female connotations of bush and forest among the Ndembu). Every day, women fetch water, wash clothes or soak manioc roots. Women also work the fields, which are predominantly located in the forest, because the soil is more fertile and crops grow much better there than in the bush.

The field forms part of the 'warehouse' which is the forest, and the forest as female and nutritional space is compared to a mother's womb. Similarly, numerous proverbs and sayings compare the female genitalia to a field, to be cleared by the men's 'machete'.

The space of the forest carries other connotations too: it is a space that negatively mirrors the world of the village and, again, expresses the more ambivalent connotations of the feminine world. Because of its 'low' and 'downstream' figurations, the forest is also associated with ominous death and rotting, with the qualities of the night, the untamed, the chaotic and the disruptive. At the installation of a local title-holder, for instance, he is publicly told by his fellow-villagers 'not to turn his eyes to the forest, but watch over the villagers instead'. Whereas the bush is to some extent a pre-cultural space, the forest retains qualities of the sub-cultural and, as such, is opposed to the social space of the village.

It is within the village's communal life and space (*pool*) that a muLuund feels at home and safe, 'like the bird *kasakal* (African or yellow-vented bulbul) in its nest'. The village itself consists of a varying number of autonomous residential family units or 'fireplaces' (*majiikw*, singular *jiikw*), which constitute a shelter and a place of security and solidarity for its members. For children and youngsters, the *jiikw* is the space and horizon of their socialisation. It is a place of support and solidarity, defined by differential reciprocal relations that crystallise most clearly in the space of the house, which may also be referred to as 'fire' (*kasw*) and which is an intimate space defined by relationships of commensality, conjugal sexuality, and reciprocal bodily intimacy and physical contact.

The intimacy of the household unit and the various activities which take place in it, such as cooking, are conceived as analogous with the corporeal processes inherent to the female body. Indeed, the house itself is conceived of in terms that are also used in relation to the maternal body, and the uterus in particular. The house's inner space (*muunz*), which mirrors the intimacy and warmth of a mother's womb, is also a space where familiarity and mutual support between 'those from the same womb' (i.e. those from the same matrilineal descent group) are established. This support is expressed in terms of physical closeness and bodily intimacy, such as 'touching', 'holding' or 'leaning upon each other', or 'stepping in each other's footsteps'.

The house as womb and life-giving space is also the scene of legitimate conjugal sexuality. It is the place where husband and wife meet and 'look each other in the eye' or 'intertwine legs', to use two Luunda euphemisms for sexual intercourse. It is a feeling of 'pudeur' and 'potential shame' (Riesman 1977: 136), referred to as *nsany*, that confines the intimacy of conjugal life to the nocturnal privacy of the household. It is only under the roof of the house, significantly called 'the shame of the house' (*nsany di chikuumbw*), that the bodies of husband and wife may 'merge into one another'. Conjugal sexuality is referred to as 'to be knotted into one another'. It ties together and interlinks husband and wife in a life-giving bond which is the opposite of the disintegrative, life-taking 'knotting' of sorcery (just as the husband 'eating' his wife is the opposite of the sorcerer 'eating' his victim).

Idioms of nurturing, eating and heating are used to express and define, within the space of the household, bonds of commensality, (physical) reciprocity, solidarity and conjugal sexuality, which are a prerequisite for and make possible the transmission of life. In this way, the interplay of metaphorical associations and transformations that draw on the domains of food production, cooking, feeding, gestation and birth-giving signify the women's most essential contribution in the process of life transmission. Luunda notions of female personhood, body and self, which usually focus on the heart, the abdomen and the belly or womb, highlight a woman's role as genitrix, mother, cultivator and cook, as having 'two arms and a vagina'. All of these roles are marked by essentially relational capacities. Through the food they produce and prepare, through their bodies and the process of 'being with two bodies' during pregnancy, through the space of the house as a social extension of the female womb, through their own spatial movement from the group of bride-givers to bride-takers, women create strongly physical and social ties between consanguines and affines, and interlink and mediate between the sexes, between agnatic and uterine, between living and dying or giving and taking. As such, women compare themselves to a needle, 'repairing' or 'sewing' (-teend, a verb which also means 'to nurture' or 'to raise') the social network.

The intimacy between people within the household is in marked contrast with the distant and detached attitude that characterises the relationship between husbands and wives and, more generally, between all men and women in the public domain. The public gender segregation is reflected in the division of labour and other strongly gendered public activities, and in the social topography.

To a large extent, women meet one another at the periphery or outside of the village and the public sphere of male influence and social control: at the river, at the pond where the cassava roots are soaked, or in the forest fields, all of them elementary (low) domains of female subsistence activities, overlooked by the (high) village, constructed on the hilltop. Within the village, the contacts between women generally take place within the defined boundaries of the household, usually at the back of the house, an exclusively female domain where children gather, women sit, food is prepared, firewood is stored and manioc or groundnuts are dried in the sun. The mortar and the sieve for preparing manioc – implements which, like the hoe, frequently recur as important constituents of female fertility within a ritual context – are also kept at the back of the house, in the area where the women pound the manioc roots into flour (twiil).

A man's social contacts, on the other hand, are much wider. They take place at the level of the village, and also include translineage contacts. Unlike female social meetings, these contacts take place almost exclusively within the space of the village, in front of the house or at a central meeting point in the village, in the men's parlour hut (choot). The front of the house is a predominantly masculine space, delineated and reaffirmed every day when the family head sweeps his courtyard in the morning. It is also at the front of the house that visitors are welcomed, news exchanged and household problems solved by the men of the unit. At the choot, men from different residential units meet and discuss their daily affairs, or hold councils and palavers. These male-dominated discussions and meetings are frequently followed from afar by the women, but only rarely do they publicly join their husbands, fathers or uncles in these conversations.[4]

During the daytime and in public, the interaction between the gender categories is thus defined in terms of male authority and social control. Through an elaborate behavioural pattern of avoidance and submission, women learn to show respect, obedience and subordination towards their husbands, fathers, brothers and elders in the public domain. The mixture of respect, subservience, distance and public embarrassment that characterises the attitude between the sexes, and especially of women towards men, is strongest between those whose relationship is defined in terms of sexuality and (possible) motherhood or fatherhood, those who are physically and emotionally the most intimately related and united. As genitors and social reproducers, childbearing women are perceived as having an accessible or 'open' body (or, metaphorically, an 'open' house or 'open' field). Through avoidance, submission and the behaviour of 'potential shame' related to the notion of *nsany*, with its confining connotations, such women close and cover up their 'open-ness'. By contrast, post-menopausal women, 'who have come at the end of birth-giving', are perceived as bodily 'closed' or 'plugged', which allows them to open up at the social level and structurally become more like men. This shift in status is spatially translated in these women's progressive movement from the back to the front of the house, where they will occasionally join in the men's conversations.

The representation of space: the archi-texture of Luunda lived worlds

How does the 'Luunda' structuring of space, their production of *representational* space (in terms of centre/periphery; right/left; up/down; high/low; front/back) connect to a more general *representation of space*? In other words, how does the Luunda production of space and place integrate such structures – or, to use a Luunda metaphor, knot or weave them – into a wider variety of wholes or, to borrow a notion from Lefèbvre, 'textures'? How does the Luunda socio-cultural and political architecture become an 'archi-texture'? As Lefèbvre states:

> A texture implies a meaning . . . for someone who lives and acts in the space under consideration, a subject with a body – or, some-times, a 'collective' subject. From the point of view of such a 'subject' the development of forms and structures corresponds to functions of the whole. Blanks (i.e. the contrast between absence and presence) and margins, hence networks and webs, have a *lived* sense which has to be raised intact to the *conceptual* level.
>
> (Lefèbvre 1991: 132, original emphasis)

With regard to the Luunda, Lefèbvre's notion of 'texture' is a rather fertile one as it coincides with the aLuund's own conceptualisation and experience of their lived space. This Luunda notion and practice of texture, of weaving, knotting or interrelating (between individual bodies, the social body, the natural environment and cosmology) is itself connected, amongst other things, to the central image of the tree. In order to illustrate this, we have to turn to Luunda notions of male elder-hood.

The immobility of elders and trees

Luunda men view the ideal male body and self as a self-contained, autonomous entity. This ideal is embodied by the senior man, the elder, the family or lineage head and, in the most exemplary way, by the paramount. In growing towards the status of senior elder, a man 'becomes a person' (*-b muntw*), a socially important individual who knows how to assume his responsibilities. A 'true person' or a 'true man' is someone who is courageous, firm and brave, who has self-restraint and shows perseverance, strong will, character and a sense of responsibility.

The progressive appropriation of 'personality' (*wuuntw*), again metaphorically expressed through cosmological images of verticality and 'uprightness' (*nteendeend*), implies an increasing bodily erectness, strength, autonomy and containment, and sets a man apart from others. A man is characterised by his 'capacity to stand up', a notion that also implies moral uprightness, straightforwardness and physical hardness. A man has to be hard as a bullet (*nteend*). Male hardness is also expressed through the image of the tooth. It is said that 'ordinary men do not have teeth in their mouth', and that 'it is good to have teeth behind one's lips'. More specifically, teeth refer to a man's capacity for manipulating the word. All these male qualities are expressed by the encompassing notion of erectness (*maandaand*). To be a 'male' is to be a 'strong and erect person' (*muntw wa maandaand*), a characteristic that is displayed in the elders' *musaangw* sword dance, the stylised performance of the Luunda history of conquest, danced individually in a fierce and upright way.

The process of growing towards the status of senior man, and towards the acquiring of erectness, is paired with the appropriation of wisdom (*manaangw*). A process of learning is required to 'complete one's wisdom'. Mature adult men are said to have 'trapped' this wisdom (*-pit manaangw*), which is rooted in ancestral knowledge. Wisdom covers outstanding male capacities such as alertness, perspicacity, sagacity and judgment, firmness, discretion and foresight.

All these qualities find their ultimate expression in a man's oratory abilities, which are highly valued but difficult to attain. A true elder has the word of a responsible person. He is 'like a drum', and raises his voice to treat the problems of the family unit, the lineage or the village. To possess rhetoric ability and the quality of *chiyiil*, the skill to bring a palaver to a satisfactory conclusion, is both the privilege of the senior man and a prerogative for the full attainment of his status as elder. Speech is what sets one man apart from the others. Essentially, being a 'man' and a 'person' implies the capacity of conversing, making meaning, and 'causing the words to come out'. Through his speech, the elder is associated with beginning, the rising sun, the east, the ancestral source of wisdom.[5] In this respect, the verb *-teet*, which connotes female birth-giving, also relates to male speech. The verb *-teet* may refer to the peeling of groundnuts and beans, or the hatching of an egg, and thus also evokes the idea of parturition. In addition, it also refers to the cutting of the umbilical cord. The passage from life to death is equally denoted by this verb: a dying person 'cuts the vital life-flow' (*-teet/-kechun mooy*). In general, the verb is used in the sense of 'to chop', 'to cut' or 'to cleave', as for the cutting of wood. It is also used in the sense of cutting or slicing the knot of discontent in a palaver (*-teet muloong*), or 'giving birth' to a solution in a divinatory session (*-teet ngoomb*). In both these contexts *-teet* is also used in the sense of 'talking straight'. In this way, speech is a male equivalent of female processes of birth-giving. For a man to speak is to make or 'awaken the world', and give birth to solutions to dissolve conflicts and strengthen ties of solidarity and support. Especially with regard to divinatory discourse, the symbolic equivalences between the diviner's speech as a process of world-making, and corporeal processes of impregnation, gestation and parturition, clearly stand out (see De Boeck and Devisch 1994).

The progressive growth towards ancestral wisdom and gerontocratic authority, and the gradual appropriation of a meaningful social body as elder, implies an increasing sense of autonomy and containment, expressed in images of verticality. It also connotes a growing interconnection and interrelatedness with others, whether they be one's own family members, one's descent group or co-villagers. As he grows older, a man acquires more wives and children and engages in new relationships through his children's matrimonial alliances, and through his professional and ritual skills. A man's growth towards individuation and self-appropriation is thus achieved by means of a growing optimisation of his relational and intertwining social abilities.

Luunda conversational practice and use of formulaic greetings clearly express this verbal reciprocity. Conversations usually converge around a still centre, a central, 'tree-like' person, usually a family head or elder, who initiates the talking and to whom the 'words return' after each intervention. Performing the common gestures of greeting, this elder claps his hands twice, lowers the right hand to the ground, brings it to the left side of his chest and claps his hands again twice (thereby performatively expressing the significance of the notion of *mooy* as interconnection between right and left, male and female, and between living and ancestors), while inviting the interlocutor to 'sit straight' and voice his opinion or relate and 'put down' the news. On the second hand-clapping, the interlocutor joins in, claps his hands simultaneously with the first elder's hand-clapping, and then in turn repeats the same gestures of greeting after which he starts to talk, 'to finish the news together with the interlocutor'. When he has finished talking, he repeats the same gestures once again while uttering specific formulae 'to redirect' the words towards his interlocutor, 'to make the news enter' and 'give' or 'share' it with him. At the second hand-clapping, the person who directs the conversation joins in again and says: 'I take the news'. Thereupon, this central person invites a third party to relate his news or voice his opinion, while clapping his hands for the second time. In this way, the conversation moves in a circular manner, each time returning to a central 'tree-like' point, the elder, who bridges between the interlocutors and interconnects their words.

Colloquy and the exchange of news 'opens the village', which was previously 'closed'. Disputes 'make a wound in the village tree', causing the sap to flow away, that is, disrupting the village's unity. In the palaver, the council of elders reunites, through speech, what was separated. The weaving of words makes people 'talk to one another'. Significantly, the word *muloong* denotes both a palaver, and the spool or spindle of the weaving loom, which men use in the making of raffia tissue. The word *muloong* also means 'line' or 'row'. Just as the raffia fibres are connected and put in line by the act of weaving, so the words are ordered and 'knotted', or intertwined, into a sentence through speaking. Very often the speech of the elder, and especially the judge, is generated by means of the rhythmical hand-clapping of the other participants and onlookers in the palaver, indicating the rhythm and the duration of the speech. It is through this stimulating cadenza that the words are drawn out of the speaker's mouth and that arguments are structured and put in line. In this sense, the word of the elder and the judge is also a very physical word, which interlinks speaker and listener in a shared rhythm of 'birthing' as a male equivalent of female birth-giving. As such, the capacity to speak also implies the responsibility to make connections, to maintain the social tissue of the group's unity and to dissolve possible sources of conflict.

Although men's speech has a very outspoken combative quality (as the semantics of *-teend*, 'to quarrel' and 'to crow' reveal), the word of the elder reaffirms reciprocal relationships, expressed through images of growth and commensality (*-teend* also means 'to rear', 'to raise', 'to nurture'), implying the mutual 'opening up' of the body. Reconciliation (*-buluk*, 'to reconcile': see the related verb *-bulul*, 'to open up') takes place while drinking palm wine together, as a token of taking away the misunderstanding and as a means to re-establish mutual confidence. As the aLuund say: 'to sit together causes the frictions to disappear'. Even the quality of the wine a man offers to others during a palaver may be indicative of his positive or negative intentions, and of his will to bring the palaver to a good end. Someone who offers good palm wine will also bring 'good words' and 'wise', or 'upright', 'solid', and 'firm' language. A poor quality wine indicates poor, or 'twisted', directionless speech. The reference to palm wine again links male speech to gestation: palm wine and sperm are both referred to as 'white water', and just as sperm is heated in the womb to transform it into a child, so palm wine is made to boil (by women) before consumption (mostly by men).

A reciprocal relationship is established through speech, but also through a man's capacity to listen. Listening is a body-centred activity that highlights the essential qualities of male personhood, of which the head forms the corporeal locus. Male autonomy, expressed by images of verticality, is modulated through listening into a more horizontal and reciprocal relationship with others, as a prerequisite for talking. Speech, understanding, interpretation, and thus wisdom, can only be achieved through listening. The ears are therefore referred to as the 'lord of the head' (*mwaant wa mutw*). The dynamics of interlinked Luunda practices of listening and speaking convey a double movement which shapes and expresses the way in which aLuund 'knot' relations. The interiorising movement of listening is a withdrawal into oneself by means of a reception and integration of, and participation in, the world of others. The more ties a man has with the fellow members of the group for which he bears responsibility, the more his behaviour is characterised by this process of interiorisation (on similar notions of interiorising listening see Devisch 1991, 1993).

A man's growth towards self-containment (and full socialisation) is marked by his increasing immobility and internalisation, conveyed by the image of the tree. Gradually he becomes the fixed centre of the group for which he is responsible. As I have shown elsewhere, the paramount title-holder's immobility exemplifies this to the highest degree (De Boeck 1994). The elder stands in the middle of the relationships that are being knotted around him, and of which he becomes the constituting focal point and nexus. It is said of a family head that 'he sits in the middle', just as the king 'is in the middle of power', quite literally immobilised, 'rooted like a tree' in his court. Similarly, the family head or elder, seated in front of his house, is compared to a tree firmly rooted in the earth. Of a very old and shrivelled man it is said that he is as 'a tree which loses its sap and dies'. More generally, an elder may be referred to as *shin ikuny* or *shin dia mutoond*, 'root-man' or 'foot of the tree'. Continuity between the present cultural order and its primeval origin is conveyed by the notion *ku mashin*, 'to the base of the trees', while the related notion of *kwishin* (like *kool*) denotes a point of origin, a source. His increasing immobility thereby also serves to root a senior man in the ancestral past. As such, he is associated with the rise of the sun, the east, the beginning. As the elder becomes older, he approaches the apex of descent and is increasingly associated with the lineage's ancestors and ancestral wisdom.

The tree-like immobility of elders exemplifies the ideologically important 'unchanging continuity' of the societal order, against the transformations of society as it is lived in everyday life. This is also one of the meanings implied by the invocation to trees, whether it be the *muyoomb* or certain other trees: 'The tree has ears, children do not have ears' (see De Boeck 1994). Elders (trees) have the capacity to listen, acquired through immobility. As such, they assure the conjoining of the individual, social group and cosmos, and thereby maintain and perpetuate the ideal cultural order.[6]

To summarise, the central botanical metaphor of the tree highlights the metaphorical patterning of the male body. First of all, it combines the vertical imagery of erectness, hardness, stiffness and rootedness (through its manifold associations with the rising sun, the cock, the trap, the bow and other features) with the more horizontal imagery of interiorisation/exteriorisation, exemplified by the tree's 'listening' capacities which, metonymically, include a man's other properties such as 'hearing', 'seeing' or 'speaking'. The elder, through his identification with the tree and, more specifically, with its roots exemplifies ideal male life-transmitting powers rooted in and springing from the ancestral past, and rendered through the vertical, phallic imagery of the root,[7] the rising sun or the rain.[8]

The tree metaphor expresses masculinity and male life-giving powers, but also expands in various other directions, through pervasive metaphors of knotting, tying and intertwining. A whole series of Luunda 'knotting' structures of metaphorical directional movement weaves relationships between a fixed and immobile centre, and wider concentric circles of relatives, lineage members, villagers, affines, visitors, title-holders and strangers. Hence, for example, the reference to the royal village as a central 'knot' (*mpuund*) of a socio-political 'archi-texture', weaving relations between the villages of the *ngaand* and beyond and interconnecting them by means of an intricate network of pathways, could be likened to the 'tree-like' judge, sitting in the centre and weaving the words between various parties during the palaver.

The image of the tree, and the image of the elder as tree, both convey the deeply political identity of the aLuund as 'lords' (*amaant*). In this sense, the planting of the *miyoomb* as 'living' ancestral shrines is a deeply political act, comparable to the planting of the flag. It denotes the king's role as political *dominium*, the domination of space by means of war, armies, state-building and political power. The Luunda king as tree, as living shrine, is evidence of this dominated space. In addition, the dominant traditional political ideology is characterised by words and by speech in a strongly 'vertical' and public masculine discourse. This discourse is typified by a sequential, linear narrative trajectory; it is rooted in a memory typified by a diachronic and historical conception of time, as foregrounded in the royal charters and genealogies recited at the royal court.

The symbolism of the *muyoomb* tree is thus closely linked to concepts of elderhood and political power. This symbolism also conveys the title-holder's more cyclical, feminine and regenerative side, placing the king as ultimate tree or elder outside linear time, in a cyclical and euchronic time, a time out of time that is manifested in the ritual space-time as privileged reality for the unfolding and developing of inner growth and maturation. As a representation of the ancestors in the ancestral shrines, the *muyoomb* tree does much more than convey erect masculine power and sexual prowess. It also becomes a symbol of lineage continuity, and especially matrilineal descent, represented by the avunculate. Therefore, the *muyoomb* tree is said to have been 'planted' and transmitted by the maternal uncle who, as representative of the uterine location of the vital life-force, *mooy*, is commonly referred to as 'the guardian of the *muyoomb*'. 'To plant the *muyoomb* tree left by the mother's brother', or 'to push the tree' are commonly used euphemisms for sexual inter-course. As such, the *muyoomb* is equally linked to concepts of elderhood, political power and historical awareness, as it is to concepts of life-trans-mission and the continuation of the lineage – or, in the case of the king, the *ngaand* in its totality. Here, the stress shifts from the king as political overlord to the king as identified with the soil; from the domination of (public) space, transformed and mediated by political technology, to the identification with the land. As such, the creation of place, of an intimate sense of deep belonging, is realised in the appropriation of directly expe-rienced space. Such space is essentially private or 'shell-like' (see Bachelard 1957). Place is the space where home coincides with (female) body and cosmos. In this context, the relationship between man and environment borders on identity. It surpasses the acts of domination, of taking possession of space, of constructing or producing space through military architecture, fortifications or strategic networks of alliance. As Lefèbvre (1991: 164ff) rightly points out, property, in the sense of possession, is at best a necessary precondition, and most often merely an epiphenomenon of appropriative activity. This is why aLuund state that the king 'does not own the land', even though, politically speaking, he dominates and controls the space of the *ngaand*.

The construction of dominated space has very deep roots in history, for its origins in *kool* coincide with those of political power itself. The cyclical and regenerative 'euchronic' quality of kingship, however, taps a different source. There, sequential linear history, exemplified in the royal genealogies and charters recited at the court and in the construction of the dominant Luunda political space, is replaced by a more gestational praxis. Such 'world-making' corresponds with the Luunda villagers' immediate lived experience. Lived experience unfolds in cycles struc-tured, for example, by the movements of sun and moon, seasonal alternations and related agricultural activities, death and birth, and the cyclical passing on of life-flow (*mooy*) between generations (exemplified in the recycling of names between grandparents and grandchildren). It is at this level that the elders' speech surpasses the level of historical discourse or of political lobbying and networking in the public space. Their words acquire different 'knotting' or weaving qualities. Their speech becomes the male equivalent of maternal processes of birthgiving which find their source in the private domain.

The symbolism of the *muyoomb* tree, in terms of this maternal and regenerative sense of 'world-making', of 'hatching out', of 'giving birth', is clearest in relation to divinatory practices (De Boeck and Devisch 1994: 115ff). Being seated 'in the middle of the bush', the diviner is a *muyoomb* tree, planted on a fixed spot. Like the elder or the title-holder, who forms the middle of the relations that are being knotted around him, the diviner, identifying with the *muyoomb*, is the constituting focal point or nexus through which words are passed around or 'woven' between interlocutors. Spatially, the divinatory séance proceeds in the same way as the palaver, with the diviner in the middle and the consultants seated around him in a semi-circle. In practice, his final interpretation of the events may lead to more conflict. On a performative and symbolic level, however, his presence reaffirms reciprocal relations expressed through images of commensality. The association with the *muyoomb* relates the diviner to his ancestors and, thereby, to the matrilineal source of life. In fact, the planting of the *muyoomb* during the erection of the divination shrine is in itself an act of making or regenerating life. As noted above, the expression 'planting the *muyoomb*' refers to sexual intercourse or 'the lifting of the leg' (*-saangun*). The verb *-saangun* is also applied to the diviner's lifting up of the divination basket, and to the raising of his rattle (*luzeenz*) when he addresses the *ngoomb* divinatory spirit at the beginning of and during a séance. The *luzeenz* rattle contains the seeds of the fruit of the *mwiinzeenz* tree (*Acacia polyacantha*). In ritual contexts, the related term *chizeenz* refers to a nest of red ants, which signifies the source of feminine regenerative powers (while also referring to the place of death, *kaluung*). The shaking of the *luzeenz* rattle is accompanied by the diviner's cosmogonic speech which, in many respects, mirrors the title-holders' speech in front of the *muyoomb* shrine, but which is situated in 'euchronic' time, as a form of birthing. In this sense, the act of divination does not recall past battles and genealogies, but renders the awakening of a regenerative flow, cast in strongly sensory and corporeal terms of copulation and orgasm. In fact, the diviner is to the divination basket as a husband to his wife; he passes the basket between his legs (*-silweesh ngoomb*) as if it were a female body and womb, to render it pregnant with meaning. The accompanying sound of the rattle awakens and rhythms the spasms of life-transmission and life-flow through orgasmic sexual communion, in tune with the cyclical rhythms of the world. Divining reminds the audience how much the uterine flow of life is a maturational process which escapes full agnatic and patriarchal dominium: life's inner and passionate impetus from the uterine life source vitalises the social weave that extends through the successive generations of uterine filiation (De Boeck 1993; De Boeck and Devisch 1994: 127).

Place as landscape of memory and body of remembrance

> Place is what takes place between body and landscape. Thanks to the double horizon that body and landscape provide, a place is a locale bounded on both sides, near and far.
>
> (Casey 1993: 29)

The Luunda sense of locality and belonging is crystallised in a space-time that interconnects masculinity and femininity, real chronology and euchronic time, domination and appropriation, (political) history and cosmic rhythm, product and nature, structure and process, change and invariability, institutions and events, head and heart, white and red. *Pool*, 'place' in its fullest sense, is the space in which all complementary opposites are in some way overcome and united in a global texture. Place is both cosmological, natural and societal. It is social space, produced through Luunda constructs of representational space (body, house, land, village, graveyard, as rendered meaningful through spatial axes such as left and right, up and down, centre and periphery, front and back). At the same time, the Luunda representation of space and time links social space to nature through the image of the tree. In this process, social space stops being a cultural product and becomes instead a site of births. The spatio-temporal, cosmological rhythms inform social practice, which in turn transforms them. Again, the image of the tree links both together, while apprehending time at the very heart of space. By means of the image of the tree, and the elder as 'tree-man', each place shows its age and 'like a tree trunk' bears 'the works of the years it had taken it to grow' (Lefèbvre 1991: 95). As such, diachronic Luunda history, especially in terms of its political economy, that is in terms of migration and the elaboration of a politically inspired tributary network, is a history of space. Through space, history is crystallised synchronically in each particular place, each particular village and, ultimately, in each particular elder, for time and space become intertwined in (and through) place: place is engendered by time and, therefore, always actual and synchronic.

The synchronicity of space and time is undoubtedly also the genius behind the Luunda systems of perpetual kinship and positional succession. As Cunnison pointed out, in this concept of structural time 'the historical events which have become diffused are those which define political relationships within the whole society, and these in turn set the perception of the distant past in terms of present-day social and political structure' (Cunnison 1957: 30). As Kopytoff (1987) has shown, this allows for an intricate combination of structural invariability, and a set pattern of repetition or replication, enabling the reproduction of traditional society. In Kopytoff's understanding, African political culture is partly regarded as a given, but it is also a force of transformation which, in transforming, strengthens continuity and conservation. Kopytoff takes change for granted, but postulates a primacy of structure over content as a means of maintaining continuity amid disruption. The making of the frontier consists of spatial withdrawal, but with the capacity to carry with oneself the rootedness of one's own social structure in a social transcendence of purely physical facts, and the domination of physical space by social space. As such, the frontier may act to conserve, reinforce and revitalise the central values of the regional political culture. The formation of the frontier thus becomes a process of cultural self-reproduction on a regional scale.

Although I greatly appreciate Cunnison's insight about Luunda 'structural time', as well as Kopytoff's attempt to stress structural continuity amidst change, I feel that they both overemphasise the aspect of structural reproduction, and overlook what Hirsch (1995: 22) refers to as the 'processual' aspect of landscape, or what I would call the aspect of 'birthing' and spontaneous processes of growth. The history of natural rhythm positions each Luunda community in resonance with the cosmic regenerative rhythm of the vital life-flow (*mooy*). This life-force has cohesive, integrative, relational and connecting powers. It unites and merges social, cosmological and corporeal dimensions. It integrates the individual into the ongoing generational succession, and relates them to the people with whom they share a common ascent or residence. The driving force of the process of social reproduction lies in the domination of physical space; and that physical space, certainly in so far as it conjoins the body of the tree with that of the elder, informs and feeds this process. Physical space is thereby transformed into a structural social reproduction within a political space and architecture of conquest (the planting of the *muyoomb* as conquering act). At the same time, it is also moulded into a 'world-making' process of lived experience, thus defining the content of male and female identity and the rhythms of gender relations, labour divisions, and physical and social reproduction in general.

Landscape and memory converge through the intermediary of the tree and, by extension, the bodies of elders. Luunda notions of remembering and forgetting seem to suggest an intricate interrelationship between body, speech, knowledge and memory (see De Boeck 1995). To a large extent, Luunda remembering, and the 'knowing' linked to this remembrance, represent memory and knowledge 'in the flesh'. Such embodied remembering and knowing deals, in the first place, with the production of relation, the dimension of 'world-making', expressed through images of knotting and weaving. In rituals of remembrance, aLuund thus performatively generate relationships between bodies, people and the cosmos which cannot be fully captured by the discursive, the representational, or the level of exegetical meaning. The speech of Luunda elders, for example, is more than simply representational. Their words surpass the expression of the mimetic reproduction of the social norm, because they also spring from a highly embodied dimension, to become the male equivalent of female powers of gestation, birthgiving, nurturing and growth. Even the root -*vul*, which primarily alludes to a cognitive, reproductive memory, also contains references to this processual aspect of birthing, for it denotes male fecundity in terms of rain (*nvul*) (see note 8) and also in terms of growth, multitude and plenty (*kuvul*).[9] In this sense, the words of the elders 'grow' social memory as their bodies grow older, rooted like trees in the land (for a Melanesian comparison see Küchler 1993).

Conclusion

The bodies of elders merge with space through their identification with the land. They thereby give a place its rootedness, and weave it into the wider networks and pathways of socio-cultural and natural textures. In the 'living' ancestral shrine of *miyoomb* trees, as in the elders' bodies, places are no longer mere replicas of reproduced structures but become instead living entities which are each born, grow and wither in their own unique way, just as do trees and male bodies themselves. In and through the elder and the tree, 'place' is defined as both immediate and mediated, engendered and engendering space in which the distinction between vertical structure and cyclical process, or socio-cultural production and nature, dissolves. 'Place' among the aLuund is reproducible, and allows for the repetition of social relationships. It is thus a cultural product, while also stemming from natural production, in natural time, which is the time of growth and withering. In this anthropology of a combined socio-historical and natural rhythm, the choice between structure and process, invariability and change, institutions and events, dissolves. In such an approach, place becomes ontological since it no longer metaphorically generates, symbolically represents or performatively actualises the meaning of locality and belonging in representational space. Body and landscape, as boundaries of place, present themselves as coeval epicentres around which particular places pivot. Bodies become landscapes of memory, and landscapes become bodies of memory, mapping out places of belonging in the intertwined processes of individual and societal birthing, growth and history.

Acknowledgements

* The data presented here derive from field research (1987–89, 1991, 1994) among the aLuund of the Upper Kwaango (region of Bandundu, zone of Kahemba). Research was made possible thanks to the Research Fund of the Catholic University of Leuven, the 'Vlaamse Leergangen' and the Belgian National Fund for Scientific Research (NFWO).

Notes

1   The vertical and hierarchical character of his rule is further indicated by the way in which the Nzav title is passed on. Unlike the titles of the *ayilool*, which are predominantly inherited according to a matrilineal principle from mother's brother to sister's son, the paramount title of Nzav is inherited from father to son.

2   Before dawn, some *miyoomb* shoots are collected from the forest to be planted in a number of holes, in which the title-holder first deposits some kaolin and red earth, together with two 'knots' or rings made of grass (*nkat*). Then a libation of palm wine and animal blood is poured into the holes. The animal blood that is used cannot derive from a domestic animal or a wild boar (which is associated with sorcery), but should be from game with a monochromatic or smooth and even skin, such as that of the black-faced duiker (*kabuluk*, *Cephalophus nigrifons*), the long-tailed monkey (*nkim*, *Cercopithecus ascanius*) or the *mpuluumb* monkey (*Colobus polykomos angolensis*).

3   This ambivalence is evident, for instance, in the colour symbolism linked to the right and left sides. Whereas white is associated with the right, the more ambivalent colour red is associated with the left. The ambiguity of red is further demonstrated in the different qualities attributed to various kinds of 'female' blood, which will have positive connotations in the context of birth-giving, referred to as 'the bleeding of children', and negative connotations in relation to menstrual blood

4   The front/back, male/female opposition is mirrored in the sleeping position of husband and wife. The husband sleeps 'turned towards the fire' (*kwijiikw*) whereas his wife sleeps 'behind his back' (*kwinyim*).

5   The animal metaphor of the cock summarises the associations between male speech, the rising sun and the awakening of the world. aLuund see many similarities in the behaviour of men and roosters. Like men, cocks are 'admired for their speech' when, standing on one leg, they announce the beginning of the day and the appearance of the sun. The cock's crest is explicitly compared to the red colours of the rising sun. At the same time the

(white) cock's obvious sexual prowess metonymically elaborates the theme of masculine life-giving powers. aLuund say that 'there can be no village without a white cock [a senior elder]'. White cocks connote masculine generative powers, linked to ancestral times and the origin of the world, whereas black cocks are associated with the world of the sorcerer.

6   The tree metaphor denoting immobility also expands to the domain of hunting. 'The hunting trap', it is said, is a tree (*mupit mutoond*), in that it does not move. As one hunter explained to me: 'The name of Keendaang [the hunting trap's name in the esoteric language of the *uyaang* hunting cult] means that the trap does not move or walk. It is the animal that walks and finds the trap, not the trap that walks in search of the animal. The hunter walks morning, noon and evening with his gun to search for animals, but Keendaang remains in one spot. This is what the elders have told us: Keendaang stays in one place, one cannot surprise it. This is the way in which Keendaang [the tradition of trapping] has been handed down to us'. By means of their metonymical relation with the tightening of the trap's rope, the hunting trap and the art of trapping (*khoondzu*) also signify a man's fierceness, hardness, erectness and endurance. In *kaleepu*, the ritual treatment of a paralysed arm or leg, for example, a trap's rope is tied between hand and shoulder, or foot and waist, folding the arm or leg 'like a bow'. A miniature bow is put on the folded arm or leg, together with the rectrices of a cock. The treatment itself takes place at dawn, in order to transfer the vertical movement of the sun to the body parts that require the same erectness.

7   The metaphorical connection between masculinity and roots is most strongly expressed with regard to the tree *mulooz* (*Caesalpiniaceae, Daniella oliveri*), a tree with one large root which deeply penetrates into the earth and with sticky sap, likened to seminal fluids. The *mulooz* plays a crucial role in hunting rituals, and it is also at the foot of this tree that many ritual treatments of female infecundity (*wuumb*) take place. Bark scrapings from the *mulooz* will also be used in the treatment of male impotence (*ukob*). The tree refers to the same power that establishes a man both as a hunter and a genitor and, thus, as a contributor to the continuity of the social order of Luunda society.

8   Rain is referred to in paternal terms as *shanvul*, the prefix *sha-* denoting fatherhood. The verb *-vul* means 'to multiply', 'to become numerous' or 'to be many'. Significantly, a newly circumcised boy is compared to the rain. Through circumcision, he acquires the powers to transmit life. Life-transmission in its more masculine aspect is symbolically also represented by the *muleemb* tree (*Moraceae, Ficus sp.*) which, like the *muyoomb*, is planted in the courtyard of every important title-holder and, most prominently, in the courtyard of the paramount title-holder, since the royal title is transmitted patrilineally. Therefore, the paramount title-holder will pass the first night after his enthronement with a leaf of the *muleemb* tree on his head and, together with other ritual substances, under his tongue. The *muleemb* signifies the unity of the agnatic group, and agnatic ties in general. After finishing a meal, for example, the paramount title-holder normally tears to pieces a *muleemb* leaf in remembrance of his father, and a leaf of the *malopw*, a water lily, in memory of his mother's side. The *muleemb* also signifies male potency

and fertility. In the esoteric vocabulary of the circumcision ritual, *muleemb* refers to the erect penis. Furthermore, the circumcision masters frequently draw a circle in the air with a finger. This movement, which reminds the boys of their painful circumcision, is also referred to as *muleemb*. *Uleemb* is also the name of the poison that Luunda hunters apply to their arrowheads, and the arrow, again, is a meaningful constituent of male sexual prowess.

9   *-vul*, *-vulijaan*: to multiply, to become numerous, to reproduce; *kuvul*: plentitude; *-vudi*: many.

References

Appadurai, A. (1995) 'The Production of Locality', in R. Fardon (ed.), *Counterworks. Managing the Diversity of Knowledge*, London: Routledge.

Bachelard, G. (1957) *La Poétique de l'Espace*, Paris: Presses Universitaires de France.

Bustin, E. (1975) *Lunda under Belgian Rule. The Politics of Ethnicity*, Cambridge, MA: Harvard University Press.

Casey, E.S. (1993) *Getting Back into Place. Toward a Renewed Understanding of the Place-World*, Bloomington, IN: Indiana University Press.

Cordemans, E.L (n.d.) *Notes Ethnographiques sur les Indigènes Habitant la Région de Kulindzi, Territoire Kahemba*, Unpublished manuscript, Archives Terr. Kahemba et Distr. Kikwit.

Crine, F. (1964) 'Aspects Politico-Sociaux du Système de Tenure des Terres des Lunda Septentrionaux', in D. Biebuyck (ed.), *African Agrarian Systems*, London: Oxford University Press, 157–72.

Cunnison, I. (1956) 'Perpetual Kinship: A Political Institution of the Luapula Peoples', *The Rhodes-Livingstone Journal* 20: 28–48.

—— (1957) 'History and Genealogy in a Conquest State', *American Anthropologist* 59(1): 20–48.

De Boeck, F. (1993) 'Symbolic and Diachronic Study of Inter-Cultural Therapeutic and Divinatory Roles among aLuund and Chokwe in the Upper Kwaango', in K. Schilder and W. Van Binsbergen (eds), *Ethnicity in Africa*, special issue of *Afrika Focus* 9(1–2).

—— (1994) 'Of Trees and Kings: Politics and Metaphor among the aLuund of South-western Zaire', *American Ethnologist* 21(3): 451–73.

—— (1995) 'Bodies of Remembrance: Knowledge, Experience and the Growing of Memory in Luunda Ritual Performance', in G. Thinès and L. de Heusch (eds), *Rites et Ritualisation*, Paris: Vrin.

—— (1996) 'Postcolonialism, Power and Identity: Local and Global Perspectives from Zaire', in R.P. Werbner and T.O. Ranger (eds) *Postcolonial Identities in Africa*, London: Zed Books.

De Boeck, F. and Devisch, R. (1994) 'Ndembu, Luunda and Yaka Divination Compared: From Representation and Social Engineering to Embodiment and Worldmaking', *Journal of Religion in Africa* 22(2): 98–133.

Devisch, R. (1991) 'Symbol and Symptom among the Yaka of Zaire', in A. Jacobson-Widding (ed.), *Body and Space: Symbolic Models of Unity and Division in African Cosmology and Experience*, Uppsala: Almqvist & Wiksell, 283–302.

—— (1993) *Weaving the Threads of Life: The Khita Gyn-Eco-Logical Healing Cult among the Yaka*, Chicago: Chicago University Press.

Hirsch, E. (1995) 'Landscape: Between Place and Space', in E. Hirsch and M. O'Hanlon (eds), *The Anthropology of Landscape: Perspectives on Place and Space*, Oxford: Clarendon Press.

Kopytoff, I. (ed.) (1987) *The African Frontier. The Reproduction of Traditional African Societies*, Bloomington, IN: Indiana University Press.

Küchler, S. (1993) 'Landscape as Memory: The Mapping of Process and its Representation in a Melanesian Society', in Barbara Bender (ed.), *Landscape: Politics and Perspectives*, Providence, RI and Oxford: Berg.

Lefèbvre, H. (1991) *The Production of Space*, Oxford: Blackwell.

Riesman, P. (1977) *Freedom in a Fulani Social Life. An Introspective Ethnography*, Chicago: University of Chicago Press.

Turner, V.W. (1967) *The Forest of Symbols: Aspects of Ndembu Ritual*, Ithaca, NY: Cornell University Press.

—— (1969) *The Ritual Process. Structure and Anti-structure*, Ithaca, NY: Cornell University Press.

Chapter 2

Wild gods, containing wombs and moving pots

Emplacement and transience in Watchi belonging[*]

Nadia Lovell

This chapter examines the way in which the Watchi of southeast Togo[1] conceptualise their relationship to the locality which they inhabit, and how such relationships are mediated through the use of nature. Related theoretical questions concerning the concept of nature itself, the transformation of landscapes into habitat and the dynamics involved in shaping notions of belonging are also explored. While the chapter explores mythologies and symbolic typifications of landscape and nature, this goes beyond the scope of sheer representation as the sociality of these concepts is firmly contextualised within the framework of social, cultural and historical localisation of collective identities.

The creation of belonging, which is inherently tied to notions of identity, to a differentiation between 'us' and 'them', is itself multi-faceted and stratified: who 'we' are depends on context, on historical shifts and (re-)constructions, and on contextual definitions. For this reason, the argument extends further to incorporate notions of gendered space, and the differentiations which arise as a result of such dynamics and shifts in meaning. This far from implies that the Watchi fail to identify who they are as a group, but that the group itself constitutes, and re-presents, its identity at several levels, which operate both simultaneously and in a desynchronised fashion, thus creating coordinated yet at times also competing discourses around identity. In so doing, movement across territories and the creation of new settlements become possible, while maintaining the mythical and cosmological fundaments which underpin a common Watchi understanding of belonging and locality. Yet, if notions of identity and community are rarely hegemonic, the same must be said of the understanding of nature itself. The concept of nature, therefore, has to be seen in the context of the various discourses of which it becomes a constitutive part, and which it also helps arouse. Complementary or competing images of nature have to be considered in relation to one another, in the field of power relationships if necessary, but also in terms of various groups' different claims on territories of knowledge.

The construction, maintenance, negotiation and transformation of boundaries which pertain to nature, the human body, cosmologies or identity are all processes which are instrumental in the definitions of these concepts in the first place. The motion by which nature is created, appropriated, imbued with meaning(s) and transformed into a socially significant category mirroring images of human identity tends to emphasise the malleability of such a concept, which is, I believe, why such associations are so fruitful in the first place and so conducive to human interference. The amorphous characteristics of nature, and of humans in nature, make them particularly pregnant with meaning because they can be given almost any shape, and come to be moulded and mirrored in one another in a multiplicity of contexts while allowing for constant transformations and modifications.

The notion of nature has also come under renewed anthropological scrutiny in the context of gender studies, where the long-presumed relationship between women and nature has been examined. Although I shall return to this association later, suffice it to say at this stage that the predominant focus has been on the criteria which are believed to constitute gender *per se*, and the notion of nature as a category has remained relatively unexplored in these theoretical debates. I propose to examine how women help create an identity both of and for themselves and, simultaneously, mediate in the creation of a particular image of nature which is instrumental in shaping religious discourses and power relations. Closely tied to this construction of identity and notion of belonging is the way in which the Watchi relate to their gods, and the memories they create around them. These are needed for a community to be properly established.

The Watchi seem to be using nature through its association with divine beings in order to appropriate and lay claim to specific territory and to emphasise the legitimacy of locality. Hence the history of their original settlement into this region of Southern Togo, which is primarily a history of migration (see also de Medeiros 1984; Gayibor 1986), recounts their arrival on the site, with the founding members of the village, a man and a woman, carrying conjoined male and female deities. These intertwined deities had been removed from their original site after an internecine dispute, and this group of Watchi in flight were able to appropriate their new, uninhabited (so it is claimed) territory by installing their two deities in this new location. Although no major resettlement of the Watchi has occurred in recent times, new, more localised settlements and movements are established in an identical fashion: the expansion of a crowded household is made effective by the installation of a shrine for a deity, and the identification of a god that has 'fallen to earth' from its cosmos requires the building of a shrine which, inevitably, leads to the expansion of a household into previously unclaimed territory. Territory or space, however, is defined both as a metaphysical domain and as a terrestrial entity. Deities are believed to dwell on another plane, but also need to have their presence manifested and anchored on earth in order for humans to propitiate them properly. In its physical manifestation, the appropriation of a territory thus associated with a deity can involve pragmatic and ethereal forms and considerations. Settlement, in this sense, stretches beyond the confines of the strictly terrestrial and encompasses the sea, rivers, trees, wild animals and the sky. Through this association with their deities, humans also appropriate part of a metaphysical, cosmological landscape (see also Århem, this volume).

It is in this context that Watchi perceptions of their own and their gods' existence is conditioned through locality. The notion of place is primordial in the manifestation of Watchi identities, in the way in which they construct their cosmological beliefs and in the dynamic processes involved in creating and maintaining a sense of belonging to a place, while remaining malleable enough to incorporate new dimensions and the transformation of already existing identities.

Locality is constructed through the intermediary of deities which are themselves extensions of natural and environmental features. By providing these deities with names, a place is created for humans to dwell in, and the gods are simultaneously provided with an identity and place of their own. In both cases, the process of grounding deities for worship assists in providing that particular deity with an identity of its own, distinct from the generic and amorphous mass to which it belongs at a metaphysical level. The action of naming a deity therefore imbues a space with a sense of place, no longer an anonymous feature in the environment. Yet, the identity of humans and that of their gods are intricately linked, as is their relationship with nature.

Humans, clay and localising discourses

Watchi religious beliefs focus around deities called *vodhun*. A *vodhun* is one god among others in a cosmological order notable for its complex polytheistic structure. *Vodhun* are all given personal names, depending on their gender, individual characteristics and parentage. Like humans, they are believed to entertain kinship ties with one another,[2] and their origin will thus partly determine their individual identity. Some ethnographers have been busily involved in trying to identify as large a number of *vodhun* as possible, positioning them in a hierarchical and archaic relationship depending on such parentage, in relation to a cosmological order defined through myths of creation. The earlier the appearance of the god in the cosmology, the more powerful it was deemed to be by virtue of its chronological and genealogical pedigree. Maupoil (1943) and Verger (1957) have estimated that there might be more than 2,000 gods, hierarchically organised, while others (Rivière 1981; Augé 1988; de Surgy 1981, 1988) have indicated that the contemporary *vodhun* pantheon could easily accommodate more than 1,000 such deities (see Lovell 1993 for a fuller discussion).

The present chapter focuses on what the Watchi consider to constitute the identity of a deity and its instrumentality in delineating definitions of place, territoriality and their domestication, and how these processes contribute to endowing humans and gods with distinctive, overlapping and localised identities. I begin with a brief exploration of four narratives of origin and settlement intended to provide an embryonic imagery of Watchi concepts of place and landscape. There is, of course no such thing as a hegemonic origin, nor do such mythical narratives displace other histories of settlement and migration. These accounts are used for methodological rather than structural purposes, inasmuch as the focus is primarily on how these narratives promote a method for structuring important Watchi concepts, rather than providing a universal theory of mind and cognition à la Lévi-Strauss. The focus then shifts to how such narratives are shaped by, and feed into, particular notions of Watchi sociality, individual and social experience, and relationships to nature.[3]

Vodhun are believed to possess a spiritual existence in the cosmological sphere, as precursors to their human counterparts. One narrative portrays Mawu, the supreme god, as having preceded the existence of *vodhun*[4] and subsequently created these deities in order for them to give life to human beings. Mawu, also referred to as Mawu-Lisa, is most often ascribed a dual-gendered identity. Unlike *vodhun*, Mawu possesses no human form. It is likened to the wind, an amorphous and undefined yet powerful element which imbues terrestrial existence with its essence and vitality. I have heard informants describe its gender in temporal terms, referring to its primordial existence as female and subsequently acquiring a co-existing male identity.[5] In these accounts, *vodhun* come to occupy an intermediary position between Mawu and humans, both conceptually and physically. Deities are believed to be located in the cosmos, yet perceived as leading lives very similar to those of humans. *Vodhun* have spouses and 'children', although they do not, like humans, procreate in the proper sense.

Several other overlapping myths of origin are employed to explain the accession of humans – and of the Watchi in particular – to their present territories. In one such myth, the source of life is attributed to a male original creator appearing as a palm tree (*hunde*) said to have descended from the sky in order to populate the earth with its seed. The trunk itself is considered male, and said to be very deeply rooted in the soil. This imagery is translated in everyday contexts, where men refer to this tree when invoking their moorings to a particular place and settlement: 'planting a *hunde* in your dwelling shows that you are deeply rooted', and its branches are described as stiff and hard, conveying typical and ideal attributes of masculinity.

This image of the *hunde* is opposed to that of other palm trees whose branches are said to sway in the wind, thereby connoting their soft nature.[6] Eating the nuts of a *hunde* signifies the end of the household, and is equated to an act of cannibalism, to 'eating one's own children'.

The nuts of this palm tree are – historically and contemporaneously – all conceptualised as being female. Indeed, the original *hunde* is said to have carried sixteen nuts (metaphorically representing the first sixteen wives of this paradigmatic creator), who subsequently bore children, established the first sixteen original settlements and became the apical ancestresses of all the current clans populating the region. Significantly, while the tree trunk itself is considered as unequivocally male, it shares in the essence of femalehood in more than one way: its nuts are female, as just described, but the roots of *hunde* are also said to be unable to grow if a clay pot (*eze*) is absent from its base.[7] The presence of the pot in the ground is said to have preceded all other forms of existence, and it is believed to represent the essence of life itself. In addition, all the nuts deriving from this tree have to be collected in a clay pot, lest the picker dies.

In yet another narrative, the existence of both *vodhun* and humans is ascribed to the powers of a cosmological bird (a chicken, to be precise) which would have roosted on the world in order to make it come alive. This chicken hence stands as the creator of the world as it appears to humans, the originator of both divine and human life. Significantly, the earth itself is represented as a cooking pot, containing all living things. The pot is made of clay stemming from the earth, which represents yet another source of existence.

Finally, the Watchi at times also locate their origin in a landscape called *bome*, a place likened to a wide field of red clay, where humans return upon death in order to be remodelled and recycled back to human existence by *bomeno*, the mother of clay, who subsequently returns them to the world of the living. *Bome* is thus another original source of life whose existence is sometimes attributed to the deeds of Mawu-Lisa (the dual-gendered supreme being). *Bome* itself is associated with the female gender, and is presided over by a woman who is instrumental in the perpetuation of all human life.

Some recurring themes can be identified, such as the references to conjoined, shifting and overlapping notions of gendered identity prevalent in the first two accounts, while the latter two refer to the world as essentially female. Features of the natural landscape such as clay, nuts, trees and other significant landmarks convey a vivid imagery through which existence is both explained and mediated. The last two accounts also converge in at least one other respect: while the female nuts of the male *hunde* present the basis for all divination and legitimate the existence of the sixteen original clans to populate the earth (see note 6), the chicken which roosts the world into being also provides an archetypal imagery for divination. The grating motion of chickens on the ground as they scratch for food (referred to as *ka*) parallels the gesture made by diviners when marking their divination board in consulting the Afa oracle. A last twist has to be added: when women dance for the *vodhun* in rituals, they perform certain steps which are likened to those of chickens, and are indeed said on occasion to dance like chickens, thus evoking the origins of both human and metaphysical existence, enacting and embodying cosmos at one and the same time.[8]

Vodhun are generally characterised by their 'natural' features, and their closeness to what is perceived to lie outside human control. They are fundamentally tied to natural and pre-social habitats located outside of human settlements, in the wild bush (*gbeme*) which constitutes the primary dwelling places of untamed animals hunted for meat. For instance Sakpata, *vodhun* of smallpox or other outwardly similar diseases causing eruptions on the skin, is said to reside in the earth. Some of my informants would show me the ground, or grab a handful of dust, when talking about him. Significantly, Sakpata is also referred to by the name *vodhun* Anyigbato, the 'owner of the earth', and is closely associated with new settlements, and also with displacements of population. As a disease, smallpox is believed to reside in the earth, and former epidemics affecting large numbers of the population were attributed to the wrath of Sakpata, often leading to the relocation of entire communities seeking refuge elsewhere. *Vodhun* Toxosu is associated with fresh water, rivers and waterways, and is believed to cause encephalitis and other forms of swelling, while Mami Wata is said to dwell in the sea. Others seem on first examination to be less directly associated with place, such as Hevieso, linked to thunder, lightning and violent storms; Eda, represented by the python but also by the rainbow, and Ga, the deity of iron. These latter more abstract links to locality far from preclude such *vodhun* from becoming highly localised and situated on earth. As god of thunder and lightning, Hevieso is said to manifest itself to humans in the shape of monolithic stones strewn across the landscape, Eda the python and rainbow straddles the universe by planting its tail in water while grazing the earth for food, and a find of iron ore will indicate the presence of Ga. Such relationships to natural features of the environment are iconographic and also metonymic. Material features such as these are used to represent deities at a metaphorical level, but they are in themselves also imbued with the power of the god. The relationship is therefore dualistic and interactive since the material object itself is both essence and representation.

In their cosmological manifestation, *vodhun* are said not to be of much use to humans. They are neither particularly vengeful nor benign in their intentions, but possess a propensity for mischief and the infliction of misfortune. Yet *vodhun* cannot be invoked or propitiated by humans in this original, neutral, state. Prayers cannot be offered, nor sacrifices be made, to a deity in this free-floating, cosmological ether. In order to become more accessible to the needs and demands of humans, and in order for its own expectations to be satisfied, a *vodhun* must be brought to earth, and grounded in particular locations for its wrath to subside and its powers to be fully brought to bear on humans. The action of situating the gods in this way has to be performed by humans themselves, and involves gods and humans in a mutual process of creation. This grounding process is achieved primarily through the installation of a shrine acknowledging the location of the deity on the site, an action which also incorporates the use of clay, plants, animals and medicines in the making of an effigy of, and for, the deity. As a result, the dialectic relationship whereby humans situate their gods on earth implicitly and explicitly engages the former in a relationship that portrays the socialisation of nature, and whereby the positioning of a *vodhun* partly signifies the appropriation of nature, in the form of clay, plants, and animals. However, nature is more than simply socialised in the process and for the purpose of creating cosmos, since it is simultaneously transformed into a habitable landscape and serves, by the same token, to locate humans in a metaphysical and cosmological landscape. The identities of nature, humans and *vodhun* are all transformed through these exchanges of substances. How, then, is a site selected? What does the installation of a shrine involve?

When the Watchi recount incidents where they have suffered the wrath of their gods it is, they say, because the *vodhun* sometimes feel the need to be remembered. The most common occurrence described is that of a *vodhun* manifesting itself through punitive action. The Watchi often make reference to violent possession trances, to unknown and lengthy episodes of illness, or to unexplainable misfortune and loss of wealth as finally being attributed to the interference of a *vodhun*.[9] Other equally dramatic incidents can alert humans to a deity's presence. For instance, some may manifest themselves directly, without the use of illness or possession as an intermediary. Informants have recounted how, when out walking, they may have stumbled across a Neolithic stone which proved to be Hevieso (the object is believed to have fallen from the sky during a storm), or come across a natural axe blade signifying the presence of Ga, god of iron. Mami Wata is encountered in waterways, in the guise of a white mermaid, and the sighting of a python in a baobab tree reveals Eda, the rainbow. In all such cases, shrines for the deity concerned will need to be erected in a relevant location, defined partly by the action or event related to the identity of the *vodhun* itself (the location of a shrine to Hevieso, for instance, could be designated as the place where a thunderbolt has struck) and partly by the mode of its manifestation.

Once a link between deity and human has been indicated in one such way, the installation of a shrine will normally be required. A diviner will direct the afflicted individual to an already established cult leader who will, for a fee, help establish a new shrine in the client's name. Although this process of establishing shrines technically and originally duplicates the identity of the already existing deity and its cult leader, *vodhun* do over time evolve personalities of their own, a process tightly linked with the identities of their human counterparts.

Containers, keepers and the warmth of locality

The processes involved in grounding *vodhun* on earth, making them amenable to worship and propitiation and responsive to humans' quest for protection, is partly intended to domesticate the unpredictability of deities, transforming their primeval association with the wild and undo-

mesticated bush into a relationship where humans yield enhanced
control over their gods. This process is in itself highly gendered as it
engages Watchi men and women in distinctly codified relationships
with their deities, while also transforming human identities through
this contact. Thus far we have explored the association of *vodhun* with
natural features of the landscape, such as the earth itself, trees, rivers,
stones, and natural phenomena such as thunder and lightning, and how
humans conceptualise locality through the use of a wide category of
nature. This process has been described as necessary for the communication of humans and deities, but also as a precondition for human
settlement. We now turn to other aspects of nature, which also provide
material for the conceptualisation of space and which are also gendered.

The notion of clay located in *bome* is all-encompassing since it provides
the raw material for all humans (as is also evidenced in the other narratives
presented earlier). Clay is used to make earthen pots (*eze*), where food is
cooked and transformed by women for human consumption. These pots
are also metaphorically associated with a woman's belly or womb (*fo*),
where humans are made and cooked by the woman's body during gestation. The pot and hearth of the house are both equated with a woman's
body, and are seen as the essence of the household as a unit. 'This is where
my pot is' (*ezenye li fia*) is a commonly used euphemism expressing the
longing felt by men having to be absent from their household and separated from their wives for long periods of time. The pot represents the
pragmatic and emotional centre of human existence and settlement, and
is associated with belonging in more than one way. The cooking
performed by the women displays and enacts their caring and nurturing
character, and is used as a metaphor to invoke the warmth and comfort
provided at the heart of the household. Keeping one's pot and one's
cooking wholesome thus ensures success in marriage, fruitful pregnancies
and healthy progeny. The cooking pot needs to remain in one piece in
order to ensure the continued survival of the household. Likewise,
women's pots as wombs need to remain intact and unbroken[10] in order to
secure the fertility of the household and its perpetuation. It is said of a
woman who cannot cook that she will be unable to keep either husband or
children, and that she will be prone to miscarriages and to loosing her children in infancy.[11] For a woman to be unable to cook when she reaches
adolescence connotes a certain degree of carelessness, flightiness and
indulgence, and an unwillingness to comply to expectations of responsibility. It also tacitly implies a propensity for sexual meanderings. A woman
who does not cook for her husband might be suspected of cooking for
someone else – a euphemism indicating infidelity – even if such suspicions

remain unfounded. Likewise, the act of cooking for someone, particularly of the opposite sex, is considered so intimate that a married woman who would indeed cook for another man might be accused of infidelity or, at least, of expressing her inclination or intention to do so. The action of cooking could therefore be seen to ground a woman's sexuality within the domestic sphere, in the same way as her other 'pot', her womb, grounds the fertility of the household. Both convey ideal images of nurturing, stability and fecund existence. During one of the most important parts of initiation into a *vodhun*'s secret society, female devotees are made to sit on four upturned pots with outstretched legs as confirmation of their fitness to carry forth the *vodhun*'s ideal of embodying the world. If one of the pots cracks or breaks, the devotee will be banished from the shrine, and is said never to be able to procreate. It should come as no surprise that the Watchi (and many other Ewe subgroups) refer to their descent in terms of locality: to share a common ancestral belonging implies sharing the same womb, and the term *fome* (translated as lineage in many ethnographic accounts on the Ewe, see for instance Nukunya 1969; Verdon 1983) literally translates as '(being) in the womb'.

Beside these associations between women and pots activated through the processes of cooking essential to the earthly existence and perpetuation of the household, and the link between women and 'pots' expressed through the procreative forces of gestation and pregnancy, women are also the makers of clay through their relationship with *bomeno*, the archetypal mother of clay, whose being they synchronically represent and contribute to shaping. Women are moulded in her image and with her metaphysical assistance help create life and shape human beings into existence on earth. This exclusive link imparts upon them the power of handling clay. As potters in a pragmatic sense, women transform the earth into cooking utensils for the general use and feeding of the community. In metaphorical terms, women as potters process the essence of life itself, turning it into a perpetually recyclable substance.

If clay provides the idiom for ensuring the existence and regeneration of all earthly human life, the pots produced by women serve another purpose outside the strictly domestic realm of nurturing. The universe itself is imaged as an upturned pot, containing deities, humans and all natural elements, and all *vodhun* shrines are topped with an upside-down pot representing this containment. Clay pots are in addition an essential element in shaping the cosmological and terrestrial existence of *vodhun* themselves, as they are used in the constitution and grounding of deities in the human community. They constitute the primary material object used in the process of locating the gods inside the shrines erected on their behalf. This point will be discussed further below.

Yet the metaphor of pots extends further, and in another direction. Women's wombs as pots are filled, through the procreative act, by male semen, which is then cooked in order to produce a healthy progeny. A pregnant woman will refer to herself as 'having a full pot' (*ezenye dogba*) and as having been plugged by a man's penis (*edeto lekpeun setunu ne ve*). The latter also refers to sexual intercourse in general, although a more common idiom describes this act as 'having someone inside one's flesh' (*do lãme ne*). Yet semen is only added to a substance inherent in a woman's womb, and with which it is subsequently made to mix. The blood located in the womb is primordial to the process of growth, and its existence has to precede the act of copulation in order to ensure fertility. The redness of pots is not conjectural, as it represents and mirrors the redness of the womb. Pots come to embody the shape, colour and processual changes which occur in women through their monthly and life-cycles, while also being fundamentally shaped and modelled by them.

Significantly, the sexual idioms used to describe the conjoining of men and women at their most intimate are extended to encompass one of the most important relationships in the religious domain, namely that between devotees and *vodhun* during acts of possession. Women who are possessed consider the gods to be their partners in a cosmological marriage, and they are readily penetrated, having their flesh 'entered into' and mounted by the deities. Devotees are described as the spouses (*vodhunsi*) of the gods, although such unions do not preclude human alliances. Yet if women are invaded in this way, possession remains one of the most potent avenues for grounding the deities among humans, and involving them in acts of communication. Women become the pots into which the *vodhun* descend and are contained, allowing gods to dwell inside in an act of expressive and regenerative copulation enabling the perpetuation of cosmos through human action and cooperation, while the human universe is ensured continuation through divine intervention and approval. By the same token, women are able to 'speak their gods' (*fo vodhun*) during possession, entering into an altered state of consciousness which allows them to perceive and convey the wishes of their gods and, more poignantly perhaps, to acquire their identities through the merging of bodily and spiritual substances. Indeed, women devotees are sometimes referred to, and directly addressed by the name '*vodhun*', indicating a total amalgamation and appropriation of conjoined identities (see Lovell 1997).

Vodhun abduct their devotees in the same way as men are said to abduct their future wives. The twist, however, is significant: women may be abducted by their gods during possession, leading to a lack of control and submission to the whims of the gods, but *vodhun* in their shrines are themselves contained in pots made by women, and women also become their containers when possessed, thus making this relationship highly dualistic and malleable. The generation and re-enactment of the world through acts of cosmic copulation neutralises gender in order to merge and transcend human and divine gendered identities (see Lovell 1997).

The nature of initiates' and devotees' relationship with their deities, which is primarily enacted through initiation and possession, sets them very much apart from uninitiated members of the Watchi community. Nevertheless, all women are considered potential targets of the *vodhuns'* attentions, and some 60–70 per cent of women adhere to secret societies. Seen in a wider context, possession is a mode of expressing a specific locality (Werbner 1977). In this case, the exclusive relationship between women and *vodhun* is an extension of their involvement in creating a sense of belonging to the territory which the Watchi appear to have occupied since the seventeenth century. Identifying locality and maintaining a sense of belonging are highly predicated upon female possession.

Women could perhaps best be described as the containers of life and, to an extent, of cosmos, since they provide the raw material for the (pro-)creation and perpetuation of the life of human beings, while also representing the ultimate containers for the gods. However, they are more than simple receptacles of male semen and cosmic *vodhun*, since they themselves provide the original container and substance through which *vodhun* and men are created in the first place, namely the blood of procreation whose redness is mirrored in the pots which they carry, represent and create; all reflecting processes orchestrated by the rhythmic recycling of *bomeno* herself.

The processes establishing cosmological beings such as *vodhun* amongst the community of the living are directly paralleled in Watchi sociality when new settlements are established or households segmented into new residential units. Each household needs to be grounded by the same principles as the ones which surround the instalment of a shrine. Each household will therefore become situated in its new location by the erection of a shrine for a *vodhun* associated with that particular clan, moulded into a pot kept in a hut at the entrance of the settlement, indicating its legitimacy and ensuring its proper protection. Significantly, the segmentation of a household or the anchoring of a completely new and larger settlement evolves around the setting up of a new *fome*, or new womb, and will focus on the identity of a new *vodhun* shrine established on behalf of a woman, who will subsequently be deemed the apical ancestress of the segmented household; although descent in the generations that follow will tend to be traced in the male line until a new resettlement or segmentation occurs. The *fome* or womb of a woman therefore serves to establish the original settlement while the house itself, generally headed by the most senior man of the settlement, provides legitimacy in the male line for descending generations. The erection of a *vodhun* shrine within the settlement will, as a result, be accompanied by the instalment of a hut sheltering the stool of lineage ancestors traced in the male line, but not including the apical source of life herself. She remains firmly ensconced in the hut of the *vodhun*, and cannot be dislodged from its structure. The male descendants in turn will follow the stool, but this in itself is not enough to legitimate either new settlements nor proper cosmological security. A household without a *vodhun* to ensure its well being is doomed to incur the wrath of the gods, and will therefore irrevocably fail to thrive and procreate.[12] The planting of the *hunde* palm tree, discussed earlier, outside a settlement can thus be seen to root the male household (*afe*) in its new location provided the red clay pot representing the female womb of the apical ancestress is present at its base.[13] The tree thus penetrates and fills this original primordial pot in the same way as a man's penis fills a woman's womb during sexual intercourse.

While women most blatantly embody this notion of cyclic containment and contribute to the appropriation and representation of nature through these associations with *vodhun*, clay, pots and wombs, some men are also involved in the process of grounding the gods and locating them on earth for settlement and the general benefit of the community. Women may be seen as containers for the gods, but these receptacles also need to be filled with substances that are primordially handled by men. Most shrines are in the hands (literally, *vodhun li asinye*, 'the god is in my hand') of male keepers or guardians, who act as custodians of the *vodhun* and also perform healing.

As already mentioned, divination may be used to identify a deity causing misfortune to an individual, and the requirement for an already established healer to help in the installation of a new shrine. The keeper of a shrine will therefore impart on the sufferer and future shrine keeper a knowledge of herbs, animals and other substances required for the installation of a new shrine for *vodhun* Sakpata, for instance. Identical in origin, the old and new shrines will both be modelled on the knowledge of the original custodian, making both *vodhun* in effect identical in personality, temper and constitution. However, as the novice expands his knowledge of the botanical and animal worlds through time, this new shrine will come to acquire an identity quite separate from its original foundation. The constitution of the *vodhun* is also transformed in this process, bringing it closer to the identity of its current holder. Shrines may also be inherited, which perpetuates knowledge while also allowing for continued modification. These relationships to knowledge are translated in territorial terms, as powerful shrines tend to expand physically across compounds, and spiritually by attracting increasingly large numbers of followers. Shrines established on behalf of a *vodhun* which has fallen to earth are cared for by the person who first stumbles across them, and allow their keeper to expand their territory to appropriate the god.

Plants (*ama*) are considered potent agents in the general treatment of illnesses, but their use depends partly on their individual properties, and partly also on the effect they might achieve when combined with others in medicinal concoctions. As a result, although most Watchi share in a relatively extensive knowledge of their use in the treatment of everyday ailments, specialised medical knowledge is derived from an individual's ability to devise new recipes for the treatment of illness and constitutes well-guarded secrets rarely divulged to outsiders. The status of healers is therefore constructed partly around their own ability to combine plants appropriately, and from the secrecy that surrounds such practices. The pinnacle of knowledge is associated with *vodhun*, where the use of animal parts, particularly the skin, head and vital substances deriving from the liver, heart and pancreas, taken from creatures such as chameleons, cobras, alligators, antelopes, lions and certain birds such as parrots, is also included. All these substances need to be inserted into pots when establishing a *vodhun* for the first time. These plants must subsequently be renewed regularly in order for the power of the gods to be boosted and revitalised.

Plants and animals are thus used as repositories for male knowledge, as they act as mediators between the identities of keeper and deity, engaging them both in a mutual process of definition where remembering and forgetting is part and parcel of the deal (McCarthy-Brown 1989; Barnes 1989). Plants and animals provide the essential corporeal elements for worship and mediate in both the creation and dereliction of the gods. Indeed, shrine keepers refer to their deities as 'being in their hands' (*li asime*), and to themselves as 'making the gods exist' (*vodhun li*) (see also Barber 1981, 1990)

If *vodhun* are therefore associated with nature in its raw, uncontrolled and dangerous form, their domestication and localisation involve nature in reversed form: the use of plants and specific animals, which are also taken from the wild (*gbeme*), neutralises the destructive forces of the gods while making them simultaneously accessible and controllable. However, while the deities' immediate association with nature excludes humans from the equation, their taming incorporates them as agents through the use of nature itself.

Of wild gods, knowledge and the transcendence of territory

The territory of female knowledge invokes unmediated associations with and encompassment of *vodhun*, directly mapped onto and located in women's bodies and enacted through an immediate reflection and appropriation of cosmological locality and natural landscape. Women in general provide and reflect the raw material of existence in the form of unmoulded clay and blood-filled wombs. More particularly, initiates and devotees of secret societies take these associations one step further by becoming direct embodiments of their gods during possession (see Lovell 1997). Indeed, they are called '*vodhun*', and acquire particular forms of initiatic knowledge where these links are made more explicit in songs, enacted rituals and possession itself. Territories of male knowledge involve the custodianship of *vodhun* yet remain partly constrained by their gender, since male shrine keepers cannot accede to the secret knowledge imparted on women during initiation, which is almost exclusively a female affair.[14]

Ceremonies marking the end of initiation of female novices into secret societies attached to *vodhun* shrines provide a good illustration of the association between gender, nature and locality. The particular focus here is on the performance of a dance, carried out in the public space just outside the enclosure surrounding the most sacred area of the forest in which the *vodhun* dwells. This area is located between the inhabited space of the village and the bush, along the path leading away from the inhabited centre and into the bush. It is therefore best characterised as a space between the sacred (the forest itself) and the everyday contexts. It is also a space that is inherently 'void' (see Parkin 1991). The heart of the forest is inhabited by *vodhun*, while the centre of the village obviously represents the core of human everyday activity. This normally void space, which is usually only passed through when walking from one hamlet to another, is particularly well suited to this kind of performance precisely because of its lack of definable status in the Watchi idiom. It is neither male – represented by male settlement and village life – nor female – as evidenced by the female activities enacted in the sacred forest. In addition, this space is neither entirely public – again, as reflected in village life – nor unconditionally private and secret – as propounded by the *vodhun* inside the shrine and forest themselves. It is referred to as the space outside of the sacred forest (*hunkpame*, literally 'the enclosure of blood'), or sometimes as the space outside the village, but it has no name of its own. The initiates perform their dances here at the very end of their seclusion in the sacred enclosure of the *vodhun*, where they have spent most of their time during initiation.

The end of initiation is marked by a ceremony which lasts four nights and three days, and which involves the initiates in activities over which their level of control varies greatly. It is clear that their active participation increases as the ritual proceeds. They see themselves being acted upon (being fed, dressed, asked to dance, sacrificed upon, being made to drink the blood of sacrificial chickens) in the beginning, while their own contribution to all these activities is more marked towards the end of the ritual. I focus here on an event which takes place on the third day, at dusk, and continues until the final day of the ceremony.

The novices, held in seclusion inside the sacred ground where they have undergone initiation for periods ranging from three months to a few years, are joined in this part of the performance by fully initiated members of the secret societies. Most of them are female , but one male novice and a handful of male initiates are also present (see note 12). The dance that is about to be performed provides the novices with the first opportunity since their initiation started to display their skills to the general public. Female novices and devotees dance in pairs, or in groups of four. They move down the length of the dancing ground (about 100 meters) and back again, keeping pace with one another. They return to where they started, and are then replaced by another group of female dancers. Having exchanged their loincloth for a new, more colourful one, the first group resumes its dance. This part of the performance continues, groups of dancers succeeding one another, displaying their skills and being cheered on by members of their families and the general public, all of whom are keen to comment upon what they see.

The ground suddenly empties, the paraffin lamp illuminating the scene is extinguished in a hush, while the drums continue to beat. The music then speeds up, the drummers playing with all their might. In complete darkness, the empty ground is suddenly and noisily invaded by the female novices and the devotees, who leap out of the bushes surrounding the sacred forest, chanting, shouting and ululating. They dance energetically, running in all directions, carrying small bushes on their heads. Their movements are highly disorganised and uncoordinated, their dancing and running markedly contrasting with the structured display of their earlier performance. They run out of the central ground, some towards the forest, others towards the village which they are not allowed to enter. The male devotees, and the only male novice, suddenly spring out of the bushes too (they themselves do not carry any shrubs on their heads), bouncing into the central ground, and dance around the women while attempting to encircle them. They slowly bring all of them into the middle, where the women fall silent and motionless to the ground. The men continue to run around them, in ever smaller and constrained circles.

This part of the dance was likened to a hunt. Informants referred to the men as *adelā*, hunters, and to the women as *alōlā*, animals of the wild. The reference to wild animals and their association with women is common among the Watchi, and indeed echoes other ethnographic data from West Africa and beyond. Women are often associated with wild meat (*gbeme lā*) and, by extension, with the bush (*gbe*) or uninhabited areas. Thus a woman who has been unfaithful to her husband is said to 'have put her foot in the bush' (*edho fo gbe*), a reference which indicates her close association with an unruly state to which she is constantly drawn and to which she may also return. Women are sometimes likened to bats (*aguto*), another animal of the wild, and are said to 'fly and hang on other trees' (i.e. men) if dissatisfied or unhappy in their relationships. Significantly, discourses held by men about women parallel many of the idioms used when referring to *vodhun* which are also viewed as wild, untamed, unruly and potentially unpredictable and fickle in their attachments.

Yet where men are concerned, nature, women, gods and the wild also represent the highly fertile landscape where game can be acquired and prestige achieved. And while the wild areas of the bush are populated by *vodhun*, game and, potentially, women who always show a propensity for preferring such a habitat, the pinnacle of culture is also associated with these areas. Women have a privileged access to knowledge of *vodhun* through the very nature of their identity as women, and are therefore elevated precisely through this association with the wild. The bush may well be pre-social and unruly, but power also inheres in chaos (see Parkin 1985). By locating herbs in clay, trees in pots, *vodhun* in shrines and children in wombs and blood, men enact their attempts at containing what might always run away. *Vodhun* might suddenly abandon a community, and women cut across territories through the various tasks they perform

– such as collecting wood, tending to fields, fetching water at streams – through virilocal marriage or by being taken away and becoming the spouses of *vodhun* (or other men). Men and *vodhun* thus compete with one another for the attention and devotion of women, but men ultimately always comply with the wishes of their gods, since these provide the ultimate legitimacy for settlement. Paradoxically, although the earthly nurturing nature of women as pots is constantly propounded through the imagery of clay, blood and fertility present in *vodhun* rituals, women (whether devotees or not) regularly desert their households when ritual ceremonies take place, temporarily leaving behind their usual domestic tasks of cooking for and nurturing others in order to emphasise aspects of their fertile association with the gods.

The relationship between genders is itself multivocal, and mirrors the discourse relating to locality and belonging. While women are sometimes referred to as wild animals which need to be hunted down by men so that order can prevail, such metaphors also involve the men in hunting in new, unknown and potentially dangerous territories. Only through women can territories be expanded and male trees be planted, since the grounding pot of descent and emplacement, and the founding womb of *fome* as place of gestation and as locality for settlement are unequivocally embodied in women. The analogy extends to *vodhun* themselves, since they too are essential to the establishment of settlement and the provision of cosmic blessing and approval. The fixity of *vodhun*, like the fixity of women, determines locality and belonging by virtue of male legitimate settlement and the appropriated and located sheltering properties of the house. Yet the non-fixity and movement of both deities and women are also essential elements in securing access to new – earthly and cosmological – territories and fertile procreation. The clay of pots and wombs used to locate and make effigies of the gods is also pervasive as it can be found anywhere in Watchi territory. Pots and wombs thereby demarcate belonging, but they also embody movement and the containment and expansion of history itself. Women may be chased by men since they belong to the wild, yet they also embody the epitome of 'culture' and knowledge through their association with cosmology. Through their close link with *vodhun*, women are being hunted not only to be controlled, but also in order for the men who hunt them to have access to the space which they, as women, inhabit but which is also the natural dwelling place of the gods. The transformative processes involved in the dialectical relationships between humans and nature thereby positions culture in 'places in between' (Bhabha 1994), since *vodhun* cosmology highlights this inherent mobility across potentially habitable territories. By chasing women (or wild animals), men are also relinquishing power to the hunted since they, the 'prey', always lead the way. The association of women with wild animals is, therefore, a double source of prestige: women, like animals, provide meat in the form of sexual intercourse, and in the form of children. But one property to be hunted is much more elusive to the hunter: knowledge of the *vodhun* itself, in its unmediated and experiential form. This remains inaccessible. When asked about their relationship to men and male keepers of shrines, a group of female initiates engaged me in the following song:

> The knowledge of *vodhun*
> He cannot understand
> He will not know
> He guesses in the enclosure
> So that he (can) hear the knowledge
> The knowledge of the *vodhun* is frightening
> He cannot understand

Conclusion

Associations between deities and natural features in *vodhun* religion have prompted Augé (1988) to seek to understand the reasoning behind what he calls the worship of inanimate objects (la matière) as a universal religious propensity. What motivates Man (Augé's idiom) to devote his attention to stones, pieces of wood, rivers, the sea and the earth? Why do such objects become deified? Augé's argument is ultimately structuralistic, but he also uses a healthy dose of Cartesian inspiration: Man, he claims, is able to worship stones because they provide a sounding board for his own thoughts about himself and about the world. Material objects are therefore 'good to think', à la Lévi-Strauss, because man is constantly involved in making sense of the world, and in classifying its features. Thinking about the world thus not only makes it more intelligible, but provides a means of control over one's environment. However, Augé goes further and investigates how this propensity of the mind to structure one's surroundings also involves reflexivity and auto-reflection: by objectifying nature, man proves to himself that he has the capacity to think (Je pense donc je suis), thus reifying his human existence and identity. The process is a conscious one, where man's ability to create the world in his own thought materialises this world, making it more present through its subjugation and objectification.

While Augé focuses on what he refers to as pagan representations of nature through the deification of matter (*la matière*), others (Douglas 1966, 1975; Descola 1994; Århem in Chapter 3 of this volume) argue that the propensity to use and transform nature in such ways seems to be universal, albeit in culturally specific ways. All cultures appear to reify elements of nature, either through religious and ritual forms such as the Ndembu's use of the *mudyi* tree, or through environmental awareness in the form of pressure groups. Like Augé, Descola ponders over the universality of such characterisations, and although he agrees that the relationship with nature may take different forms cross-culturally, giving rise to distinct notions of 'nature' itself, certain features of the natural environment seem to be acted upon universally, not so much because they act as archetypes (in a Jungian sense), but rather because human sociality appears to focus ontologically on certain key features of the environment which become conducive to the emergence and development of fruitful social praxis. Nature is thus appropriated by humans in order for it to be socialised, while serving as a focus for socially significant human interaction. The objectification of nature, in this sense, is a necessary means to its domestication and socialisation through its incorporation into the human domain. The process is thereby inherently social in character. Nature needs to be socialised in order for it to be understood, and only through this appropriation can it be of any use in 're-presenting' human sociality. In this view, the externalising process is also essential in creating a human identity distinctive from nature. Descola's interpretation, through its highly sophisticated rendering of nature and the social, is also inherently problematic: what he terms the objectification of nature must remain a highly ambiguous exercise, since objectification *per se* also involves an artificial distance between the human, which is alive, and the object, which is rendered closer to inanimate matter. Nature and human identity are seen as ontologically distinct categories, rather than transformative and interactive processes. If seen as discursive action, the socialisation of nature is bound to alter the essence of nature itself and, by the same token, of human identity *per se*.

The belief in the existence of ontological classifications is itself problematic, since their presence can neither be confirmed nor denied, and the argument therefore relies on a circularity which is difficult to disentangle. Douglas engaged us in an early and similar discussion relating to universal perceptions of the body and its products (1966, 1975). Admittedly, in the quest for human universals, such notions appear appealing. However, they rely on an externalising concept of nature where nature is, in itself, a thing which needs objectification (either in order to become fully social, as in Descola's interpretation, or in order to prove man's capacity to think and reflect upon his environment, as propounded by Augé or, before him, Lévi-Strauss). Neither view focuses on the 'making' of nature. Nature either provides raw material, is constituted of matter (*la matière*), is the product of human thought or is endowed with natural symbols. These things are assumed to be already there. Moreover, such interpretations tend to view nature as external to, and distinct from, 'human nature'. Humans act upon nature as privileged creation in order to understand and socialise it, remaining distant from and domineering over natural processes, rather than being part of them.

Trying to resolve the issue by focusing on the materiality of nature appears to be missing the point, and is ultimately an unanswerable conundrum. Nature, like ethnicity, does not possess an essence which makes it inherently meaningful. An understanding of nature, based on the notion of a raw material, is bound to be as misleading as an understanding of ethnicity based on the assumption of race. Concepts of nature are connected with boundaries, as Douglas and others (Scheper-Hughes and Lock 1987; Boddy 1989) have repeatedly pointed out, but these boundaries are not fixed. The construction, maintenance, negotiation and transformation of boundaries pertaining to nature, the human body or ethnicity are all elements which are instrumental in the definition of these concepts in the first place (see also Stokes 1994 on a phenomenology of music, and Weiner 1991 on poetry). Only by focusing on these dynamics can nature be better understood. The process by which nature is created in the first place, appropriated, imbued with meaning and transformed into a mirroring image of human society would emphasise the malleability of such a concept. Nature is indeed 'good to think', but only inasmuch as it provides the means for a socially dynamic exchange which involves human sociality as well as a phenomenological positioning of humans within place. The concept of nature is itself bound to be affected in the flow of information about and around it. Thus the objectification of nature does not bring nature into the social sphere, but rather involves it in a dialectic relationship where nature does more than simply reflect society (such as in totemism). Nature is itself acted upon in order continually to transform its meaning, in relation to social, moral and experiential codes. Nature becomes socially meaningful because it provides the means through which humans can recognise identities and places, and transcend these when necessary.

Watchi notions of locality, and of its construction, are at best multifaceted. The *vodhun* contribute to a sense of belonging to the place of settlement, and provide a subsequent justification to such a claim, but they are not alone in doing so. Humans are dialectically involved in the shaping of the identities of their deities, and in allowing their presence on earth in the first place. The processes involved in the shaping of *vodhun*'s identities, shrines and receptacles such as pots also involve humans in the direct shaping of their environment and in the appropriation of nature. Creating a cosmology positions gods in the human community, legitimising claims on territory and movement through time and space, and ensuring the continuity of human life itself; but it also maps out cosmological territories which humans come to inhabit through their association with *vodhun*. Knowing the world therefore implies a direct knowledge of earthly territories transferred onto metaphysical landscapes of belonging, enacted and made implicit by virtue of knowledge itself. Nature is not objectified through this process, nor is it simply socialised to bring it within human bounds. Nature in this sense does not exist simply in society, but it is also viewed as society. The image of nature within human society is thus matched by an image of humans within nature.

Acknowledgements

* I am indebted to David Zeitlyn and Wenonah Lyon for comments provided on earlier drafts of this paper.

Notes

1 The Watchi are most commonly linked with the wider Ewe group, which stretches westwards from this region of Togo across the border into the southeast of Ghana. They also share important similarities with the neighbouring Fon of Benin, most particularly in the domain of religion.
2 And indeed, some of these kinship ties are also mediated through their relationships with humans, although I shall not dwell on this point here for lack of space.
3 Again, the stress in this context is on how narratives fuse with phenomenological experiences of the 'lived' world. Jackson saliently points out that 'Unlike theoretical explanations, narrative redescription is a crucial and constitutive part of the ongoing activity of the lifeworld, which is why narrative plays such a central role in phenomenological description. Moreover, narrative activity reveals the link between discourse and practice, since the very structure of narrative is pregiven in the structure of everyday life' (1996: 39) and, quoting MacIntyre, 'stories are lived before they are told' (MacIntyre in Jackson 1996: 39).
4 I refer to these narratives as one aspect of how the Watchi perceive their world, temporarily, when prompted by ritual occasions or the enquiries of a

curious anthropologist. It does not signify that all Watchi conceive of their existence as overly cosmological, nor for that matter is their cosmology homogeneous.

5 In most contemporary Christian or Christianised discourses, Mawu has acquired an unequivocally male character. The Ewe translation of the Bible equates Mawu with God in contemporary discourses (see Greene 1996 for a historical overview).

6 Witchcraft is said to be unable to perch on this tree, thus making the dwelling secure and protected for its inhabitants. The oil from its nuts are used in sacrifices to ward off evil.

7 The nuts used in divination always stem from this particular palm tree, and are referred to as the (generally male) diviner's wives. The many combinations of the Ewe divinatory system known as Afa (and closely akin to Yoruba Fa divination), are subdivided into 255 possible combinations, the first sixteen of which are considered female, and represent the origins of the world, and the founding clans (*fome*, which literally translates as 'in the womb'). These sixteen combinations are also considered the mothers of divination. All subsequent permutations are described as male, and are treated as the children of the first sixteen mothers.

8 It is no coincidence that chickens are the primary sacrificial offering in *vodhun* rituals. Women often consume the blood of these birds before possession, just as the *vodhun* is supposed to mount its devotees.

9 Several courses of action can be recommended at this stage, but I shall focus only on the installation of shrines in the present context.

10 This process of keeping the pots intact and in good condition has nothing to do with abstinence from premarital relationships. Watchi adolescents are relatively free to engage in amorous pursuits and experience sexual relationships prior to marriage, as long as these do not lead to unexpected or unwanted pregnancies. This would, indeed, make the 'pot' unsound.

11 These same idioms of infertility are used to describe witches, who are said to feed on their own children in the womb, preventing their growth and well-being. A woman who cannot cook and is unable to nurture husband and children appropriately is thus associated with a broken pot, and therefore runs the risk of being accused of witchcraft, eating her children and possibly bewitching her husband instead of imbuing them with life.

12 Such is the power of deities that when a new market, intended by the Togolese government to be one of the largest in West Africa, was commissioned and built in Lomé in the late 1980s it quickly fell into disuse and is now derelict due, people say, to insufficient sacrifices to the gods. A venue of that scale requires human sacrifice, and the government allegedly refused to be involved in such practices since this would have attracted adverse international attention. It is said that the scale of the project nevertheless elicited persons with vested interests to abduct and kill several people in the area. As even this was insufficient to properly propitiate the gods and invest the territory with appropriate powers, the market never thrived.

In addition, during recent fieldwork among a group of Anlo-Ewe in Ghana, a whole community was said to have abandoned its settlement some fifteen years ago due to an unresolved dispute over the guardianship of a *vodhun*'s shrine. The police had to intervene after violent clashes broke out between various factions of the community. The site is said to remain derelict but under constant police supervision.

In another such dispute, in the town of Anlogan, a prominent trader undertook the construction of a very large house in the centre of town in the 1940s. When I enquired about its unfinished state (in 1996), one of my informants simply pointed across the road, where a *vodhun*'s shrine was located in a courtyard. I was told that as the new two-storey house would have overlooked the shrine, 'exposing its genitals' for the new residents to see, the *vodhun*'s dissatisfaction had inflicted countless misfortunes on the proprietor, who eventually dropped his project and let the house stand unfinished. Thus if *vodhun* are essential in helping establish a locality, they can also restrain its expansion and act as powerful agents in human conflicts over land rights and religious conflicts, particularly in contexts of modernity.

13 Ancestors and *vodhun* are kept strictly separate. Anyone associated with the shrines of *vodhun* in the capacity of cult leaders, healers, devotees and initiates of *vodhun* secret societies where possession takes place, are never to enter the cycle of ancestorhood. They are said instead to return to life anew in order to feed the cosmological sphere by providing new cult leaders, healers, devotees and so on, thereby creating a descent line of 'returnees' (*amedzodzo*). People who become ancestors, by contrast, lead ordinary lives, and are not involved in *vodhun* in any systematic or structured fashion. The functions of chiefs and cult leaders are incompatible, since the first are intended to reach ancestorhood, while the latter are to be recycled into *vodhun* cosmology.

14 A few boys and men are nevertheless included, and are incorporated only by virtue of following a female line and being subsumed in their mother's blood. They perform important functions such as sacrifices (which women cannot do). However, shrine keepers are precluded from becoming initiates; see Lovell 1993, 1997.

References

Augé, M. (1988) *Le Dieu Objet*, Paris: Editions Flammarion.

Barber, K. (1981) 'How Man Makes God in Africa: Yoruba Attitudes towards the *Orisa*', *Africa* 51(3): 724–45.

—— (1990) '*Oriki*, Women, and the Proliferation and Merging of *Orisa*', *Africa* 60(3): 313–38.

Barnes, S.T. (1989) 'Introduction: The Many Faces of Ogun', in S.T. Barnes (ed.), *Africa's Ogun: Old World and New*, Bloomington, IN: Indiana University Press.

Bhabha, H.K. (1994) *The Location of Culture*, London: Routledge.

Boddy, J. (1989) *Wombs and Alien Spirits: Women, Men and the Zar Cult in Northern Sudan*, Madison, WI: University of Wisconsin Press.

Descola, P. (1994) *In the Society of Nature: A Native Ecology in Amazonia*, Cambridge: Cambridge University Press.

Douglas, M. (1966) *Purity and Danger: An Analysis of Concepts of Pollution and Taboo*, London: Routledge & Kegan Paul.

—— (1975) *Implicit Meanings: Essays in Anthropology*, London: Routledge & Kegan Paul.

Gayibor, N.L. (1986) *Les Peuples et Royaumes du Golfe du Bénin*, Lomé: Institut National des Sciences de l'Education, Université du Bénin.

Greene, S.E. (1996) 'Religion, History and the Supreme Gods of Africa: A Contribution to the Debate', *Journal of Religion in Africa* 26(2): 122–38.

Jackson, M. (1996) 'Introduction', in M. Jackson (ed.), *Things as They Are: New Directions in Phenomenological Anthropology*, Bloomington, IN: Indiana University Press.

Lovell, N.I. (1993) 'Cord of Blood: Gender, Medicine and Social Dynamics among the Watchi of South-East Togo', unpublished Ph.D. thesis, School of Oriental and African Studies, University of London.

—— (1997) 'Unleashing Spirits and Unbounding Gender: Vocal Gods and Polyvalent Discourse in Watchi Possession', *Ethnos* 62(3–4): 79–106.

Maupoil, B. (1943) *La Géomancie à l'Ancienne Côte des Esclaves*, Paris: Institut d'Ethnologie.

McCarthy-Brown, C. (1989) 'Systematic Remembering, Systematic Forgetting: Ogou in Haiti', in S.T. Barnes (ed.) *Africa's Ogun: Old World and New*, Bloomington, IN: Indiana University Press.

Medeiros, F. de (ed.) (1984) *Peuples du Golfe du Bénin*, Paris: Editions Karthala.

Nukunya, G.K. (1969) *Kinship and Marriage among the Anlo Ewe*, London: Athlone Press.

Parkin, D. (1985) *The Anthropology of Evil*, Oxford: Basil Blackwell.

—— (1991) *Sacred Void: Spatial Images of Work and Ritual among the Giriama of Kenya*, Cambridge: Cambridge University Press.

Rivière, C. (1981) *Anthropologie Religieuse des Evhé du Togo*, Paris: Les Nouvelles Editions Africaines.

Scheper-Hughes, N. and Lock, M. (1987) 'The Mindful Body: A Prolegomenon to Future Work in Medical Anthropology', *Medical Anthropology Quarterly* 1: 6–41.

Surgy, A. de (1981) *Géomancie et le Culte d'Afa chez les Evhé*, Paris: Publications Orientalistes de France.

—— (1988) *Le Système Religieux des Evhé*, Paris: Editions l'Harmattan.

Stokes, M. (1994) 'Introduction', in M. Stokes (ed.), *Ethnicity, Identity and Music: The Musical Construction of Place*, Oxford: Berg.

Verdon, M. (1983) *The Abutia Ewe of West Africa: The Kingdom that Never Was*, Berlin: Mouton Publishers.

Verger, P. (1957) *Notes sur le Culte des Orisa et Vodun à Bahia, la Baie de Tous les Saints au Brézil et à l'Ancienne Côte des Esclaves en Afrique*, Dakar: Institut Français d'Afrique Noire.

Weiner, J.F. (1991) *The Empty Place: Poetry, Space and Being among the Foi of Papua New Guinea*, Bloomington, IN: Indiana University Press.

Werbner, R. (ed.) (1977) *Regional Cults*, London: Academic Press.

Chapter 3

Powers of place

Landscape, territory and local belonging in Northwest Amazonia[*]

Kaj Århem

Notions of landscape, territory and local belonging are, on the whole, little explored in Amazonian ethnography.[1] It is as if the apparently undifferentiated vastness of the lowland tropical forest has discouraged anthropologists from studying local landscape phenomenologies, and as if notions of territory and tenure are assumed to be irrelevant or poorly developed in this scarcely populated vastness. In fact, the Amazonian environment is exceedingly diverse and differentiated (Moran 1993), and is perceived as such by its human inhabitants. Northwest Amazonia is particularly interesting in this regard. Here, elaborate 'shamanic geographies' coexist with patrilineal descent systems and explicit notions of ancestral territories.[2] In many respects, Northwest Amazonian cosmologies, like those of the Australian aborigines, are landscape-based (Morphy 1993). Myth and shamanic discourse – the authoritative idiom in which knowledge is codified – are grounded in the local landscape, and the segmentary social organisation is spatially articulated in a distinctive territorial system, identifying exogamous descent groups with particular ancestral territories. The precise nature of this territorial bond, and the subtle connections between cosmology and socio-political organisation – in particular, the relationship between the idea of territory and the practice of tenure – remains, however, largely unexplored.

Two largely opposed views can be discerned in the literature: one where descent ideology and shamanic notions of territory are divorced from tenure and control over subsistence recourses (Goldman 1963; Jackson 1983; Reichel-Dolmatoff 1986); and another where territorial control is seen as a functional aspect of descent and thus pivotal to the working of the social system (Hill and Moran 1983; Moran 1991; Chernela 1993). Drawing on ethnographic material on the Pirá-Paraná groups of the Colombian Amazon, principally the Makuna, the present chapter suggests an alternative interpretation of Northwest Amazonian territoriality, allowing for a reconciliation of these conflicting views. The picture that emerges is a complex one, where shamanic knowledge and ritual control over land and its creative potential – including river territory and river resources – play a central role in mediating between a descent-derived notion of territorial 'ownership' and effective tenure. In the concluding section of the chapter, the narrow ethnographic focus is opened up towards a broader, and theoretically suggestive, comparative horizon.

Ancestral territory

Subsisting on shifting cultivation, fishing and hunting, the Tukano-speaking groups inhabiting the Pirá-Paraná river system in central Northwest Amazonia display the features conventionally associated with Tukanoan social organisation, notably patrilineal descent, symmetric alliance and linguistic exogamy. Pirá-Paraná society forms a tightly knit but open-ended social universe of some six to eight named exogamous groups, each ideally constituting a distinct language unit.[3] The various groups relate to each other in terms of single-generation relationship terms such as 'elder/younger brothers', 'affines' or 'mother's children'. Groups related as 'brothers' do not intermarry, while those classified as 'affines' are potential or preferential partners in marriage-exchange. 'Mother's children' represent an intermediary and ambiguous category in the system; intermarriage is infrequent but does occasionally occur. Each exogamous group is symbolically associated with a particular cosmic domain – Earth, Sky or Water – so that their integration into the wider Pirá-Paraná society expresses the wholeness of the cosmos.

The normative mode of marriage, as codified in the idiom of the agnatic ideology, is the balanced exchange of women between groups of affinally-related men.[4] Dyadic sets of affines tend to develop close relations of intermarriage. The Makuna, inhabiting the lower part of the Pirá-Paraná river and a section of the Apaporis river, comprise one such pair of closely intermarrying exogamous groups. The two groups, referring to themselves as Water People (*Ide masa*) and Earth People (*Yiba masa*), share a contiguous territory and speak a common language, thus violating the Tukanoan ideal of linguistic exogamy. The long history of intermarriage between the two groups has contributed to the forging of a common and largely endogamous identity which, in important respects, supersedes the categorical identity of each of the component exogamous groups. The profile sketched here of Pirá-Paraná society is seen from a Makuna horizon and, more specifically, from the perspective of the Makuna living on the Komenya river, a left-hand tributary of the Pirá-Paraná river.[5]

The dominant form of settlement among the Pirá-Paraná groups is the large, multifamily house, the 'maloca'.[6] Serving as dwelling, meeting place and temple, the 'maloca' is the centre of Pirá-Paraná social and ritual life. Two basic types of 'malocas' predominate in the region, both of majestic proportions: the rectangular longhouse and the conical roundhouse. Socially, the 'maloca' comprises a core of closely related male agnates: a father and his married sons, or a set of brothers and their wives and children. Marriage is virilocal, and the adult male members of the 'maloca' constitute the lowest-order segment of the descent system. The headman, or 'owner' (*ühü*) of the 'maloca' is typically a senior member of this agnatic core: the eldest son, or the most senior of a set of brothers. Apart from headmen and occasional local leaders, who wield modest and usually ephemeral authority over local clusters of settlements, influence is exercised by prominent ritual specialists, particularly protective shamans (*kumua*) and chanters (*yoamara*).

The exogamous group is internally segmented into named clans, ranked in order of seniority as elder and younger 'brothers' (*bai masa/kien masa*). The clan ancestors are conceived of as 'sons' of a single 'father', the eponymous ancestor of the entire exogamous group. This ancestral figure, like the ancestor of each of the component clans, is depicted as a Spirit Anaconda (*hino*) and referred to as the 'grandfather' (*nyikü*) of all living members of the group. Each exogamous group is associated with a bounded river territory, or Water Path (*ide ma*), and a specific ancestral birth place, called the House of Awakening of the ancestors (*büküa masa yuhiri wi*). This Spirit House is conceived of as the dwelling of the ancestral anaconda, and as the home and ultimate destination of the souls of all deceased members of the exogamous group. Upon death, the souls of the deceased travel to this invisible house where they are reborn as 'spirit people' (*rümüa*).

The exogamous group also holds what may be described as corporate sacred property, including tangible ritual goods (musical instruments, ornaments), sacred substances (blessed coca, tobacco, red paint and beeswax), and intangible spiritual wealth, such as chants, songs and a specific set of personal names which circulate among its members in alternate generations. The most important tangible symbol of the group is the set of sacred palmwood flutes – the Yurupari instruments (*he büküra*) – which are said to embody the ancestors. The flutes are brought into the longhouse during important collective rituals, particularly in connection with the male initiation ceremony. In its essential, spirit-form this sacred property, described as 'weapons' and 'defences' (*küni oka*), is said to be kept in the House of Awakening of the group. Shamans and other ritual specialists draw on these spiritual 'weapons' and 'defences' to protect the living against disease and other dangers arising from predatory spirits and enemy peoples.

Each of the (ideally five) ranked clans constituting the exogamous group is associated with a specialist function – chief, chanter, warrior, shaman and servant – in descending order of seniority. This notion of complementary specialist roles, largely pertaining to the domain of ritual and shamanic discourse, amounts to a vision of the functional integration and socio-cosmic unity of the exogamous group. Each clan recognises a proper ancestor and a distinct ancestral birth place, thus duplicating the structural features of the exogamous group as a whole. The hierarchical ordering of clans is articulated in their spatial distribution along the river associated with the exogamous group, so that senior clans are associated with the mouth and lower course while junior clans are associated with the headwaters and upper reaches. The string of mythical birthplaces along the river thus ideally forms a single descent line with its apex at the mouth, close to which the House of Awakening of the entire exogamous group is located.

In shamanic imagery the river territory of the exogamous group is identified with the ancestral anaconda itself, the winding course and flowing waters of the river constituting the living body of the ancestor with its head at the mouth and tail at the source. The territory of each clan corresponds to a segment of the ancestral body, the chiefly clan representing the head and the last-born the tail. The river territory of the exogamous group as a whole is also described as a House in which the different clan sections correspond to the compartments strung out along the central hall of a single great longhouse. House, river and anaconda thus merge into a single, commanding image of the unity and internal differentiation of the exogamous group.

The senior or 'chiefly' clan of the exogamous group is referred to as 'owner' or 'guardian' of the ancestral territory (*riaka ühü*, literally 'owner/guardian of the river'). Since the senior clan tends to be identified with the larger group of which it forms a part, territorial ownership is associated with the exogamous group as a whole. The Earth People are recognised as 'owners' of the Komenya river, and the Water People are similarly 'owners' of the Toaka river on the lower Pirá-Paraná, their original home and ancestral territory. The analogy with 'maloca' organisation is transparent: just as the senior of a set of brothers is the headman and 'owner' of the house, the first-born clan is collectively recognised as 'owner' of the river territory, itself conceived of as a House. Also, just as individuals identify with the house they inhabit, the settlements and localised clan segments along a single river identify with the river that literally and metaphorically connects them, thus expressing their essential relatedness.

The resulting pattern of territoriality conceptually divides the Pirá-Paraná river system into a multiplicity of discrete and internally segmented territories. Each such territory, comprising a major tributary or river section and the adjacent land it drains, is 'owned' by a particular exogamous group and identified with a distinct, named ancestral anaconda. Like language and sacred property, then, territorial ownership is a feature of the descent system. It implies a relationship of identity between ancestral river and exogamous group, and connotes belonging rather than politico-jural control over land and resources. Territorial ownership 'places' the group in social and cosmological space.

River community

Pirá-Paraná territoriality provides a normative model for conceptualising spatial order, but does not account for the actual composition of socio-spatial groups. The concrete, on-the-ground organisation of Pirá-Paraná society can best be described in terms of the systematic articulation of descent and marriage, producing a particular variety of segmentary organisation elsewhere referred to as a 'segmentary alliance system' (Århem 1981). Characteristic of this system is the progressive dispersal of the exogamous group and the concomitant spatial concentration of intermarrying segments from different exogamous groups. By repeating marriage alliances over generations, affines are turned into consanguines, thus transforming the reserved and often tense affinal relationship into one of closeness, solidarity and trust. In effect, the residents of a single tributary or river section form a relatively bounded, coherent and autonomous community of intermarrying clan segments. Each river community is in turn segmented into highly endogamous, consanguineal local groups, structured around strong and stable alliance relationships. Such composite and localised communities – from the cluster of neighbouring settlements to the larger river community – effectively form the building blocks of Pirá-Paraná social and spatial organisation.

The Makuna on the Komenya river provide an instructive example of this articulation of descent and marriage. At the turn of the century, harassed by white rubber hunters and divided by internal conflicts, a segment of Water People on the Toaka river moved up the Pirá-Paraná to the Komenya where they joined a group of Earth People, their traditional allies and 'owners' of the Komenya river.[7] The move was above all an effort to resist (or evade) the onslaught of the whites, but it also represented a manifestation of the strong solidarity among closely intermarrying groups. Today the Water People and the Earth People on the Komenya identify themselves as a single river community. The merging of their related but originally distinct languages expresses the profound sense of community emerging out of close intermarriage and territorial contiguity.[8]

The Makuna make a clear conceptual distinction between the 'river community' as a concrete, localised *group* and the 'exogamous group' as a fundamental social *category*. The distinction is linguistically expressed: a river community or localised population in general is identified by attaching the suffix *gana* to a place name or geographical location, most commonly a river or river section as in *Komenya gana*, 'the people of the Komenya river'. The exogamous group, by contrast, is invariably identified by the suffix *masa* (meaning 'people' or 'humans'), as in *Ide masa*, 'Water People', or *Yiba masa*, 'Earth People'. This distinction between category (*masa*) and community (*gana*) is particularly clear in the contrast between 'owners' and 'residents' of a particular river territory, where 'ownership' is a function of the descent system and 'residence' refers to membership in a localised group or river community. The distinction is socially significant and has crucial practical implications, for while ownership connotes an inalienable spiritual bond between a group and its ancestral territory, residence confers mutable use rights over the resources of the inhabited territory.

In concrete terms, membership of a river community implies the right to cut gardens, to fish and to hunt practically anywhere in the territory. No individual (or group) can claim exclusive rights to potential garden land or to any particular hunting or fishing ground. Communal access to forest and river resources is limited only by metaphysically motivated restrictions on hunting and fishing, which apply to 'owners' and 'residents' alike (see p. 94). Within the loosely bounded locality occupied by a cluster of settlements, the gardens belonging to the different settlements intermingle and the exploitation of hunting and fishing grounds overlap, but between one locality and another such overlapping is rare. This differentiation of territory with respect to resource use is, however, tacit, discreet and informal; nothing prevents a man from one part of the territory from clearing land or hunting or fishing in another. Indeed, men make sporadic fishing expeditions into sections of the river inhabited and exploited by other local groups, precisely in order to demonstrate their presence and reaffirm their claims to the common resources of the territory. Usually such journeys are combined with social visiting; they may be preludes to a joint ritual, a means of restoring fractured relations, or of creating new alliances. This pattern of intense social and ritual interaction within and among local clusters in a single territory serves to shape and consolidate the river community as a cohesive social, political and territorial unit.

Stephen Hugh-Jones (1995) has suggested that Tukanoan society is best understood in terms of two alternative and co-existing conceptual models, which correspond to gendered readings of the 'maloca' as metaphor and social category: the 'maloca' as a fundamental agnatic unit in the descent system (male reading), and as a consanguineal group of men and women – a procreative unit and reproductive social body, metaphorically associated with the womb (female reading). Both models are ritually underpinned. The Descent House as all-male agnatic reality is epitomised by the Yurupari ritual (*he wi*) in connection with male initiation, when women and children are excluded and the male participants are identified with the ancestors, embodied in the sacred Yurupari instruments. Initiates are made to 'die' and are then reborn as adult men and full members of the descent group. The whole ritual can be seen as a reaffirmation of the descent system and the spiritual unity of the exogamous group. Analogously, the Consanguineal House as procreative, female body and commensal community is given ritual expression in the Food-giving ritual (*bare ekari wi*), during which a highly formalised exchange of food between kin (hosts) and affines (guests) is progressively transformed into a joint feast with distinct sexual overtones. Categorical distinctions are thus symbolically dissolved, and the 'maloca' turns into a community of consanguines. This ritually created Consanguineal House supplies the conceptual model for the formation of the endogamous local and territorial groupings, constitutive of Pirá-Paraná socio-spatial organisation. Contextually symbolising the unity of agnates and the community of consanguines, the 'maloca' thus embodies the entire range of Tukanoan notions of human sociality. Indeed, the House is metaphorically made to encompass the whole world.

The *maloca*-cosmos

The Pirá-Paraná groups conceptualise the cosmos as an immense 'maloca', a World House with doors, posts, beams, walls and roof. The sky is the roof, the hills and mountains are the supporting posts and protective walls, and the earth is the floor. Along the middle of the 'maloca' cosmos runs the Milk River, debouching in the Water Door in the east. The Water Door is the entry to the World House, the point of creative beginning and the source of all life. The Door of Suffering in the west is the exit and opening into the underworld, associated with death and decay. The model of the 'maloca' cosmos is mapped onto the major features – the hills, rivers and rapids – of the local landscape. Each major river basin in the region is conceived of as forming one such localised world – a World House – structured by the river system that traverses it, and enclosed by the surrounding hills and uplands separating one river basin from another. The Pirá-Paraná landscape is thus imaged as a nesting series of houses within houses, from the Houses of clans and exogamous groups, identified with single rivers and their sections, to the World House of an entire river basin.

The extent and precise boundaries of such a localised world vary from one group to another. From the point of view of the Makuna, the Apaporis river is the axis of the world. The Pirá-Paraná basin forms one side of their 'maloca' cosmos, the other side comprising the southern affluents of the lower and middle Apaporis, inhabited by the Letuama, Tanimuka and Yauna groups. The Makuna say that 'their' world (*güa sita*; literally 'our earth') begins at the falls of La Libertad (Yuisi *gumu*) on the lower Apaporis, and ends at the Jirijirimo falls (Hasa hudiro) in its upper reaches. Yuisi *gumu* is the Water Door, the entry into their House. Hasa hudiro is the exit, their Door of Suffering, where the souls of the dead leave the House of the living. The centre of the 'maloca' cosmos is said to be close to the source of the Komenya river. Uninhabited and rarely visited, this site is called Tabotiro, the Place of White Grass. Those who have seen it say it is an open, treeless area in the midst of the forest, covered with shining white grass. At Tabotiro, the Makuna say, there is an invisible cosmic pillar, reaching to the uppermost sky and extending deep into the underworld, along which shamans travel between the different layers of the cosmos. This is the wicker pot-stand in the centre of the 'maloca' cosmos, holding the gourds of coca and snuff of the ancestors.

The Makuna see themselves as living in the middle of this World House. They refer to themselves as *güdareko gana*, 'the people of the centre'. The groups on the upper Pirá-Paraná – Barasana, Taiwano, Tatuyu and others – are referred to as 'headwater peoples' (*hode gana*), while the Yauna, Letuama and Tanimuka peoples living on the lower and middle Apaporis are referred to as 'downstream peoples' (*roka gana*). More remote peoples, living at the edge of the named and known world

– the Tukano, Cubeo, Cabiyarí, Yukuna and Witoto – are referred to as 'peoples of the margin', *tünima gana*. They belong to other Houses, other worlds. Their territories are, in cosmological terms, little known and potentially perilous.

A sequence of cosmogonic myths accounts for the creation of the cosmos and provides the key to Pirá-Paraná notions of landscape. The myths centre on two principal ancestral beings, Romi Kumu (literally Woman Shaman) and Ayawa, the eldest of a group of heroic brothers (Ayawaroa). Woman Shaman, usually represented in the singular, is the original procreator and Mother of the World (*ümüari hako*). As her name suggests, she is attributed with the power of shamanism which today is the prerogative of men and male ritual specialists; in fact, she is a 'woman' with male powers, an androgynous – or rather presexual – self-sufficient, self-reproducing being, a world unto herself. Ayawa is her 'male' counterpart, usually standing for the phratric set of primordial ancestors, the Male Creators, embodied in the Yurupari instruments. According to myth, Woman Shaman was originally alone. She was consubstantial with the world; the world was her body. A mythic episode referred to as 'the creation of time' (*rodo meni*) describes, in metaphorical terms, the onset of her menstrual cycle, equated with the cyclical alternation between the dry and the wet seasons of the year. Time – as manifest in the annual and menstrual cycles – was created, and the earth made fecund. Plants and animals emerged directly from Woman Shaman's exceedingly fertile womb.

Another set of images describes creation in terms of the maturing bodies of the Male Creators, and as the outcome of their heroic deeds and creative craft. Various myth fragments describe the primordial ancestors travelling across the earth in search of its centre, which is the domain of Woman Shaman and contextually identified with her house, body or womb. Encircling the world and walking in line, the ancestors named and appropriated the land for the peoples that were to inhabit it. As they walked on the soft and level earth, singing and playing the Yurupari instruments, mountains were formed from the sound of their flutes, and the rivers emerged out of the saliva dripping from the orifices of their instruments. At various points along the way, they stopped to masturbate in the cavities of trees and to prepare their ritual ornaments. The trees bore fruit, and animals of all kinds emerged from the wastes of their work. Arriving at the centre, the ancestors 'measured' the world by extending the principal Yurupari instrument (called Gekero) in the four cardinal directions, and upward and downward. Then, they placed their stools in a circle around the centre and sat down to rest. Thus they created the world in the form of a huge 'maloca', illuminated by their radiant feather crowns and shining ritual ornaments. At the centre was the pot stand, holding the ancestral gourd of coca.

This 'male' sequence accounts for the creation of space and the physical features of the landscape. Earth, water, rocks and mountains, just as plants, animals and artefacts, are one with the ancestors. Again, the process of creation is identified with bodily change. As the young ancestors travel from margin to centre they mature into sexual beings, overflowing with male potency and uncontained desire. Reaching the centre, they 'measure' the world by actually 'pushing' it into its present spatial extension; they make 'room' for their descendants to occupy it. The very process of creation is here represented as a transforming act of erection and ejaculation. The Yurupari instrument is the divine phallus, the epitome and supreme image of male generative power. The formation of rocks, hills and mountains metaphorically alludes to the progressively hardening bodies and swelling penises of the ancestors, and the imagery of river formation – the saliva dripping from the orifices of their sacred instruments – evokes the image of ejaculation and the discharge of divine semen. The phallic formation of space and landscape, and the uterine creation of time and seasonal change, thus together form two gendered and complementary images of creation. The world is at the same time house and body, male and female.

The culminating event in the cosmogonic account is the portentous encounter between Ayawaroa and Woman Shaman. The gendered images of creation merge, and the creative process is brought to full fruition. The Male Creators appropriate the ritual goods, originally in the possession of Woman Shaman, and impregnate her with their potent semen, thereby fertilising the world. Thus deprived of her 'male' powers, androgynous Woman Shaman becomes woman, the primordial procreator in control of sexual reproduction. The Male Creators, on their part, gain control over the ritual goods and shamanic knowledge and thus acquire the secret of immortality. Male supremacy is established. Woman Shaman-turned-woman is forced to leave her original domain in the centre, and travels to the Water Door in the east to give birth to the ancestral anacondas, progenitors of all current life-forms on earth, including humans. Cosmos is gendered, life engendered. As they mature, the ancestral anacondas swim upriver towards the centre, each taking possession of its proper place and establishing the ancestral territories of the different exogamous groups. Having completed their work, the ancestors ascend to the sky, each occupying a distinct level, thus creating the different layers of the cosmos.

In the same cosmogonic move, the ontological disjunction between the physical and the spiritual realms of the cosmos is established. Sky and earth, the ethereal realm of spirits and the earthly domain of mortals – humans, animals and plants – are separated. Life on earth becomes physical and corporeal, and sexual procreation becomes the generative principle of the gendered universe. The trophic chain of eaters and food, and the biological processes of birth, maturation, decay and death are established as the ordering templates of life.

The cosmogonic myths provide the legitimising charter for the descent system and the mythological context for 'reading' the landscape. Hills and mountains are spoken of as the houses or stools of the ancestors or, alternatively, as their petrified bodies. The names of the hills encircling the Pirá-Paraná basin – Sun, Star, Jaguar Head, Stool, Metal Ornament, White Fish, Curassow and so on – all refer to attributes, possessions, bodily parts or transfigurations of particular, named ancestors. In the vision of shamans, mountains are the ancestors who, in turn, are metaphorically depicted as the supportive house posts and protective walls of the 'maloca'-cosmos. Therefore, Makuna say, shamans look after the hills and mountains just as the headman of the 'maloca' looks after his house and the people inhabiting it. By offering coca and snuff to the hills, shamans feed the ancestors and ask for their protection.

The Pirá-Paraná and Apaporis river systems trace the precise itinerary of the ancestors as they travelled from margin to centre, creating the world and populating the earth. Extending through time and space, they connect the ancestral past with the living present. Referred to as 'the paths of the ancestors', rivers embody the mythic memory of each exogamous group and its component clans. Rivers, Makuna say, are like the colouring of the anaconda: spotted, divided and segmented. They are strings of names, each telling a distinct story of ancestral deeds. Through their names and places, the rivers narrate the story of creation from beginning to end, from mouth to source.

The river-narrative begins at the Water Door. At Yuisi gumu, the gateway to the Makuna cosmos, the story comes alive and gains experiential momentum; from here to the centre, every name and place – every bend and stretch of the river, every rapid, pool and tributary – is known and charged with meaning. The story describes, indeed creates, the semantic topography of the Makuna territory, thus constituting it as meaningful landscape. The names of the rivers allude to the Houses of Awakening of particular clans and exogamous groups, and of the birth houses – the 'wombs' and 'fertility gourds' – of animals. Above all they speak of the creative deeds of the ancestors: the place where the creators felled the Water Tree, the trunk and branches of which turned into the upper Apaporis river and its affluents; the place where they killed the Man-Eating Eagle; the point where they prepared and drank potent 'yagé' (a hallucinogenic drink);[9] the House of Smoke where the 'god-children' of the ancestors were burned to death by the heat from the sacred instruments, and so on. Each ancestral deed left its mark on the landscape: from the poisoned blood and urine of the dying Eagle various streams were formed; where the gods drank 'yagé' a pool of still, dark water appeared, containing the ancestral 'yagé'; and at the site where the ancestral initiates were burned to death, the water contains the fire of the burning Yurupari instruments – cooled only by a trickle of wholesome water flowing from a small stream higher up the river, created by the ancestors from the sweet juice of the *tomü* fruit. The narrative ends at Tabotiro in the centre of the earth. From there, a small, dark rivulet, formed from Woman Shaman's menstrual blood, flows into the Komenya river. It is said to be deadly poisonous, as are the fish that swim in its waters.

Makuna topographic names encode ancestral events and literally turn them into places. Each named place embodies particular powers emanating from the ancestors and their creative work, and every story conveys the fundamental message that the land is potent because it is part of the ancestral body and the result of primordial creation. The ancestral beings are present and incorporated in the landscape: rivers, rapids, hills and mountains are their physical manifestations and visible traces. For shamans, the trunk and branches of a river system, and the ring of hills encircling it, are 'paths of thought'. When they perform protective shamanism in the midst of the 'maloca', their minds travel along the circle of hills and follow the course of the rivers from mouth to source, repeating the creative journey of the ancestors and turning the world into a protective House. By means of their silent chanting, and by the power of their thoughts, shamans rebuild the 'maloca' cosmos and create the world anew. In Makuna shamanic idiom, they 'maintain the world' (*ümüari wano*).

Food and eaters

An appreciation of the trophic relationship between eater and food, as imaginatively elaborated in Pirá-Paraná shamanic discourse, is essential for an understanding of local notions of human–land relatedness. According to the Makuna, plants and animals share in the powers of creation. They contain the primordial substances from which the world was made, and by means of which it is continuously recreated. In the process of creation, each class of being 'received' and incorporated the particular powers which allow it to sustain and defend itself in its appropriate habitat. By analogy with the spiritual property of the exogamous group, these powers are conceptualised as 'weapons' and 'defences', and are represented as ritual gear and other powerful objects and substances. Each life-form has its own distinctive set of 'weapons' that objectify the creative powers that brought it into being.

Soil, water and plants, say the Makuna, contain the potent semen and blood of the creators, the 'celestial fire' of the primordial ancestors (associated with the light of the sun) and the 'vaginal heat' of Woman Shaman (associated with domestic fire). Stinging insects, snakes, scorpions and spiders were born from Woman Shaman's poison gourd and contain her potentially lethal menstrual blood. Game animals and fish along with ants, termites, grubs and caterpillars emerged as a result of the transformative work of the ancestors. Different varieties of fish were born from the down and feathers of the ancestral feather crown, and from the different parts of the primordial Yurupari instruments. The fish thus 'received' and incorporated the feathers, splinters, down, clay and colours from which the ancestral artefacts and sacred goods were made; these are their 'weapons' and 'defences'. Other animals received the 'pepper of the sun', the 'snuff of the sky', the body paint and the dart poison of the creators, and so on. To each kind of plant and animal, the ancestors allocated the particular powers that constitute them as beings.

Animals, by contrast to plants, are conceptualised as prototypical 'eaters'; they are constituted as much by what they eat as by the creative processes that brought them into being. The 'weapons' contained in plants are incorporated in the bodies of plant-eating animals, and the 'weapons' of different kinds of prey animals similarly re-incorporated in their predators. The constitutive powers of each species are thus successively re-incorporated at ascending levels in the food chain. Because of the foods they eat, animals are considered potent and potentially harmful as a source of food for humans. The most powerful animals of all, the predators at the top of the food chain, are not considered food at all; they are classified as prototypical non-food (*bare mehe*), epitomising the shamanically important category of 'man-eaters' (*masa bari masa*). In fact, top predators such as the jaguar and the anaconda are attributed with immortality and thus, symbolically, identified with powerful spirits and ancestral beings.

In Makuna shamanic discourse, the universe of living beings is conceptually construed as an elementary food chain composed of three

trophic levels: 'man-eaters', 'humans' and 'food', where the intermediary category contextually includes (non-human) animals as well as
humans. The scheme is relativistic and 'perspectival' (Århem 1990);
from the point of view of any class of beings, all others are either 'predators' or 'food'. The 'predator' category is labelled after the supreme
predator, the jaguar (*yai*), and the 'food' category after the prototypical
male-procured food, fish (*wai*). By identifying the top predators with
the ancestral beings, this classificatory scheme is turned into a cosmological model in which plants, (non-human) animals, and humans are linked
to powerful spirits in a hierarchy of trophic relations at the apex of which
are the creative and predatory spirits – the ancestors. In this cosmic food-
web the ancestors prey on humans, just as humans prey on animals and
plants. From the point of view of predatory spirits, humans are their privileged prey.

The model of the cosmic food-web amounts, in important respects,
to a 'prescriptive food system' allocating a class of proper food to every
category of eater. In Makuna shamanic idiom this relationship is
couched in terms of 'ownership' and 'belonging': the eater 'owns' its
proper food, and the food 'belongs' to its legitimate eater. A key feature
of the model is the notion of predation as a creative act. As a human
being dies, the soul is captured and 'consumed' by the ancestors and
returned to the House of Awakening of the exogamous group to be
reborn as a complete spirit person. Similarly, when a human hunter kills
and consumes his prey, he returns the constitutive essence, the 'soul', of
the slain animal to its place of origin – the 'birth house' of the animal. By
shamanic means, he empowers the species to reproduce and multiply.
Predation, then, is a 'male' mode of procreation (cf. Århem 1996). In
effect, the notion of the cosmic food-web is a model of the distribution
of power in the larger universe of beings, an ecology of the cosmos.

Much of Makuna shamanic discourse revolves around the contextual
distinction and identification between eater and food. Human food
(*masa bare*) comprises four major categories of beings: cultivated plants,
ote (particularly low-growing plants and tubers of the garden, prototyp-
ically manioc); tree fruits, *he rika* (particularly wild forest fruits); fish,
wai; and game animals, *wai bükü* (literally 'old' or 'mature/big fish').
In the context of food shamanism, all edible plants and animals are
classed as 'fish'. The classificatory distinctions between cultivated
plants, tree fruits, fish and game are suppressed and subordinated to
their shared features as human food. From the point of view of humans,
a fundamental conceptual boundary is thus drawn between the human
eater (*masa*) and his food (*wai*). However, in the wider context of

cosmological classification, the perspective shifts. From the point of view of ancestors and large predators, humans and their animal food are grouped together as prey; their common destiny is to be killed and consumed. The notion of *masa* is thus extended to include all living – and hence mortal – beings. The fundamental distinction is redrawn between immortal spirits (*yaia*) and their mortal prey (*masa*).

In this inclusive sense, the concept of *masa* stresses what all living beings have in common: the property of life itself. All apparent taxonomic distinctions between living kinds turn into sociological boundaries between different 'peoples', evoking a model of the natural world as a grand society in which each class of being is defined analogously to the subdivisions of human society. Natural beings are thus contextually assimilated with human society, dissolving the classificatory distinction between 'nature' and 'society'. Plants and animals become 'social others'. This inclusive notion of 'people' is invoked in rituals and in preventive and curative shamanic practices to stress the relatedness of all living beings. While the 'human' aspect of plants is tenuous and weakly elaborated, fish and game animals are depicted as pronouncedly 'human'; they are people in another reality-dimension. Just as fish and game are conceived of as transformations of one another, animal life-worlds are seen as permutations of human sociality (see Århem 1996).

By close analogy with human social groups, plants and animals are seen as forming local populations, associated with particular places, territories and cosmological domains. Cultivated crops belong to the female domain of the garden, closely associated with the house as a female, procreative space. The garden is the 'womb' of the cultivated crops. Similarly, animals and tree fruits belong to particular, localised 'houses' in the forest and the rivers where they are said to breed and multiply. Each species and local population has its own house where its regenerative powers are located. The birth houses of fish, metaphorically described as gourds, baskets or pots and compared to wombs, are strung out along the rivers from mouth to source, while the houses of game animals are located in hills and saltlicks in the forest, radiating from the centre towards the margins of the earth. Each local population of a species forms a distinctive group, identified with a specific birth house and constituted by the creative powers and metaphysical properties associated with the locality it inhabits.

The plants, animals and people of a particular territory are significantly related. They are all seen as vital manifestations of the creative power of the ancestral anaconda, progenitor of all life forms and ultimate Owner of the river territory it embodies. The contextual identity of animals and humans is particularly elaborate and is expressed in a totemic, classificatory scheme in which the 'natural' distinction between fish and game is reiterated in the social division between Water People and Earth People (see Århem 1996). Game animals, epitomised by the tapir, are closely associated with the Earth People, while fish (particularly *Brycon spp*) are associated with the Water People. The ancestor of the Water People is also conceived of as the mythical progenitor of the fish inhabiting the rivers of the Water People territory. Similarly, the ancestor of the Earth People is simultaneously described as procreator of the fructivore game animals living in the Earth People territory. Animals and men thus have a common origin and share in the same ancestral essence; the Houses of Awakening of humans are also the birth houses of animals. Such symbolic associations between humans and animals serve a supremely significant purpose in Pirá-Paraná cosmology, as they instruct people of their ultimate role in the ecology of the cosmos. Water People and Earth People are, respectively, the 'fish' and 'game' of the ancestors.

This play on identities also sheds light on a fundamental aspect of Pirá-Paraná territoriality. The inclusive and mythically constituted territory of the Water People clans corresponds to the migratory route of the *Brycon* population that spawns on the lower Apaporis. The fish seasonally migrate between their breeding place on the Apaporis and their feeding areas along the tributaries of the lower Pirá-Paraná. Similarly, the ancestral territories of the Earth People clans correspond to the feeding routes of localised populations of tapirs converging on particular saltlicks and breeding places in the forest. According to the Makuna, these routes and trails of the tapir are rivers on land, connecting Earth People settlements to their Houses of Awakening along particular streams and in specific saltlicks in the forest. Localised populations of fish and game thus supply models for the conceptualisation of ancestral territories. In effect, Pirá-Paraná notions of territoriality emerge as elaborate cultural constructs inspired by a precise knowledge of animal territoriality.[10]

Animals are not only considered intrinsically localised but also fundamentally protean. Their essential identity varies according to time and place. Fish, for example, are said to transform from one place to another, and to take on or discard powers ('weapons' and 'defences') according to the cosmological definition of the particular river section where they swim or feed. The river itself, say the Makuna, constantly changes; in some parts the water is 'heavy' and 'bitter', in others it is 'light' and 'sweet'. Depending upon place and season, the fish incorporate the potent 'yagé' of the creators, the rage of the ancestral warriors, the sadness of death, the down and left-over feathers of the primordial feather crown, the splinters and chips of the sacred Yurupari instrument, or the fire of the ancestors. The same is true of game animals roaming in the forest. In shamanic classification, the constitutive identity of animals is contingent upon local and seasonal environmental conditions. Accordingly, Makuna 'biology' is less concerned with the immutable properties of the 'species', than with the variable properties of local populations and individual organisms – particular animals killed or plants collected – thus stressing the intimate connection in Pirá-Paraná thought between being and place, organism and environment.

This cosmological differentiation of the landscape constitutes the territory as a metaphysical force-field which humans must carefully navigate if they are to survive. Rivers, in particular, are minutely segmented into parts and sections, each with its specific implications for human resource use. Depending on the metaphysical properties associated with it, each place is believed to be either harmless or harmful. Fish swimming in harmful ('bitter') waters are said to be dangerous to eat because they cause illness and pain. In such places, appositely called 'places where the fish cause pain' (*wai huno*), fishing is prohibited. Other sections, where the water is 'sweet', are said to be harmless because they are associated with benevolent deeds of the ancestors. In this way, the forest and rivers of any territory are finely differentiated into parts that can be used and others that cannot according to a shamanic geography, the fundamentals of which must be known by each and everyone.

A territory of knowledge

According to Makuna world-view, all edible plants and animals are ambivalent and powerful. They sustain life and give strength, but may also kill and cause disease. Because of the 'weapons' they contain, all beings are potentially lethal to human eaters. Animals are considered particularly potent because they are human-like; they have the powers and capacities of humans. Eating, in Makuna imagery, involves a metaphysical battle between eater and food where the animal killed and the food consumed have the capacity to defeat the human eater. Illness is described as the 'cost of eating' (*bare waha*). To make it safe to eat, humans bless their food. By means of food shamanism (*bare keare*), men – and men only – convert potentially harmful beings and substances of nature into life-sustaining food. The blessing of food could be described as a form of preventive therapy, a mystical means of removing or evading the dangers of eating. As such, it is a constant feature of everyday life; at all times and in every place men silently chant and blow spells over a piece of food or a gourd of liquid. Each class of food demands its proper chant, and animals or plants from one part of the forest or river require different treatment from those from another part. Because the same class of food differs in its constitutive essence and metaphysical properties from place to place and according to seasonal changes, the shamanic treatment varies accordingly. The process, however, is fundamentally the same: in his mind and by means of his silent chant, the blesser collects the 'weapons' of the edible plant or animal, ties them together and returns them to their place of origin – the birth houses of plants or animals.

The chant recounts the origin of each species and local population, and lists all the 'weapons' contained in the edible organism, including the powers of place and season that constitute its essential identity. In the case of animal food, the shamanic treatment is said to transform the meat into harmless plant food, such as manioc bread or other garden fruit. In the process, the blesser not only removes the 'weapons' incorporated into the animal through the food it eats, but he also averts the danger deriving from the carnivores which feed on it, and from the animals that live in association with it, its 'owners' and 'helpers'. The same applies to the blessing of forest fruits, which also have their animal 'owners', the fructivores. For each kind of edible plant or animal, the blesser must, in his silent chant, cover the entire food chain in which it participates, including the animals with which humans compete for food. As he removes the 'weapons' from the food and sends them back to their origin, the blesser returns the 'soul' of the edible plant or animal to its birth house, thereby enabling its subsequent rebirth. In this way, he protects the human eater from the danger inherent in the organism, while also ensuring its generic reproduction. Food blessing, then, is a regenerative ritual act, the procreative culmination of male predation.

The blessing of food is a necessary condition for living the Makuna way. It presupposes detailed knowledge of the environmental features of the territory – the fruits in season, the feeding and breeding habits of fish and game, their dens, movements and tracks – and also of its shamanic geography, its names and places and the mythic stories these convey. To subsist in their local environment, people must be able to handle and harness the powers of the land and make it safe for living. This knowledge forms part of the 'defences' of humans; it belongs to the spiritual legacy of the clan and exogamous group. As such it is localised, intimately tied to the ancestral territory of the group. As 'owners' of a particular river, men are endowed with the power and knowledge to sustain themselves in the territory with which they identify. However, territorial ownership also entails ritual power over local plants and animals. Men 'own' their proper 'food', the edible plants and animals of their territory. Empowered by their shamanic knowledge and ritual possessions, men ritually control the birth houses of plants and animals and, thus, the fertility of the land. During repeated fertility rituals focused on the birth houses of fish, game and forest fruits, shamans and knowledgeable elders ensure the continuous reproduction and multiplication of edible plants and animals. Thus, the spiritual legacy of the exogamous group allows its members to sustain and defend themselves in their territory, and simultaneously impels them to ritually renew its creative potential.

Ritual control over land and resources can, however, also be acquired. If, in principle, shamanic knowledge is part of the descent property and an aspect of territorial ownership, in practice it is a feature of tenure and, thus, a property of the river community. Tenure presupposes familiarity with the local environment and the competence to bless food and maintain the fertility of the land. When the Water People took up residence on the Komenya river, they quickly acquired knowledge of the new territory from its owners, the Earth People. Their arrival was ritually blessed and sanctioned through a series of ritual exchanges, and the Water People were invited to bring their sacred Yurupari instruments – their ancestors – from their ancestral home on Toaka. Through the transfer of their ritual possessions, their permanent incorporation into the Komenya river community was publicly confirmed and legitimised. By virtue of their numbers, political strength and ritual skills, the Water People gradually assumed many of the ritual responsibilities towards the land originally pertaining to the Earth People. Eventually they came to be seen as ritual 'guardians' of the territory. In effect, the Water People are today 'co-owners' of the Komenya river.

By learning the names, places and stories of the land, and by incorporating its creative powers, residents progressively identify with the territory they inhabit and make it socially and experientially 'their own'. While territorial ownership is permanent and exclusive, tenure is negotiable and inclusive. Shamanic knowledge – shared and exchanged among close allies – is the mediating factor between ownership and effective tenure. By allowing for the transfer of knowledge and power between individuals, groups and territories, this intangible and detachable quality of sacred property injects a measure of elasticity into Pirá-Paraná territorial organisation, fundamental to its smooth operation. To the Makuna, the significant territory is essentially a 'territory of knowledge'.

Conclusions

The peoples of the Pirá-Paraná river basin think of the world as a house with many rooms, each room in turn constituting a house on its own, with its proper 'owners' and 'dwellers'. The river basin as a whole is the World House, the 'maloca' cosmos embracing the entire Pirá-Paraná social universe. Each of its major rivers represents a discrete territory, a smaller House or Water Path, 'owned' by a distinct exogamous group but actually inhabited by a largely endogamous community of kin and affines. Territorial ownership implies identification with a bounded river territory, ritual control over the edible plants and animals of that territory, and the shamanic obligation to maintain its creative potential. As an aspect of the descent system, territoriality is part of the foundational ordering of the cosmos. Tenure, however, in the sense of effective control over land and river resources is vested in the river community. As such, it is a function of locality. The articulation of descent and marriage works towards the formation of localised, endogamous communities. Locality and the sharing of territory produces, as it were, commensality and consubstantiality, a common tie to the land and a deep sense of consanguineal community. As a metaphor for unity and relatedness, the House is expanded to embrace both consanguines and agnatic kin, the endogamous river community as well as the fictive unity of the exogamous group.

Local belonging is thus construed in terms of both descent and locality, identification with an ancestral territory and membership in a fluid and composite river community. In an experiential sense, home is the House one inhabits and in which one feels secure, the familiar territory and local landscape one occupies and uses for a living. Usually it is the territory where the sacred Yurupari instruments of one's clan and exogamous group are kept, where one's parents and grandparents have lived (and died), and where one expects to be buried at death. And yet this 'lived' House, protected and blessed by trusted shamans, is only meaningful in relation to that ultimate resting place of one's soul, the House of Awakening in one's proper ancestral territory. This imagined house of the ancestors is the origin and destiny of all members of the exogamous group, the repository of their immaterial sacred property and life-sustaining powers. Even for those who have never lived there, nor ever visited it, the ancestral river territory is their spiritual home in the cosmos.

In a more inclusive sense, the Pirá-Paraná peoples also see themselves as dwellers in the World House, inhabitants of the wider territory embracing the entire Pirá-Paraná social universe. This is the known and named world 'maintained' by protective shamans and ritually recreated in sacred ceremonies. While ordinary men enlist their own knowledge and shamanic powers to sustain themselves and their families in their immediate, local environment, shamans have the wider responsibility of protecting and maintaining the 'maloca' cosmos.[11] In their acts and thoughts, shamans thus transcend the social and territorial boundaries of the groups to which they belong. They are guardians of the World House.

The protective role of shamans is currently gaining renewed significance. Since the mid-1980s, gold miners have invaded the Taraira river valley and surrounding uplands on the southeastern fringe of the Pirá-Paraná basin, and several mining towns have emerged in the area. As a result, forests are being destroyed, rivers and streams contaminated and the wildlife increasingly depleted (Århem, in press). Pirá-Paraná people react variously to the outsiders and the dramatic changes they have brought about. Some see the gold mining in Taraira as an opportunity to obtain coveted trade goods. Others, including the mostly young and literate leaders of the emerging indigenous movement in the area, see the invasion of miners as a threat. By organising themselves politically, they seek new ways of asserting and defending their rights to land and local self-determination.[12] In remote settlements and villages, however, knowledgeable elders and ritual specialists interpret the events of the day in a different light, and devise their own strategies of defence. To them, the Taraira hills are the supporting posts and protective walls of the 'maloca' cosmos; in their eyes, then, the miners literally threaten to tear down the entire cosmos. Confronted with this disconcerting scenario, local shamans intensify their protective spiritual labours, and ancient rituals are performed with renewed fervour to fortify the crumbling 'maloca' cosmos. Under the mounting pressures from the outside, and in the shadow of the Taraira gold rush, Pirá-Paraná shamanic and ritual traditions are currently experiencing a veritable renaissance.[13]

Let me end on a comparative and deliberately conjectural note. Pirá-Paraná notions of landscape and the human–land relationship are strikingly similar to those of a wide range of other indigenous societies throughout the world.[14] Such commonalities among totally unrelated peoples, with entirely different economic and social systems, suggest a unity of experience rooted in a common mode of relating to land and landscape. There appears to be a fundamental and transcultural modality of grounding identity in place that unites these different societies and ways of life, a mode of identifying with the land that springs from deep practical and experiential involvement in the local environment. The immediate sensory exposure to the landscape, and the radical intimacy between humans and their environment, characteristic of an intensely localised mode of life, would seem to generate a participatory ontological stance that manifests itself in a limited set of cultural representations of human–land relatedness. Such a set of kindred cultural representations may account for the puzzling parallels among diverse societies in different parts of the world.[15] In this perspective, the metaphorisation of the world as a House is significant. The Pirá-Paraná peoples see the world from within, in a dwelling perspective (Ingold 1995). The House as home, in all its multiple meanings, is a metaphor of intimacy and identity – an extension of self.

Acknowledgement

* I gratefully acknowledge the constructive comments on earlier drafts of this chapter from Bill Arens, Stephen Hugh-Jones, Alexandra Kent and Nadia Lovell.

Notes

1 A significant beginning towards an anthropology of the Amazonian landscape has been made by Descola (1994) and S. Hugh-Jones (1995); see also Reichel-Dolmatoff (1996).

2 For the notions of 'shamanic geography' and 'shamanic territory', see Reichel-Dolmatoff (1986); Hammen (1992). See also Hill (1996); Hill and Moran (1983).

3 Principal ethnographies include Århem (1981); Correa (1996); C. Hugh-Jones (1979); S. Hugh-Jones (1979); Jackson (1983).

4 The system is grounded in a 'two-line' (Dravidian) relationship terminology that provides the basic exchange-model for all interaction between 'self' and 'significant others'.

5 The ethnographic present is the early 1970s. At the end of this chapter, brief reference is made to the situation in the late 1980s and early 1990s.

6 'Maloca' is the (non-indigenous) vernacular term – also used in the ethnographic literature – for the traditional, indigenous dwelling. The Makuna term is *wi*, or *hahe wi* ('big house'). It should be noted that the account refers to the early 1970s; today, the majority of the Pirá-Paraná population live in nucleated village communities (see note 5 above).

7 Water People and Earth People refer to one another as *hakoa masa* ('mothers' peoples'), suggesting their close consanguineal bonding.

8 S. Hugh-Jones (personal communication) suggests that the two languages probably were more closely related than people claim them to have been; generally, and as a consequence of their normative ideal of language exogamy, Tukanoans tend to exaggerate language differences.

9 The drink is prepared from a cultivated hallucinogenic plant (*Banisteriopsis caapi*), widespread in Northwest Amazonia. 'Yagé' is the (non-Makuna) vernacular term – also employed in the literature – for the plant and the drink derived from it.

10 This affirmation is part of a longer and more general argument concerning Makuna ecological imagery to be developed elsewhere (but see also Århem 1996: 201–2). Suffice here to say that there is suggestive evidence that Pirá-Paraná sociology and cosmology are profoundly inspired by an intimate knowledge of local ecology. Indeed, I would go so far as to suggest that the notorious attention to place and local differences in Pirá-Paraná socio-cosmology is grounded in an apprehension of the extreme diversity and differentiation of the tropical forest environment of Northwest Amazonia.

11 Thus the shamanic notion of 'territory' comes close to the ethological and ecological definition of territory as 'defended area'.

12 The struggle of the local indigenous organisation, ACAIPI (Asociación de Capitanes Indígenas del Rio Pirá-Paraná) is politically and legally sanctioned by Colombia's Indian policy and the 1991 Constitution. The organisation has also been successful in gaining moral and material support from national and international NGOs (including Fundación Gaia-Amazonas, a Colombian NGO with international affiliations; see Hugh-Jones, unpublished paper).

13 This cultural revitalisation is paired with, and far from excludes, an intense concern for material progress and beneficial contact with the wider society – as is made manifest, for instance, in the current interest in ethno-education (Hugh-Jones, unpublished paper).

14 See Tilley (1994), and contributions in Bender (1993) and Hirsch and O'Hanlon (1995). Ingold (1986) and Wilson (1988) provide relevant theoretical and comparative reflections on this theme, particularly relating to material on the Australian Aborigines (see also Myers (1988)).

15 My argument here is similar to that of Descola (1996) concerning the social construction of 'nature' and human–nature relatedness.

References

Århem, K. (1981) *Makuna Social Organization: A Study in Descent, Alliance and the Formation of Corporate Groups in the North-Western Amazon*, Stockholm: Almqvist & Wiksell International.

—— (1990) 'Ecosofía Makuna', in F. Correa (ed.) *La Selva Humanizada: Ecología Alternativa en el Trópico Húmedo Colombiano*, Bogotá: ICAN/FEN/CEREC.

—— (1996) 'The Cosmic Food Web: Human-Nature Relatedness in the Northwest Amazon', in P. Descola and G. Pálsson (eds), *Nature and Society: Anthropological Perspectives*, London: Routledge.

—— (in press), *Makuna: Portrait of an Amazonian People*, Washington, DC: Smithsonian Institution Press.

Bender, B. (ed.) (1993) *Landscape, Politics and Perspectives*, Oxford: Berg.

Chernela, J.M. (1993) *The Wanano Indians of the Brazilian Amazon: A Sense of Space*, Austin, TX: University of Texas Press.

Correa, F. (1996) *Por el Camino de la Anaconda Remedio: Dinámica de la Organización Social entre los Taiwano del Vaupés*, Bogotá: Universidad Nacional/Colciencias.

Descola, P. (1994) *In the Society of Nature: A Native Ecology in Amazonia*, Cambridge: Cambridge University Press.

—— (1996) 'Constructing Natures: Symbolic Ecology and Social Practice', in P. Descola and G. Pálsson (eds), *Nature and Society: Anthropological Perspectives*, London: Routledge.

Goldman, I. (1963) *The Cubeo: Indians of the Northwest Amazon*, Urbana, IL: University of Illinois Press.

Hammen, M.C. van der (1992) *El Manejo del Mundo: Naturaleza y Sociedad entre los Yukuna de la Amazonía Colombiana*, Bogotá: Tropenbos Colombia.

Hill, J. (1996) 'Ethnogenesis in the Northwest Amazon: An Emerging Regional Picture', in J. Hill (ed.), *History, Power, and Identity: Ethnogenesis in the Americas, 1492–1992*, Iowa City: University of Iowa Press.

Hill, J. and Moran, E. (1983) 'Adaptive Strategies of Wakuénai Peoples to the Oligotrophic Rain Forest of the Rio Negro Basin', in R. Hames and W. Vickers (eds), *Adaptive Responses of Native Amazonians*, New York: Academic Press.

Hirsch, E. and O'Hanlon, M. (eds) (1995) *The Anthropology of Landscape: Perspectives on Place and Space*, Oxford: Clarendon Press.

Hugh-Jones, C. (1979) *From the Milk River: Spatial and Temporal Processes in Northwest Amazonia*, Cambridge: Cambridge University Press.

Hugh-Jones, S. (1979) *The Palm and the Pleiades: Initiation and Cosmology in Northwest Amazonia*, Cambridge: Cambridge University Press.

—— (1995) 'Inside-Out and Back-To-Front: The Androgynous House in Northwest Amazonia', in J. Carsten and S. Hugh-Jones (eds), *About the House: Lévi-Strauss and Beyond*, Cambridge: Cambridge University Press.

—— (n.d.) 'A Meeting with Several Agendas: Reflections on Some Recent Developments in the Colombian Pirá-Paraná Region', unpublished paper.

Ingold, T. (1986) 'Territoriality and Tenure: the Appropriation of Space in Hunting and Gathering Societies', in T. Ingold, *The Appropriation of Nature: Essays on Human Ecology and Social Relations*, Manchester: Manchester University Press.

—— (1995) 'Building, Dwelling, Living: How Animals and People Make Themselves at Home in the World', in M. Strathern (ed.), *Shifting Contexts: Transformations in Anthropological Knowledge*, London: Routledge.

Jackson, J. (1983) *The Fish People: Linguistic Exogamy and Tukanoan Identity in Northwest Amazonia*, Cambridge: Cambridge University Press.

—— (1995) 'Culture, Genuine and Spurious: The Politics of Indianness in the Vaupés, Colombia', *American Ethnologist* 22(1): 3–27.

Moran, E. (1991) 'Human Adaptive Strategies in Amazonian Blackwater Ecosystems', *American Anthropologist* 93: 361–82.

—— (1993) *Through Amazonian Eyes: the Human Ecology of Amazonian Populations*, Iowa City: University of Iowa Press.

Morphy, H. (1993) 'Colonialism, History and the Construction of Place: The Politics of Landscape in Northern Australia', in B. Bender (ed.), *Landscape, Politics and Perspectives*, Oxford: Berg.

Myers, F. (1988) 'Burning the Truck and Holding the Country: Property, Time, and the Negotiation of Identity among the Pintupi Aborigines', in T. Ingold, D. Riches, and J. Woodburn (eds), *Hunters and Gatherers: Property, Power and Ideology*, Oxford: Berg.

Reichel-Dolmatoff, G. (1986) 'Algunos Conceptos de Geografía Chamanística de los Indios Desana de Colombia', in E. Magaña and P. Mason (eds), *Myth and the Imaginary in the New World*, Dordrecht: FORIS Publications.

—— (1996) *The Forest Within: The World-View of the Tukano Amazonian Indians*, London: Themis Books.

Tilley, C. (1994) *A Phenomenology of Landscape: Places, Paths and Monuments*, Oxford: Berg.

Wilson, P.J. (1988) *The Domestication of the Human Species*, New Haven, CT and London: Yale University Press.

Chapter 4

Origin and ritual exchange as transformative belonging in the Balinese temple

Arlette Ottino

Introduction: cultural notions of origin

This chapter explores how sentiments of belonging to a group, in the village of Trunyan in Bali, are linked to references to origin and are enacted through participation in collective activities and rituals. These references to origin are inherently represented in communal actions and shared participation in rituals, thus enhancing a sense of belonging. Yet, belonging appears more closely defined by a shared identity with the group itself as social entity, rather than by belonging to territory and landscape, although the natural environment does provide original features through which cosmologies are derived. In Bali, the awareness of origin is sustained almost exclusively in rituals to which members of the group have an obligation to participate. The relation between origin, ritual participation and the construction of sentiments of belonging from which the Balinese derive their social identity is historically complex, and it is further complicated (for the anthropologist) by the Balinese's apparent lack of interest in the past (Bateson 1970), and their culturally-specific understanding of the concept of origin.

Origin (*kawitan, kamimitan*) refers to the notion of beginning, as cause and source of present life. It is also equated with what is considered higher (than human), the sacred, the all-encompassing, that which pertains to the sky and, consequently, the divine (*luhur, kelangitan*). If it is, indeed, the source of life, it is so in a concrete yet also metaphorical sense, as expressed through the exchange of sustenance believed to take place between deity and worshippers during rituals in the temples.[1] This notion of origin includes (real or putative) descent and ancestry, residential space, the land and its resources, and past happenings which have permanently transformed the composition of the group and/or its socio-political context and, thereby, its present identity. Notions of origin take into consideration an understanding of space, historical events and land which has remained productive through the labour of many generations. These factors become as important in the shaping of contemporary identity as genealogical ties, which serve to link members of past and contemporary generations and suggest an understanding of notions of personhood which is not exhausted by a causal relationship between the past and the present.

The Balinese define the person as the nexus of a web of relations stretching into most dimensions of the world. The condition of being human is to be 'tied' (*kaiket*) to other beings, to the village, the land, the deeds of past generations, and to spiritual entities, ancestors and gods. It is eminently changeable, fluctuating according to time and circumstance.[2] Such notions of personhood reflect beliefs about the nature of the world, in particular conveying that its material, tangible outline is but one aspect of a holistic reality, in which the spiritual, intangible dimension is given greater importance.[3] Events such as political alliances, conflicts and natural disasters are perceived as manifestations (incomplete at best) of forces at play in the supernatural world. When these phenomena produce permanent transformations in the natural and social environments, they become enshrined as gods in the collective memory of the group. This transmutation brings such deified events into the domain of ritual, where their continued reality depends upon the frequency and intensity of the relations which the group will entertain with them. No longer reducible to the events from which they have arisen, the gods continue to be worshipped as the manifestations of the conditions associated with the collective identity of the group, expressed through the idiom of origin.

In a society as hierarchically organised as Bali, origin is inextricably linked with status and ranking. Society is divided into a system of castes derived from India, the *Tri-Wangsa*, which includes three castes: *Brahmana*, *Ksatria* and *Wesia*, who together make up only a small percentage of the population (about 10 per cent). In addition there also exists a large number of origin groups, with or without a title, who are all loosely included in the category of *Sudra*, and who stand outside the hierarchy of castes altogether. The *Brahmana* and *Ksatria* castes possess highly elaborate and generally reliable genealogies, perceived to connect them to illustrious Javanese ancestors who crossed over to Bali relatively recently in the history of the island (probably towards the fifteenth or sixteenth century). Other groups seldom possess such genealogies,[4] and it is therefore more difficult to evaluate their appropriate ranking in the social hierarchy since claims to a particular status, when disputed by other groups, cannot be defended by reference to an impeccable genealogical tree, as is the case with the two highest castes of *Brahmana* and *Ksatria* within the *Tri-Wangsa*. The ability to refer to prestigious deities, which serves to enhance an awareness of origin, becomes an invaluable asset for such groups since it endows them with a seldom questioned social status.

This helps to explain how, by placing them beyond the limits of what may be questioned, political claims relating to social status and prestige are made to appear legitimate by giving them permanency and endowing them with sacredness. Nevertheless, the Balinese preoccupation with origin still leaves unanswered questions such as why it is thought necessary, once the identity and status of the gods have been established – and by extension the social status of the ritual group – to hold periodical rituals whose sole purpose seems to be the feasting and entertaining of those gods. Once the status of a group has been secured by its transposition into the domain of the sacred, there appears to be no good reason why ritual relations with the origin should need to be maintained. Thus enshrined, the memory of origin could well be sufficient, all the more so since Balinese rituals as a rule do not preserve the individual identity of the gods worshipped in the temples. Indeed, with the exception of a few ritual specialists, most Balinese do not generally know the names of the gods they worship, nor do they seem to care. If temple rituals are about maintaining a memory of the past, the least that can be said is that they do not achieve their purpose, since the deities contacted during the rituals retain their anonymity for the majority of their worshippers. However, if we accept that rituals are performed to keep alive the relationship between deified origin and the temple, the apparently off-hand attitude of the Balinese towards the beings representing their origin becomes understandable, since it is the maintenance of the relation itself that is vital to the prosperity of the present group. Historical memory is thereby enshrined in the ritual relations between the community of worshippers and the gods.

Ritual exchange, and the maintaining of relations with origin

Belonging is inherently connected to participation in a ritual exchange of sustenance between humans and temple deities, which serves to enhance and perpetuate awareness of one's origin through performance and action rather than intellectual knowledge.[5] The performance of ritual exchange communicates all that is needed for individual worshippers to strengthen the sentiment of belonging to the group. Rituals bring together gods and humans inside the temple, where a meal is prepared for the gods who, in return, bestow their blessings on the assembled congregation. The concrete reality of this exchange is expressed in cultural representations relating to the nature of divine blessings as vital-ising substance, whose properties are akin to the food which is offered to gods in exchange. In this ritual context, the tutelary deities of a group are treated as the point of origin, from which life flows in a literal sense, under the form of a life-giving fluid (*amerta*), believed to be present in water (*tirta*) consecrated by the officiating priest as part of the ritual exchange, and then distributed to the assembled worshippers. Participation in this exchange implies membership in the ritual group, since it is understood that the gods' blessings are reserved exclusively for those who worship them. This is of particular importance for groups whose members have no contact with each other except during temple rituals. For such members, sentiments of belonging and shared origin, which are normally derived from shared descent or the performance of communal tasks, are sustained exclusively through ritual exchange. The sharing and trading of sustenance therefore acts as a symbolic vehicle for maintaining bonds with deities while, simultaneously, asserting belonging to groups at a societal level. If those ties were no longer sustained, the group would eventually dissolve as a social entity, since its spiritual source of origin would have been removed.

These points can be illustrated by the case of the cult to the goddess of food, *Dewi Ayu Pingit Mas Mekulem*,[6] located in the main temple of Trunyan, an isolated mountain village in northeast Bali. I have chosen this case for the clarity with which sentiments of belonging to a discrete territorial group, united by the notion of single origin, are articulated in the ritual sphere. The ethnographic material is presented in three sections. The first discusses the identity of the goddess as historical being and mythical construct. This is followed by a discussion of her position in the community of village deities. Finally, there is an examination of the composition of the groups who engage in ritual relations with her, and explore the nature of these relations.

Myth and history in the cultural construction of space

The goddess, whose temple is located in Trunyan, is the daughter of the king of the nearby kingdom of Bangli with which, at some stage in the past (perhaps not very long ago), the village of Trunyan, then an autonomous kingdom in its own right, entertained some kind of political relations.[7] None of the Balinese kingdoms exist today; during Dutch colonisation, they were transformed into administrative provinces (*kabupaten*). Nevertheless, this case treats Trunyan and Bangli as if they were still existing kingdoms, since the tutelary deities of their respective state temples are worshipped as the spirits of past sovereigns. Today, nothing is left of the kingdom of Trunyan except a large temple (*Kuil Bali Desa Pancering Jagat Bali*) located in the centre of the village; yet this temple is still the focal point of an important ritual network. The responsibility for the performance of rituals befalls the village community, which consists of several origin groups.[8] Trunyan has no written history, but possesses a rich oral lore which makes ample reference to a turbulent past of conquests, defeats, conflicts and treaties with its neighbours.

Trunyan lies above the irrigated belt. No rice is grown there now, although a variety of dryland rice known as *padi gaga* was cultivated prior to the two eruptions of the nearby volcano, Gunung Batur, early this century. Trunyan is situated high up, inside the ancient crater, on the edge of a large lake which occupies a prominent place in the ritual geography of the island, while the kingdom of Bangli is located downhill, at the foot of the southern slopes of Gunung Batur. No river actually flows from the lake, but subterranean water, providing irrigation for rice fields in the plains below, emerges from sources on the outer rim of the ancient crater, and the lake is therefore venerated throughout Bali as the original source of water in the eastern, southern and northern provinces. The lake is also symbolically treated as the source of water in the supernatural realm which ensures its flow in the natural world, principally as irrigation water for the cultivation of rice (see Lansing 1991). Through a network of temples, periodical rituals are conducted to secure the smooth flow of water from this mystical source. According to Lansing, the region of the volcano and the lake is treated ritually as 'a *mandala*, a sacred centre from which life-giving water flows in every direction, irrigating the fields below' (Lansing 1991: 73). Situated at its centre, Trunyan holds a privileged position as the (self-)appointed guardian of the lake, a position which may have arisen from its local political predominance in the past, but is entirely symbolic today and no longer accepted outside this village itself. This dominance is, in fact, hotly contested by nearby villages, in particular that of Batur which claims the same privilege. Batur is situated high on the edge of the ancient crater, where the large water temple *Pura Ulun Danu* is located, and where regional rituals for obtaining irrigation water are conducted. However, there is evidence from local traditions that, at some stage in the past, Trunyan controlled if not the actual flow of water, then at least the 'supernatural flow' from the lake to the irrigated fields below.

The notion of a supernatural flow of water is linked to beliefs about the presence of a principle of fertility in water, manifested in the natural world in the growth of plants. In a society where irrigated rice cultivation predominates, the link between water and life is amply demonstrated, and well understood.[9] Since features of the natural world and landscape are believed to originate in the supernatural realm, the capacity of water to develop and sustain the life of crops is perceived as a tangible manifestation of the presence of a subtle and abstract principle, or substance, acting on the supernatural dimension of plants. This is evidenced, for instance, in the surge of sap in plants and the green colour of well-watered foliage, as well as in the need to irrigate the fields abundantly during the first stages of rice growing. No specific name is given to this fertility principle, as it is viewed as an inherent attribute of water itself rather than an addition to its substance. Water snakes and eels are common manifestations of such representations, as are the *naga*, mythical spirit-snakes who are believed to dwell in the sacred waters of the lakes, or in the sky in the guise of rain clouds.

Since water flows freely over the landscape, and rain falls equally over every field, this principle should in theory perhaps be beyond appropriation on the part of political groups. However, since the flow of this fertility principle depends in practice on a network of temples rather than the actual network of waterways (Lansing 1987), and since these temples shelter the gods who look after the interests of the community which worships them, it becomes susceptible to political control.[10] Thus for the irrigated rice fields in the kingdom of Bangli fertility may, at some stage in the past, have depended upon a ritual connection with the village of Trunyan (if one accepts that Trunyan ever controlled its access). In the mythical tradition of Trunyan, this is expressed in terms of an alliance contracted between the two kingdoms: the marriage between the daughter of the king of Bangli and the king of Trunyan (Danandjaja 1980: 40–8; Ottino 1994).[11] According to this myth, the princess became the junior wife of the king of Trunyan, a mythical figure originating from a kingdom in Central Java, whose first wife was the tutelary goddess of the lake, daughter of the sun and a goddess of the sky. Trunyan is said to have come into being, as a socio-political realm and as the guardian of the sacred waters of the lake, as a result of this mythical union between the Javanese prince/king of Trunyan and the tutelary goddess of the lake (as first wife). The daughter of the king of Bangli arrived in Trunyan as second wife much later, during historical time, following a political conflict between Trunyan and Bangli.[12] The union was intended to heal this rift.

The nature of the conflict, and its underlying causes, remain obscure. The Trunyan myth is not clear on this point. Water stopped flowing in the Bangli fields. Then, after her marriage, the princess brought with her as her dowry a handful of iron eels given by her father, the king of Bangli, and threw them into the lake, whereupon water started flowing again and has never stopped since (Danandjaja 1980: 47). However, in the tradition of Bangli, the reasons for the drought are made more explicit. Trunyan is accused of having deliberately stopped the flow of water in the fields. This latter myth affirms that, because of differences in religious affiliations and the unwillingness of the king of Bangli to pay homage to the temple of the lake in Trunyan, the goddess of Lake Batur, as punishment, caused the water to stop flowing in Bangli (Riana 1996).[13]

It is possible to interpret these events in at least two ways. We may, in the first instance, surmise that the myth refers to a 'real' drought and that water did dry up in the rivers, causing the irrigated rice fields in the plains to wither. This is possible, since Bali is subject to seven-year cycles of droughts caused by the meteorological disruptions of El Niño, frequently resulting in shortages of irrigation water. However, the mythical tradition could also refer to a 'supernatural' drought, attributing poor crops and meagre harvests to a lack, or failure, of the fertility principle at symbolic level. That it is the daughter of the king of Bangli who, by throwing a handful of iron eels into the lake, causes the drought to cease, would support this view. Indeed eels and water snakes are symbolic of the fertility principle present in water. They are always the property of a goddess and are sometimes identified with her. The eels brought by the daughter of Bangli as her dowry in marriage would then signify that the fertility principle of water guarded by the kingdom of Trunyan, withdrawn by the tutelary goddess of the lake, was replaced by another fertility principle brought from the kingdom of Bangli, by the daughter of the king and thrown by her into the lake after her marriage to the king of Trunyan, to ensure the future fertility of the fields in her father's kingdom. This is all the more plausible as the first wife of the king of Trunyan is identified with another representation of the fertile principle of water, namely the mythical water snake or *naga*. Thus, the symbolic identification of the senior wife with *naga* and the junior wife with eels may be understood as a metaphor referring to two distinct, and complementary, sources of fertility ritually acknowledged by Trunyan and Bangli: one from the natural environment, the other from the political order. Accordingly, fertility for the fields would originate primarily from the lake in Trunyan through the intermediary of its tutelary goddess but be controlled by the political order of the kingdom headed by her husband and, later, from the kingdom of Bangli, through the intermediary of a woman whose identification with natural fertility is paralleled by her symbolic identification – as a member of the royal lineage – with the political realm of that kingdom. Since eels are considered less prestigious than *naga* as supernatural beings, we may also infer that the fertility originating from Trunyan's alliance with Bangli is of a lesser order than the fertility of the lake water derived from a woman who is the daughter of the sun itself. A quote from a manuscript kept in *Pura Ulun Danu*, where the tutelary goddess of Lake Batur is also worshipped, suggests that her power, pertaining as it does to the universal order, encompasses and transcends the power of any political system which is bound to be, by comparison, particularistic 'because (as) the Goddess makes the waters flow, those who do not follow her laws may not possess her rice terraces' (in Lansing 1991: 73). Even today, this is echoed in the common view that the king of Bangli must subordinate his will to the goddess of the lake situated in Trunyan (Riana 1996). The figure of *Ratu Ayu Pingit Mas Mekulem* may then be taken to represent a woman from the royal household of Bangli, exchanged with the king of Trunyan for access to water needed for the crops of her native village. Alternatively, she may be viewed as an iconic representation of the consequences of a political alliance contracted between the two kingdoms to ensure access to water in times of drought.

Other interpretations are also found elsewhere, which do not invalidate those held in Trunyan. Rather, they reflect different views of the political relations between the kingdoms in the region. Consequently, in the tradition of Bangli, the conflict between Batur and Bangli is well documented, but Trunyan is seldom mentioned and the daughter of the king of Bangli plays only a minor role in tradition. When she does appear in the tale, it is not as the wife of the king of Trunyan, but as the wife of his son; thus in a lesser position than in the tradition of Trunyan, where she marries the king himself. Indeed, whereas as the junior wife of the king of Trunyan, she reigns over the whole village, as the wife of his son, she reigns only over his descendants (i.e. the origin group which refers to him as its apical ancestor). Moreover, in this second option the couple does not reside in Trunyan, as in the first myth, but in Bangli with the princess's father, in a reversed form of the marriage residential settlement common in Bali known as *nyeburin*.[14]

In *nyeburin*, the husband resides in his wife's father's house, and enters her ancestral group, while his wife becomes the head of household and their progeny are included in her ancestral line. This form of reversed marriage, in which descent is traced through the wife's lineage rather than through the husband's (as is normally the case in this patrilineal society) implies that the status of the husband's lineage is perceived as socially inferior to hers. *Nyeburin*, it is said in Bali, 'transforms a husband into a woman and his wife into a man'. The reversed marriage in the tradition of Bangli reveals its perception of Trunyan as inferior in status, and helps explain why, in this version of the alliance between the two kingdoms, it is the son of the king of Trunyan (son-in-law of the king of Bangli), and not his wife (daughter of the king of Bangli), who goes to Trunyan to throw, in the waters of the lake, the iron eels obtained from his father-in-law (the king of Bangli), to whom he is, by force, subordinated. It must be remembered here that, in both traditions, the iron eels are the property of the king of Bangli. In the Trunyan tradition, the king gives these eels to his daughter as her dowry when she marries the king of Trunyan, whereas in the Bangli tradition, the king gives them to his son-in-law who returns to his father's place to throw the eels into the lake, a task made possible because of the female characteristics with which he is endowed by virtue of his patri-uxorilocal residence. This reversal of roles shifts the responsibility for the decision to put an end to the drought from Trunyan to Bangli, in the process relegating Trunyan to a secondary position in the resolution of the conflict. There is, indeed, a difference between ordering one's son-in-law – the son of one's opponent – to make water flow in one's fields, and offering the eels to this same opponent, to whom one's daughter is also offered in marriage.

Social position as identity

It is clear that the further we inquire into the details of past relations between Bangli and Trunyan, the greater the range of plausible explanations. All such explanations satisfy our criteria of historical validity, since they reflect various political and social realities, and reveal fundamental issues concerning the relationships entertained between particular kingdoms in this region of Bali. These interpretations of the past offer equally plausible theses of history, since they all refer to the mnemonic preservation of untraceable events integrating the king's daughter into the community of gods sheltered in the main temple of Trunyan. Furthermore, the identity of the princess as person, whether historical figure or mythical construct, has little bearing on what she, as goddess of food, represents in the temple today.

In order to deepen our understanding of her identity, the focus of inquiry must shift from the goddess' position of member of the royal lineage of an outside kingdom, to that of member of the community of village gods in Trunyan. This community, whose organisation mirrors the social organisation of the village, includes seventeen deities. In this deified realm, secretaries, ministers and dignitaries, each attributed specific tasks in the administration of the supernatural dimension of the village, are found alongside the triad of the king of Trunyan and his two wives. No relations of kinship exist between the triad and the other gods. The relatively recent arrival of the princess in this community of deities, her position as junior wife to the king of Trunyan and her earthly origin all point to a relatively low status. As befits a junior wife, she is entrusted with tasks reserved for low-ranking members of the family. However, as the wife of the highest-ranking deity in Trunyan, she ranks higher than those who perform administrative duties. She awakens the gods at the beginning of festivities, and prepares and serves them food when they are invited in the temple of Trunyan for the periodical festivals held during the ritual year. In addition, she also cooks each month for her husband on the night of the new moon (*tilem*). In a village such as Trunyan, the cooking and sharing of food communicate the value of commensality, in promoting a form of social solidarity modelled on the family. Food is usually not accepted from strangers, except when bought commercially. Cooking is done by women of the household for members of the family, and invited guests who share in the food are temporarily assimilated into its structure. That the daughter of the king of Bangli should be given the task of cooking for the gods suggests the recognition of her status as member of the family of the highest god of Trunyan. It also sets her apart from other gods, since it is through her agency that individual gods in the community are brought together, united as a 'family' in the sharing of the food she has prepared. The lowliness of this task, normally reserved for the younger women in the household, is contrasted with the privileged position she holds as a goddess who, through her marriage with the king of Trunyan, belongs to the small group of highest-ranking deities in Trunyan. More importantly, through her cooking, she becomes the active agent in the promotion of sentiments of village unity.

Her ambiguous status is echoed in the location of her shrine within the main village temple. This temple has five inner yards, hierarchically organised around the auspicious directions of the four points of the compass, with the highest-ranking, or innermost, yard (*penaleman jeroan*) situated in the centre. The innermost yard shelters the shrines of

the king of Trunyan and his first wife, the tutelary goddess of the lake.
The daughter of the king of Bangli is housed on the periphery of this
central yard, in a yard dedicated to the deities associated with Majapahit,
a Javanese kingdom which ruled over Bali after the fourteenth century,
exerting a profound influence over its political and social organisation.
The founders of the recent ruling houses in Bali are believed to originate
from this kingdom, and the dynastic kings in Bangli also trace their
origin to Majapahit. The location of the goddess' shrine in this yard
marks her out as member of a ruling house with which close relations
were entertained, although irresolvable differences, whose nature can no
longer be ascertained, have also endured.

   This is at least the case if we accept that the goddess of food existed as
a historical figure. Neither the functions attributed to her, nor the location of the shrine in the temple, can enlighten us in this matter. Whether
the shrine commemorates a real woman, the daughter of a historical king
of Bangli, or acts as the representation of an alliance between Trunyan
and Bangli in which Bangli recognised its subordination to Trunyan in
return for access to the waters of the lake, has little effect on her position
in the community of village gods. What is communicated is of a different
order. Her position in the community of village gods, and the tasks
attributed to her, reflect the social identity of the groups who interact
with her in rituals. A consideration of those groups, their composition
and their position in society, reveals the goddess as the personification of
values deemed necessary to transform individual groups, otherwise
sharply distinguished by notions of distinct origin, into a unified
community.

Ritual groups and notions of origin

Two kinds of ritual groups are considered here, corresponding to two
levels in the structure of the village (Ottino 1994). The first consists of
the origin groups (*dadia*), related to the goddess through notions of
putative origin and assigned functions to her shrine, and the second,
which comprises the village community at large, acts as one ritual group
for the cooking of food during the performance of temple festivals.
While putative origins single out these *dadia* as different from other
groups in Trunyan, the collective cooking of food fosters the sentiment
of belonging to a unified community.

The dadia

In Trunyan, the *dadia* is a small origin group,[15] patrilineal, patrilocal
and endogamous, venerating as its apical ancestor the son of the king of
Trunyan and each of his two wives. Danandjaja refers to the existence of
seventeen *dadia* in Trunyan at the time of his stay.[16] Every *dadia* is
related to the three main deities through putative ancestors whose
ranking in the hierarchy is determined by their place in the birth order
and the status of their respective mothers, and reflects the status of the
group within the socio-political order.[17] The apical ancestor of a *dadia*
indicates the status of the group, anchoring it into a ritual position
considered in principle to be immutable, where origin and status are
mutually reinforcing. Each *dadia* possesses a temple, built outside the
main village temple, in which a cult is rendered to this apical ancestor
and to the forebears of the (presently) living members of the group. By
contrast to the village-wide festivals, held in the main temple and in
which the whole population participates, this cult is private, involving
only the descendants of these forebears and their families. Consequently,
dadia rituals sustain a sentiment of belonging to one particular origin
group, opposing it to others, while village rituals blur those distinctions
in favour of a sentiment of belonging to a greater community of more
complex and composite origin.

Three *dadia*, belonging to the category of first settlers (groups who
trace their origin from the foundation of Trunyan), share the expenses of
looking after the shrine of the daughter of the king of Bangli. Only one
dadia acknowledges the son of the goddess as its apical ancestor. The
other two instead each recognise as their originator one of the sons of
the senior wife, the tutelary goddess of the lake (Danandjaja 1980:
116–25). Two of the *dadia* each provide a priest for the shrine. All three
dadia acknowledge the existence of a specific bond between themselves
and the goddess by fulfilling an obligation[18] to contribute financially to
the upkeep of her shrine (*nyungsung*). The term *panyungsungan*
describes the groups involved in supporting the upkeep and maintenance of a shrine, stressing the relationship entertained between the god
and the group, rather than the actual constitution of the group as such.
Thus, while a *panyungsungan* may be a descent group able to trace
genealogical links between its members and its deities, it may also
consist, as Danandjaja (1980) has shown, of a group constituted by families brought together in the discharge of ritual duties inherited through
time and across generations as part of their contribution to the village.
Since much prestige is attached to the upkeep of a deity of high status, a

group may also actively seek to appropriate for itself the upkeep of its shrine, either through sheer force or by claiming the direct intervention of the god through a trancer. This is important as it implies the possibility of social mobility through the manipulation of rituals. Indeed in Trunyan, Danandjaja reports that a sub-*dadia* did make use of this possibility, withdrawing from its mother-group and setting itself up as a separate *dadia* with a new temple and new 'son' of the first wife of the king of Trunyan (see Danandjaja 1980: part 1). To cite another example, the upkeep of the shrine dedicated to the prestigious twin brother of the goddess of the lake, tutelary god of the ancestral law, was forcibly appropriated, in the past, by an incoming origin group whose leaders for some time governed Trunyan in the name of the kingdom of Gelgel in south Bali (see Danandjaja 1980; Ottino 1994). By proclaiming the daughter of this deity as its apical ancestor, the new government legitimated its appropriation of the legislative power and secured its position in the hierarchy of status among origin groups. Although couched in genealogical terms, putative descent from a prestigious apical ancestor is often no more than a device for legitimating the status of the members of the group in the present.

The *dadia* which venerates the goddess's son as its founder maintains a particular relationship with the goddess herself. Since her son acts as apical ancestor, she herself indirectly becomes the original point of reference for that group. It is the social position of this particular *dadia* which most closely echoes the ambiguous status of the goddess. Like her, its members trace their origin from the kingdom of Bangli, yet they are also included in the category of first settlers in Trunyan in ritual contexts, when a distinction is made between the groups of first settlers who constitute the core of the village community, and other more recently arrived groups. It is plausible that they are descended from families brought in by the princess upon marriage, but present members of the group can no longer trace such a connection. However, although included in this ritually-privileged category, their political status remains insignificant. The other two *dadia*, by contrast, are considered politically powerful (Danandjaja 1980).[19]

The existence of a closer relation with a god than the one described above is required if a group is to provide a priest for its shrine. This is especially true in Trunyan, where priests are often chosen by the deity herself through trance. This mode of selection, common in the mountainous hinterlands of Bali, presupposes the existence of an affinity between the deity and the group from which the priest derives, thus highlighting links with the past, although it is difficult to obtain concise details regarding the nature of such affinity. The priestly function, which runs in the male line, is often implicitly rather than overtly hereditary, and it is rare for the deity to select someone outside the range of the close agnatic descendants – sons or nephews – of the priest. In high-ranking social groups, the status of priest can be derived simply from birth.[20] Being chosen implies a greater than average state of inner purity. To be chosen by a god is a much envied privilege, from which religious and political prestige can be derived by the priest and his immediate relatives, setting them apart from other families less favoured by the gods. This mode of selection is particularly significant for members of low-ranking groups designated by deities to become priests, since it offers alternative ways of achieving such a virtuous state. Such prestige may endure in future generations, since priests are regularly selected from the same family. Status, in this sense, is linked to origin since descent may motivate claims to greater purity.

In the case of the daughter of the king of Bangli, the claims for higher status and greater purity are partially cancelled by the fact that the two priests (*dangka*) are chosen from two origin groups which belong to different ritual moieties. The village community is divided into two moieties (*sibak*), one male and one female, solely for the purpose of preparing and conducting rituals. Included in the male *sibak* are the origin groups who do not trace their origin outside the village, including one of the two origin groups providing a priest for the daughter of the king of Bangli. The female *sibak* is made up of all other origin groups, including the one which provides the second priest. Newcomers may be integrated into the female *sibak* through ritual 'adoption' by the existing members, but integration in the male *sibak* is closed to all except the genealogical descendants of the first settlers. The two *sibak* are viewed as complementary parts of a single unit, the male division being thought superior to the female. Representatives of each *sibak* are needed to carry out all ritual tasks. The provision of two priests, taken from each side of the ritual community, echoes the position of the goddess as mediator in the rift which always threatens to split apart the groups who trace their origins from Trunyan itself and those from the outside. She thereby acts as an agent for the elaboration of a sense of village unity.

The village community

The village community acts as a single, undifferentiated ritual group. It performs well defined ritual duties on particular occasions. Each month, on the night of the dark moon (*tilem*), the goddess is said to cook for her husband. She also cooks for her husband's divine guests during the important temple festivals held periodically during the ritual year. Two households are designated each month, on a rotating basis, from each *sibak* to cook rice which is offered to the gods before being shared out among members of all the households in the village. This rice derives from two sources: that collected from each household in Trunyan, and that from the fields of the village of Jehem in Bangli (fields contributed by the princess as part of her dowry). Mixing the two rices reinforces the image of the goddess as agent in the consolidation of ties between Bangli and Trunyan. Rice is a highly valued food, equated with the very condition of being human. To eat rice signifies membership of the human species, and to consume rice grown on a particular territory implies sharing in the substance of that land and, by extension, sharing in its identity. The mixture of rice from both villages, in ritual contexts, confirms that the substance of the Trunyanese today is the product of this alliance in the past.

On a different level, the cooking and sharing of rice among all households of these origin groups fosters a sense of belonging to a higher, all encompassing community united by the ideal of partaking in the same corporeal substance. This unity, which operates only in ritual contexts, denies individual social aspirations for status and power and negates the importance of the *dadia* in other domains of social existence. Eating together implies equality between parties, and this practice affirms the ritual equality of every *dadia* in the village, while stressing the importance of placing their solidarity to the community over their individual interests. Similar values are conveyed also during the periodical festivals held in the main temple of Trunyan during the ritual year. On such occasions, rice is also prepared and offered to the gods during ritual, and the leftovers are shared among every household afterwards. As this cooking of rice for the community reproduces, in the social sphere, the task of the goddess in the pantheon of village deities, we may therefore infer that *Ratu Ayu Pingit Mas Mekulem* acts as a symbolic representation of the value of commensality in fostering harmonious and peaceful relations in the community, and in personifying the positive outcome of alliances with powerful neighbours. The ritual practice of cooking and sharing rice from the two kingdoms communicates these messages through its very performance. Nevertheless, the goddess's identity remains only a partial component of a complex notion of collective origin, expressed in ritual exchanges which emphasise the limited relevance of individual origin in the village community.

Ritual exchange and belonging

In addition to the sharing of rice amongst households of the village community, which echoes the sharing of rice amongst the gods in the pantheon, another exchange of food takes place during rituals. As discussed above, for the Balinese (in Trunyan as elsewhere on the island) origin is associated with the locus of life, in the form of *amerta*, a life-giving substance which, while subtle and abstract, is nevertheless considered real in a ritual context. While a full discussion of *amerta* would be beyond the scope of this chapter, it is important to know that rice tends to be identified with *amerta*, being endowed with the same vitalising attributes. Rice is believed to be, in the natural world, a manifestation of *amerta* in the supernatural world. Both are foods of the highest and purest kind, each acting on a different dimension of the person. Whereas rice is obtained from the earth, *amerta* is bestowed on humans by the gods. It is also believed to be present in the water consecrated by the priest during ritual, which is then distributed to all participants. The assembled community receives this consecrated water (*tirta*) as a gift from their gods, to whom a meal has previously been offered.[21] The offering of the meal, which is followed by the blessings with consecrated water, thus constitutes the first part in an exchange of food (or sustenance) which forms the core of every temple ritual. The performance of this ritual serves to enhance the identity of the community as a collective entity, through the enactment of an exchange structured upon the ideal model of the family. Food circulates among members of the community taken in the largest sense of the term, to include the gods as well as human beings (Barraud and Platenkamp 1990), in the same way as it circulates among members of the family, contributing in both cases to sustain the idea of a common substance and leading to a sense of sharing the same identity. All that needs to be known about the nature of the village community is communicated in this ritual performance. The ritual exchange serves to enhance the identity of the community as a collective entity, through the enactment of historically significant narratives and mnemonic representations. Knowledge of this communal identity is thus imparted on the group through rituals which use natural features of the environment to enhance their meaning. If and when the exchange lapses, the sentiment of belonging to the group also declines.

In this context, the individual identities of various village gods become irrelevant. Rather, they merge into a diffuse notion of collective origin which nurtures the collective identity of Trunyan as a community. These concepts of origin, which refer to food-like substances shared with the gods, and belonging, which is ascertained primarily in one's relations with a group, remain so broad that they can include transformations of the socio-political order, environmental change and natural events without altering the fundamental unity of the group.[22] In this sense, the notion of origin itself transcends territory, and allows for people to move in their physical environment without altering their adherence and belonging to their origin group. It is for this reason important for ritual exchange to be performed regularly, since interruptions in the cycle (caused, for instance, by the occurrence of a death at the time of the ritual or difficulties in meeting the costs involved) threaten the very existence of the community.

Origins, ritual exchange and modern Balinese religion

This chapter has attempted to show how sentiments of belonging in Trunyan are expressed through narratives of historical events, natural features of the environment and social relations, transmuted into personified deities and transferred into the realm of the sacred. Such transpositions turn mundane events into loci of origin, which are then used as points of reference to explain or legitimate the present conditions of the ritual group. Gods are thus made to reflect the characteristics of their worshippers. The congruence between the personality of the deity and the social identity of the ritual group endows the traditional Balinese deities with a particularistic quality, opposing them to the more abstract and universal Hindu gods of modern Balinese religion. Over the last decades and since Indonesia's independence, traditional Balinese beliefs have been subjected to a process of 'rationalisation', aiming to bring them in line with the ideals of the four world religions officially recognised by the Indonesian government.[23] This has resulted in the emergence of 'Bali Hinduism', a modern creed adapted to the needs of the well-educated and urbanised Balinese population (Bakker 1997). In this modern and hybrid religion, the highly particularistic temple gods have been pushed aside, in favour of more universalistic gods of Hindu origin such as Brahma, Wisnu and Siwa and, increasingly, in favour of the supreme god common to all official Indonesian religions, Sang Hyang Widdhi Wasa, no longer associated with notions of specific origin other than as universal creator of all life. Gradually, the identity of the old gods is being replaced by this universal, omnipresent God as new generations of Balinese are introduced to this modern creed at school. In this context, the importance of the exchange of sustenance between humans and deities in maintaining identity and an understanding of common origin, becomes extremely tenuous. It is therefore not surprising that the understanding of *tirta* has undergone considerable transformations. Indeed, the well-educated modern Balinese would balk at the interpretation given here. For them, *tirta*, the water consecrated during the temple ritual, is valued exclusively for its purifying power, while its vitalising characteristics, so important to many Balinese until recently (see, for instance, Geertz 1975b), are now understated.

Although the current public religious discourse in Bali runs counter to the argument I have presented here, ritual practices have nevertheless remained remarkably constant in the values they foster. Membership to the congregation of a temple still remains exclusive, since it prevents membership in the congregation of other temples in a similar category. In other words, notions of origin represented through the gods of one temple would conflict with those conveyed in the rituals of another, and membership of both would be akin to postulating two distinct identities, or two different ancestral origins. Only one group of origin can be validated as purveyor of individual and communal identity. As a consequence, it is impossible for a family to become affiliated to the congregations of two, or more, different *dadia* temples. Nor is it possible to participate in the collective rituals of two different villages. Membership in a ritual group is so closely related to identity, that it automatically excludes the possibility of belonging to all other ritual groups of the same kind. To do so would blur descent categories and communal belonging, both considered important indicators of social identity and status, and lead to disorder and chaos which are both conducive to sterility, disease, drought and death. The notion of belonging thus entails demonstrating respect towards the order of the universe.

Rituals help to articulate the interconnections which exist between origin, status and universal order. The ritual exchange of sustenance, for instance, contributes to the creation of an ideal image of the group, in which gods and humans reflect different aspects of this existential unity (Barraud and Platenkamp 1990). The construction of unity through ritual requires the prior separation of the two parties, where gods and humans need to be constituted as distinct entities in order for the exchange of sustenances to take place. Food derived from a common source (the fields belonging to the goddess and owned by the village community) thus acts as a vitalising substance for both parties involved in ritual exchange, in the process publicly and metaphorically proclaiming that gods and worshippers are but two dimensions of a unified reality. If the symbolic value of *tirta* (water), as the vehicle for the god's gift of life, health, wealth and fertility, stimulates the growth of rice in the fields, the two substances become intrinsically merged and feed into the sustenance of humans at pragmatic and symbolic levels. It also becomes obvious that an increased exchange of sustenance between humans and gods, through ritual performance, is perceived to result in enhanced prosperity for both the group and the gods. This may in part explain why many Balinese continue to worship in temples long after any memory of the original bond with forebears and the temple has been lost.

Notes

1 Temple congregations are seldom homogeneous groups united under a notion of common ancestry. Beyond the kin group temple (*sanggah*) of the residential houseyard and that of the corporate descent group (*sanggah gede*) which, in the past, exploited an estate of rice land collectively, in most temple congregations it is rare to find more than a few families who are aware of being united by bonds of kinship. *Pamaksaan* are mostly heterogeneous groups made up of a central core of families who have inherited from their forebears an obligation to maintain the temple and conduct rituals there, and among whom the priest (*pamangku*) is chosen. More peripheral are clusters of 'followers', families whose forebears have transmitted to them duties such as participation in money and kind to the performance of the temple rituals. The temple congregation also includes families or individuals who attend the rituals because they feel that it is 'proper' for them to do so, either because their parents or grandparents did so in the past or because they have been privately advised, by a local medium, to affiliate themselves to that particular temple. What differentiates temple congregations from other groups is that they are united solely by a shared obligation to support the temple and ensure the performance of periodical rituals in it. In other terms temple congregations are brought together in ritual circumstances only. There is no sense of a common bond uniting the members, unless of course they are related in other domains of life, for instance through kin ties, shared activities or common residence in a village. For *pamaksaan* see note 17.
2 See C. Geertz' studies on personhood in Bali (Geertz 1959, 1975a).
3 It is difficult to render adequately with words taken from our vocabulary the Balinese conceptions of the nature of the world, in particular the domain lying beyond the sphere of what is apprehensible to human perception. I have chosen to use the word 'supernatural' rather than 'spiritual' in this paper, because it describes more accurately the relation between the tangible world (*sekala*) experienced by human beings through their senses, which corresponds more or less to what we mean by 'nature', and the intangible world (*neskala*) not usually apprehended by humans because of the limited scope of their senses, which may be rendered as 'supernature'. Nature and supernature may be compared to two facets of the same reality; whatever exists in the tangible world being assumed to be reflected in the intangible world.

4 Geertz and Geertz (1975) also distinguish between noble groups who possess a genealogy (Brahmana and Ksatria), and commoner groups whose genealogical awareness is very shallow, rarely stretching further than two or three ascending generations. It may be argued, however, that even among the Brahmana and the Ksatria, the reliability of genealogies is questionable (Rubinstein 1991).

5 See Evens 1994.

6 Dewi means goddess, Ayu is a title used for women of high birth, Pingit means hidden or esoteric, Mas means gold, but may refer to an origin group of the same name, and Mekulem means to sleep. Such names describe a deity's status and function in the local pantheon. The goddess has the task of awakening the gods on the occasion of each festival.

7 Balinese 'kingdoms' resembled small chiefdoms, rather than the nation-states with which the term kingdom has become associated. For instance, the kingdom of Trunyan covered an area no wider than about 100 square kilometres, its capital being the village of the same name.

8 I am using the term 'origin group' here in the sense coined by J.J. Fox in his work on hierarchy and precedence in Austronesian societies (Fox 1990a, 1990b, 1994), to refer to a group where a distinction is made between the genealogical forebears and the apical ancestor with whom no descent tie can be traced.

9 While a full-scale discussion of the complex symbolism of water in Balinese life would be beyond the scope of this paper, it is worth mentioning the analogies made between the role of water in rice-growing and the function of vital fluids such as blood, sweat, bile, urine and semen in the human body (Ottino, forthcoming).

10 For instance, see Lansing (1991) for a study of the role of *Pura Ulun Batur* in the politics of Bali, past and present.

11 This is opposed to the mythical tradition originating from Bangli, whereby the daughter of the king of Bangli would have married the son of the king of Trunyan (Riana 1996). The different versions reflect conflicting interests which I shall treat below.

12 'Historical time' refers here to the period in the past that is recorded in the Balinese classical texts (*babad*) and other manuscripts, generally taken to mean the period after the invasion of Bali by the Javanese kingdom of Majapahit. It is an arbitrary division, used here solely for the purpose of distinguishing between the foundation of Trunyan from the union of a prince with the daughter of the sun and a goddess of the sky, and the alliance between two political realms.

13 Working from the perspective of the dynastic temple of Bangli, the Balinese historian Ketut Riana interprets the drought as meaning that the king of Bangli belonged to the Siwa Siddhanta and Buda Mahayana religious strains, while Batur was dominated by Wisnuism. However, there is no evidence to support this view other than the oral tradition available from Bangli informants today. As such the issue must remain unresolved.

14 See Ottino (1993) for a full discussion of *nyeburin* and Ottino (1994) for an analysis of the role of *nyeburin* in the foundation myths of Trunyan.

15 On average 20–25 households, but sometimes as few as two.

16 It is perhaps not coincidental that seventeen is also the number of deities in the pantheon of Trunyan.

17 In addition, one politically powerful newcomer group, descendants of ancient rulers brought to Trunyan by the kingdom of Gelgel, venerates the son of the brother of the tutelary goddess of the lake as their apical ancestor, whom their forebears are said to have appropriated by force. This group is set apart from the rest of the population, and in the past was considered purer. See Danandjaja 1980 and Ottino 1994 for a discussion of the group's appropriation of its apical ancestor.

18 The sense of obligation is conveyed by the Balinese term *pamaksaan* derived from the root word *paksa* and stressing the idea of unavoidable obligation, which is passed on from generation to generation.

19 The index for evaluating this is the number of village leaders provided by an origin group over a given period (three decades). Danandjaja gives a detailed analysis of village leadership in his ethnography. It is, of course, always possible for a member of a socially insignificant group to rise to political leadership given the right circumstances.

20 It must briefly be added that, although no members of the *Tri-Wangsa* caste-system reside in Trunyan, and although the village fosters an ideology of ritual equality, the relations between *dadia* are hierarchical. As is common throughout Bali, hierarchical differences tend to be manifested in an idiom of purity, especially as restrictions on the sharing of food. Priests are also considered purer than average and, as such, are also subject to food prohibitions. They should not, for instance, eat food cooked in the house where a death has recently occurred, nor should they eat 'heating' foods such as pork or beef. They are also polluted by food handled by impure persons such as menstruating women.

21 *Tirta* is made from water fetched from a sacred source near a temple, from rainwater collected in jars, or from water obtained from sources in the natural environment singled out as sacred, such as water from the summit of a nearby mountain. Although it is not possible to discuss them here, such sources should be mentioned, since they express the existence of ties with the natural environment which are included in the ritual construction of the ideal village community.

22 It is obvious that this ideology serves political interests. I have treated this in Ottino 1994.

23 Those religions are Islam, Buddhism, Hinduism and Christianity, both Protestantism and Catholicism.

References

Bakker, F.L. (1997) 'Balinese Hinduism and the Indonesian State', *Bijdragen Tot de Taal-, Land- en Volkenkunde* 153: 15–41.

Barraud, C. and Platenkamp, J.D.M. (1990) 'Rituals and the Comparison of Societies', *Bijdragen Tot de Taal-, Land- en Volkenkunde* 146: 103–24.

Bateson, G. (1970) 'An Old Temple and a New Myth', in J. Belo (ed.) *Traditional Balinese Culture*, New York: Columbia University Press.

Danandjaja, J. (1980) *Kebudayan Petani Desa Trunyan di Bali*, Jakarta: Pustaka Jaya.

Davies, P. (1991) 'The Historian in Bali', *Meanjin* 50(1): 63–80.

Evens, T.M.S. (1994) 'Mythic Rationality, Contradiction and Choice Among the Dinka', *Social Anthropology* 2(2): 99–114.

Fox, J.J. (1990a) 'Sisters Since the Trunk of Heaven, Brothers Since the Rim of Earth : Progenitor Lines of Origin in Some Societies of Eastern Indonesia', paper presented at the conference on *Hierarchy, Ancestry and Alliance*, Research School of Pacific and Asian Studies, Australian National University, Canberra, 25–30 January.

—— (1990b) 'Austronesian Societies and their Transformations', paper presented at the conference on *Hierarchy, Ancestry and Alliance*, Research School of Pacific and Asian Studies, Australian National University, Canberra, 12–14 November.

—— (1994) 'Reflections on "Hierarchy" and "Precedence"', *History and Anthropology* 7(1–4): 87–108.

Geertz, C. (1959) 'Form and Variation in Balinese Village Structure', *American Anthropologist* 61: 991–1012.

—— (1975a) 'Person, Time, and Conduct in Bali', in C. Geertz, *The Interpretation of Cultures*, London: Hutchinson.

—— (1975b) 'Internal Conversion in Bali', in C. Geertz, *The Interpretation of Cultures*, London: Hutchinson.

Geertz, H. and Geertz C. (1975) *Kinship in Bali*, Chicago: University of Chicago Press.

Lansing, J.S. (1987) 'Balinese Water Temples and the Management of Irrigation', *American Anthropologist* 89: 326–41.

—— (1991) *Priests and Programmers: Technologies of Power in the Engineered Landscape of Bali*, Princeton, NJ: Princeton University Press.

Ottino, A. (1993) 'Siblingship and Continuity of the Family in the Balinese Houseyard: the Case of a Commoner Group in a Balinese Village', *Canberra Anthropology* 16(1): 36–66.

—— (1994) 'Origin Myths, Hierarchical Order and the Negotiation of Status in the Balinese Village of Trunyan', *Bijdragen tot de Taal, Land- en Volkenkunde* 150: 481–517.

—— (forthcoming) *The Universe Within*, manuscript under review for publication.

Riana, J.M.K. (1996) 'Pura Kehen Dalam Folklore', unpublished paper presented at the Conference of the Society for Balinese Studies, Denpasar, 23–5 August.

Rubinstein, R. (1991) 'The Brahmana According to their Babad', in H. Geertz (ed.), *State and Society in Bali*, Leiden: KITLV Press.

Chapter 5

Spirit possession as historical narrative
The production of identity and locality in Zanzibar Town[*]

Kjersti Larsen

This chapter approaches locality as a phenomenological quality, and as an aspect of social life, in order to discuss a process through which ethnic identity and belonging are experienced and produced. The discussion is grounded in the phenomenon of spirit possession in Zanzibar, situated off the east coast of Africa. Living in a multi-ethnic society, Zanzibaris participate in continuous interactions and discourses across what may, in analytical terms, be conceptualised as ethnic boundaries. While humans are characterised in social discourse as having ambiguous and shifting relationships to locality and identity, spirits known to Zanzibari women and men are, by contrast, perceived as having clear and distinctive identities and affiliations to specific places. The opposition between the ambiguity and multivocality of human belonging, and the distinctiveness and fixity of spirits' identity, provides the ethnographic focus of this chapter.

We focus here on spirit possession as one kind of historical narrative highlighting cultural belonging. Following Lambek, this chapter examines spirit possession as active memory based on 'primary experience and routinised "forgetting" ' (1996: 242), and approaches spirit possession as a way of embodying localities and locating bodies in socially and spatially defined communities (Appadurai 1995). By treating spirit possession as an 'inscription of locality onto . . . bodies' (Appadurai 1995: 205), one may consider this phenomenon as a continuous social construction of both identity and locality. What is at stake here is what Makris has recently described as 'the "lived in" political conditions of everyday life' (1996: 175), rather than more official political discourses. Spirit possession provides the focus for the production of identity and locality in Zanzibar Town, since the convergence of human beings and spirits highlights notions of identity, as anchored in place of origin and expressed through aesthetics or style. Aesthetics is taken here to refer to bodily modes of knowledge (Jackson 1983, 1989; Csordas 1990; Howes 1991). Aesthetic experiences can be treated as avenues to the senses and, by extension, to human experiences in and of the world. Within a Zanzibari cultural universe aesthetics, in the sense of beauty and beautification, are stressed as a sign of being civilised and, hence, Zanzibari. Beauty, the beautification of bodies, and geographical surroundings are linked to smells, sounds, sights, tastes and body movements, and are central as expressions of identity and belonging to particular localities, making sensory experience significant in the marking of similarities and differences between humans and spirits. Differences in affiliation to tribe are made evident through subtle variations in ways of dressing, choice of fragrances, use of verbal expressions, music and favourite dishes, all of which conjure up a range of associations often reaching beyond Zanzibar itself. Women and men explain these differences in style by arguing that different tribes have different habits (*tabia*) and customs (*desturi*), thus linking habits and customs to place of origin. Locality also acts as a reminder of a social ranking system which was particularly palpable during British colonial rule when distinctions between categories of people were made with reference to places of origin, each group being ranked hierarchically according to wealth and social power (*uwezo*) (see also Sheriff and Ferguson 1991; Meyers 1997; Fair 1997).

As they live in a cosmopolitan and socially stratified society, people continuously discuss and compare different ways of life both in terms of habits and customs as well as wealth and social power. Women and men emphasise their Zanzibariness by referring to hospitality, friendliness, etiquette, aesthetic elaborateness, the Swahili[1] language and, for the majority of the population, their shared Muslim faith.[2] Zanzibariness is associated more with attitudes, behaviour and self-presentation than with being of the same locality. However, perceptions of the mainland (*bara*) act as a significant point of reference, and contrast, in emphasising Zanzibariness. Perceived differences between Zanzibar and the mainland in historical, political, religious and aesthetic representations, manners and attitudes are, time and again, mentioned in conversations. Being a mainlander is presented as the antithesis of Zanzibari identity. Nevertheless, despite a common stress on Zanzibariness, people also maintain that they are different from each other because they belong to different tribes (*makabila*).[3] Tribe, in this context, refers to what people see as their own or their ancestors' place of origin, often a locality beyond Zanzibar. For instance, the term *Wagasija* denotes people of Comoran origin, and refers to people from the Comoro Islands.[4]

Waarabu[5] denotes people from Arabia, while *Wapempa* are said to be people from the Island of Pemba. Thus the Swahili term *kabila* (tribe) can best be understood as referring to 'a person from somewhere', implying that people are identified primarily through a focus on place as a situated community or nation. The term *Waswahili*, meaning the 'people of the coast', is seldom used in a self-descriptive way. To be a *Mswahili* implies that a person does not know her or his place of origin and must therefore be of slave descent.[6] To be of slave ancestry remains stigmatising in most social contexts.

Locality, in a general sense, is significant since particular places beyond Zanzibar help define constructions of identity and contribute, paradoxically, to the creation of Zanzibar itself as a nation. However, an awareness of tribe and place of origin reaching beyond Zanzibar does not necessarily express a wish to return to this original locality.

Identity, locality and the presence of spirits

This focus on locality enables Zanzibaris to create historical pasts which explain and legitimate their presence in Zanzibar Town today. As Connerton (1989) suggests, people´s experience of the present depends to a large degree upon their knowledge of the past. However, it is significant to bear in mind that the past is not fixed, and that true historical narratives exist only within the scope of the memory of those who construct them. As the recent debate in anthropology reveals (Biersack 1991; Carrier 1992), what we may find through a focus on historical narratives are often alternative constructions of history.

In this context, this chapter aims to discuss the extent to which an elaborate Zanzibari spirit classification can be seen to reveal certain constructions of historical processes and historically defined positions. According to Zanzibari women and men, spirits as human beings belong to different tribes whose differences are expressed through the language of aesthetics, including ways of dressing, choice of fragrances, music and favourite dishes, body movements, the use of language and certain verbal expressions. Different tribes of spirits are also said to have access to different kinds of knowledge.

The identification with, and interpretation of, what Zanzibaris perceive as various tribes of spirits cut across ethnic designations, social and economic strata, and gender categories. Spirit possession may be experienced by any woman or man in ritual or everyday contexts. It is generally said that the spirits themselves decide when, and whom, to inhabit and that when a woman or a man becomes inhabited by a spirit, she or he is understood to become the spirit. The spirit is thus said to control and use the human body for a period of time in order to materialise in the human world. Spirits are perceived as either male or female, Christian, Muslim, Hindu or pagan and come from places beyond Zanzibar. When inhabited by a spirit, a human body may change its identity both with regard to its gender and its religious and ethnic belonging.

In this sense spirits also act, as Lambek argues, as 'vehicles of memory, rather than as frozen remnants of memory' (Lambek 1996: 241). Also important in this respect are Bloch's observations concerning the selective organisation of history, and thereby memory. In this sense, historical narratives may also be constructed in order to forget unpleasant events. Bloch argues that 'When we consider the social actor's attitude to the distant past it becomes clear that one's effort involves not simply finding ways of remembering better . . . but also, equally, finding ways to forget it' (Bloch 1996: 229). We thereby create manageable images of various pasts, and of various Others associated with those pasts. What matters is that spirit classifications, and the rituals performed on behalf of spirits such as *ngoma ya sheitani* can be understood as historical events enacted, simultaneously, at individual and societal levels. As narratives enacted within particular social and cultural contexts, spirit possession serves to constrain, yet also promote, action and thought. Spirit possession, as it is presented, represented and enacted in Zanzibar Town, simultaneously reveals and conceals ethnic stereotypes and boundaries, and provides a context where the past can be both memorised and forgotten.

In narrative terms, spirit possession is a vehicle for memory, where remembering can be seen as a symbolic practice which leaves various narratives open to continuous reformulation (Lambek 1996). Zanzibari spirit classifications relate to the presence of various groups of people, and positions held by them, on the basis of tribal affiliation. What Zanzibari women and men perceive as different tribes of spirits represent different historical and ideological aspects of Zanzibari society. The various tribes of spirits are believed to have originated from particular localities, and the rituals performed on their behalf are constructed with reference to these localities, as well as the styles, likes and dislikes of particular people or spirits.

The classification of spirits and their commemoration in ritual constitute contradictory and contestable representations of recent historical periods of Zanzibari society. The fact that Zanzibaris may become inhabited by spirits of different tribes underlines the importance of ideas of locality and belonging in personal narratives and the construction of identity. When inhabited by spirits belonging to different tribes, a body acquires more than one identity: in effect, it changes identities and becomes the site for the re-enactment of social memory. Spirit possession thereby provides the means for the negotiation of present relationships expressing ethnic identity within historical frameworks (Boddy 1989). Whether these links between the classification of spirits and historical narratives are explicit to people themselves remains unclear, since most Zanzibaris associate spirit possession to health, illness and healing.

The following section presents a brief chronicle of Zanzibar, providing a framework for understanding the historical and social associations evoked by various spirits. The account begins when Zanzibar became subjected to Omani dominance, since this event triggered intense immigration to the island. We introduce various tribes of spirits, and link these to historical and political events central to the lives of contemporary Zanzibari women and men. There is also a case study highlighting the instrumentality of spirit possession in the production of identity, locality, and discourses of belonging.

Historical events, discrimination, and place of origin

Around 1840, the then Sultan of Oman, Seyyid Said bin Sultan, transferred his capital from Muscat to Zanzibar Town and established the Zanzibar Sultanate. A period of extensive immigration followed. Merchants, craftsmen and builders from Gujarat in India, traders and fishermen from the Hadrahmout, the Comoros and Madagascar, cattle keepers and servants from Somalia and Ethiopia, and people from what are now Malawi, Mozambique, Congo and mainland Tanzania, settled in Zanzibar. In addition the slave trade, initially conducted on a small scale, increased markedly during the nineteenth century, both for export and domestic labour. When slavery was abolished in 1907, these former slaves, alongside immigrants from the mainland, became servants, manual workers, peasants, fishermen or workers on clove plantations. Gradually, people living in Zanzibar became part of a cultural universe where Islam represented ideals and values inherent in an encompassing and unifying lifestyle which also, according to Laura Fair, 'helped to create a new and inclusive national identity' (Fair 1994). Within this cultural universe there existed, from about 1840 to 1964, three officially recognised racial groups: Arabs, Asians and Africans.[7] The socio-political structure privileged Arabs, especially those from Oman,[8] while Africans, all defined as one social category, were subordinated. Nevertheless, neighbourhoods in Zanzibar Town, especially those beyond the Stone Town quarters called Ng'ambo, were not organised by ethnicity or place of origin. Instead, they formed relationships of *ujirani*, where an ideal of solidarity among neighbours prevailed (see also Meyers 1993).

As Arabness was privileged, people tended to negotiate and redefine their ethnic identities and thus became, if not Arab, at least Shirazi or Hadimu, which indicates Persian origin (see also Fair 1994).[9] A hierarchy based on ethnic identity was explicitly expressed in various ways, ultimately resulting in the 1964 revolution (see also Lofchie 1965; Sheriff 1987; Sheriff and Ferguson 1991; Meyers 1997). In the wake of the revolution, Arabness became stigmatising. Zanzibar was then ruled by a socialist government whose members were mainly of African descent. Over the years, the revolutionary government imposed constraints on the population intended to fight racism and (what was perceived as) feudalism, and aiming to create a unified, undifferentiated Zanzibari identity where all would be defined as belonging to one tribe, the *afro-shirazi*. All organisations based on ethnic identity were made illegal. Public religious rituals were strongly discouraged. Prohibition against what was defined as Western fashion such as flared trousers and long hair for men were introduced. The economic policy after the revolution also led to a shortage of imported goods which minimised all kinds of lavishness including in connection with the performance of rituals. By and large, the project failed.

The violent revolution of 1964, which was a struggle between propertied and non-propertied classes largely defined at the time in racial terms, impacted on people's lives and on the redefinition of ethnic identities and boundaries in various ways. Many endured the loss of family members, relatives, neighbours and friends, who had either been killed or fled the island. Many previously propertied Zanzibaris lost their assets due to nationalisation and land reforms. People of Arab, Asian and Comoran origin experienced general deprivation and a loss of privileges and material wealth, while those perceived to be of African origin gained access to resources previously considered scarce, such as property, education and health services. The process of Africanisation, initiated after the revolution, was intended to eliminate ethnic boundaries and bring dignity to the previously suppressed majority of the population. In 1967, all people of Asian descent were forced to leave their positions in governmental offices and, in 1971, their business licenses were not renewed. A quota system for schools was introduced, allowing intakes consisting of 80 per cent Africans, 15 per cent of Arabian descent, 4 per cent of Asian descent and 1 per cent of Comoran descent. In 1972, the Forced Marriage Act was ushered in, making it legal for men of African origin to marry women of Arabian and Asian descent without the consent of the women themselves or their families. In the wake of this act some young women committed suicide and many young couples, often cousins, were immediately married in order to prevent what they saw as forced marriages imposed by the state. The justification for the introduction of this Act was to prevent differentiation along ethnic lines and encourage hybridity. The consequence, however, led to a rather increased awareness of ethnic belonging. People of Arabian and Asian origins conceptualised this process as racial abuse. For others, the perceived necessity to introduce the Act confirmed their opinion of Arabs and Asians as immigrants exploiting people of African origin. The revolution, and the process of Africanisation following in its wake, defined as illegitimate a wide range of activities previously associated with ethnic identity, such as political activism according to ethnic belonging.[10] Ethnicity as a marker of identity was understated in all public debates and policies but remained nevertheless important in practice, in terms of self-presentation and in shaping social, political and economic networks and loyalties. In the politics of everyday life, the revolution also strengthened the mistrust between people conceptualised as belonging to Arab or Asian groups, and those perceived as African in origin.

Since the revolution, the multi-ethnic character of Zanzibar has become part of a muted discourse in the public political arena. Yet, questions of belonging have remained central to unofficial political discourses, and have often caused tension. Those who experienced the revolution still find it difficult to talk about what happened at that time. People who define themselves as of non-African descent occasionally still express genuine mistrust of those whom they perceive to be of African origin. Equally, people of African ancestry refer to slavery, and to the period before the revolution, in order to express their suspicion of those perceived as non-African. Differences along perceived tribal lines are often evoked to explain, for instance, why one cannot trust a person, why a woman does not express shyness or why a man does not show respect. Political issues discussed in informal settings are often framed in terms of affiliation to tribes. The concept of tribe (*kabila*) therefore remains a classificatory category which people use in order to establish distinctions among themselves. There still exist, for instance, contemporary discourses which reproduce social memories of slavery and the revolution. This became evident again as questions of ethnicity were brought to the fore during the recent campaign for multi-party elections. Zanzibaris immediately defined the political rhetoric of the two main parties according to notions of Arabness and Africanness: the Civil United Front (CUF) and its followers were said to be aiming for the Arabisation of Zanzibar and the (re-)enslavement of its people, while the Chama Cha Mapinduzi (CCM) and its followers were accused of wanting to Africanise Zanzibar and throw out and disempower Zanzibaris of Arab and Asian origin.[11] Such issues are directly related to distinctions made between free-born and slave, and to people's experiences, memories and understandings of the main conflicts underpinning the revolution.

People who have impinged on Zanzibar in different historical periods have become differently positioned in society. In Zanzibar Town today, no specific ranking exists of the different tribes (*makabila*), although for most people (except perhaps those of Asian origin) the notion of Arabness remains an ideal. The term denoting being civilised, *ustaraabu*, literally means 'being like an Arab'.[12] As an extension, Arabness has become associated with Zanzibariness, while 'Bantuness' is now primarily associated with the mainland. However, both remain wide categories, and carry different meanings for different people in different contexts.

Islamic ideals and values have become important in the conceptualisation and definition of Zanzibari culture (*mila*), separating it from that of the African hinterland and also from what is perceived as more Western or also, European (*-ya kizungu*). In this context, Arabness does not refer to being Arab in a genealogical sense, but rather acts as an ideological pole.[13] Arabness has thus come to refer to the adoption of customs, dress, codes of behaviour, verbal expressions and manners, which are perceived as Arab but define a general, and idealised, identity of Zanzibariness.

Images of Zanzibariness as unified identity evoke feelings of belonging to one (imagined) community. Yet, in their attempt to create a sense of sameness and common belonging opposing them to the mainland, Zanzibaris seem to have few common experiences of the past to which they can refer. Slavery and the revolution of 1964 still provide the focal points in defining the past of most Zanzibaris, and both historical events focus on differences and conflicts, rather than on similarities in ethnic affiliation. Thus, despite a shared understanding of contemporary Zanzibariness, tensions relating to ethnic identity (especially between those of perceived Arab and Bantu origin) continue to be part of people's lives.

I now turn to a description of Zanzibari spirit classification in order to illustrate how different tribes of spirits are perceived. This classification draws attention to different aspects of, and periods in, the recent history of Zanzibaris. The narratives of spirit possession draw attention to a broad field of visual imagery grounded in feelings, prejudices, information, knowledge, historical memory and contemporary experiences.

Narratives inherent in spirit classifications

Spirits are said to bear similarities to Zanzibaris, yet are all conceived as foreigners. Consequently, no spirits are said to originate either from Zanzibar Town, or indeed from the island of Unguja.[14] The various tribes of spirits come from localities which have, in various ways, been significant to Zanzibar Town in the recent past. The classification of spirits can be interpreted as enactments of fragments of the past in the present and that spirit classifications both produce and enact social memory.

The fact that Islam is a belief system and moral code shared by most Zanzibaris is reflected in the ways of spirits. All spirits, including those considered pagan, require rituals to begin with a prayer to Allah. All demand the same kind of goods: food, drink, incense, medicines and gifts, although variations in kinds of food, colour and fragrances help create differences between the various tribes of spirits. Hence, distinctions between various spirits and their respective tribes are communicated within an overarching framework of aesthetics. In addition, these distinctions extend to the social position of the spirits where some of the distinguishing criteria are those of Arabness: Bantuness, urban/rural, free-born/slave, high/low social position, and knowledge. Certain forms of knowledge are markers of ethnic identity and belonging and should be understood with reference to social hierarchies, and to what is deemed as important and prestigious insight in Islam (-ya dini). For example, while knowledge of sorcery is associated with Bantuness, knowledge of Islam is associated with Arabness. Knowledge of remedies used in healing is, however, more ambiguous and could be associated both with Arabness and Bantuness. There are four different categories of spirits whose presence in Zanzibar Town is prominent.

The first category, *Masheitani ya ruhani*, are Muslim spirits from Arabia, and are said to speak Arabic and only broken Swahili. They have typical Muslim names such as Jinni Sheik Suleman bin Mohammad bin Said, and originate from Muscat and Jiddah. Spirits of this tribe are said to prefer white clothes, red or white turbans, and golden rings with green, red or turquoise stones. Zanzibaris tend to associate these colours with religious rituals: white denotes purity, while green and turquoise are colours associated with mosques. Red symbolises authority and greatness, both of which can be achieved through extensive religious knowledge. Among *Masheitani ya ruhani*, knowledge of religion is an important marker of rank, and has a bearing on whether one can attain a high position. Hence the ritual leaders, *mwalim*, hold a prestigious position because of their Islamic knowledge. To have *kuwa na* (knowledgeable spirit) can assist a person in attaining an important social position, either as a ritual leader and/or as a medical expert whose healing practices are linked to the hidden meaning of various verses in the Qur'an. A relationship with a knowledgeable *sheitani ya ruhani* can enhance a person's social power.

At the beginning of their ritual, verses from the Qur'an are recited and, slowly, the recitation turns into the singing of various songs in Swahili in praise of Allah and the Prophet. The singing gradually turns into *dhikir*, that is, evoking the names of Allah accompanied by the repetition of *Allah hai* (God the living one), as women and men perform specific bodily movements.

Masheitani ya ruhani are as common in rural as in urban areas. They are associated with people from all social backgrounds and all the different tribes recognised by Zanzibaris. These spirits reflect the practices and attributes which people commonly associate with Arabness and being a Muslim. This Arabness is stressed by an emphasis on specific places of origin (such as Mekka, Jiddah or Muscat) and the elaborate Muslim names of spirits. The kind of food these spirits demand, and the way it is served, are also associated in Zanzibar Town with Arabness and 'being civilised'.[15]

The second category, *Masheitani ya rubamba*, are pagan spirits from Pemba, and are categorised as spirits of Swahili origin.[16] They have names such as *Muzi wa Sanda Wajinni wa Shariff wa Mkatamalini* which, to the ears of townspeople, sound like Bantu names, and are said to speak *kipemba* (Pemba dialect of Swahili). They move to the rhythm of two sticks beaten against each other, and are seen as powerful spirits. Their knowledge of healing and sorcery is considered important and attractive, yet also threatening. Ritual leaders are called *mganga*, a title associated with Swahiliness and/or Bantuness, given to a specialist in traditional health care who knows how to prepare what are seen as non-Islamic remedies, and who has knowledge of sorcery (*uganga*). The habits and traditions of *masheitani ya rubamba* are considered non-Islamic, and less civilised. They prefer the colour black which is usually perceived as impure, and are said to prefer the kind of black cloth which was commonly worn by slaves (*kaniki*), thereby drawing attention to their position within a hierarchical structure. By the standards of Zanzibar Town, these spirits want their food served in an uncivilised manner.[17] *Masheitani ya rubamba* choose as their hosts women and men from both rural and urban areas. Although people from all tribes are possessed by them, these spirits have a tendency to attach themselves to those who consider themselves as *wapemba*, *waswahili* or also *waarabu*. Hence, women and men originating from the island of Pemba and people who stress their African origin are associated with this tribe of spirits. It is also common that people who are perceived as Arab become inhabited by these spirits and thus express the interlinkages between Arabic and Bantu aspects of Zanzibari identities (see also Middleton 1992).

Masheitani ya kibuki[18] constitute the third category and are, in common with a minority of the Zanzibari population, Christian. They speak *kibuki* and broken Swahili[19] and, although considered from Madagascar (*Bukini*), are also closely associated with the Comoro Islands and often refer to localities such as Mayote and Duwani when introducing themselves. The names of *masheitani ya kibuki* such as, for instance, Damandizo Damandizuzuriwa from Mayote and Ndamusfali Ndamanes from Duwani, generally sound foreign to people in Zanzibar Town. The ritual leader is called *fundi*, an Arabic term referring to a person skilled in any art, craft or profession. To be a *fundi* implies knowledge of spirits in more technical matters, and an awareness of how to communicate with and behave towards them.

These spirits are believed to represent what is non-Islamic, and non-African, and have therefore no preference for white or black. Rather, they favour green and pink, colours associated with the bride in Arab-style weddings and thus with situations of affluence, happiness and pleasure (Larsen 1989). They enjoy hearing music from a rattle and an accordion resembling the famous Swahili Taraab music, which is first and foremost an urban phenomenon. Their ritual meal (*chano*) consists of a mixture of drinks, stimulants, jewellery and money.[20] They are said to appreciate money, to help people in their accumulation of wealth, and bring professional success. In terms of style and social rank they are associated with what is perceived as Arabness, that is wealth and social power. Yet, they are also said to be attracted to a more Western life-style, to like Europeans and things European and, during rituals, to use some French words and to prefer the French and people with blond, straight hair. Although they stress their links with Europe and Europeans, these spirits are not identified as Westerners (*wazungu*).

The preference *masheitani ya kibuki* express for Europeans and what is defined as a European lifestyle should be understood in light of the historical linkage between these spirits and people of Comoran origin. During colonial rule people of Comoran origin, due to their high literacy rate, often worked within the colonial civil service and Europeans usually hired them as overseers in their homes (Fair 1994). People of Comoran origin were thus associated with the European community in Zanzibar, and were often defined by Europeans as Arab rather than African.

Masheitani ya kibuki portray urban, wealthy life, and are only present in urban areas. They attach themselves, first and foremost, to women of Comoran origin, although they may also choose men and people from other tribes as their human hosts. These spirits stress the importance of ethnicity and social rank, and also consumerism and a desire for worldly success. This tribe of spirits is associated with a complex hierarchical social structure. Divided into kings, queens, military personnel, commoners and slaves, the social organisation appears to reflect elements of pre-revolutionary Zanzibari society, a sultanate and British protectorate where social divisions and rank were established with reference both to place of origin and position within the urban system of production.

Finally, the fourth category comprises of *Masheitani ya habeshia*, Christian spirits from Ethiopia (*Habash*) said to speak *kihabash*, whose ritual is called *Zaar*. The term *Zaar*, which is exclusive to this tribe of spirits, underlines their foreign character and exoticism. These spirits have a preference for music from three drums marked with a cross. The fact that the language of these spirits is not understood illustrates that they are seen as more foreign than the other spirits here described. Their ritual meal consists of popcorn and *halua*, coffee and ginger tea, only food that is luxurious and associated with times of pleasure.[21] *Masheitani ya habeshia* are divided into two opposing types: refined royalty and unrefined slaves.[22] The kings and queens speak in the human world and introduce themselves by their full names, while the commoners have no individual names but are attributed categories of names which are invoked only in songs. They only accept the colour red, the Sultan's colour, and are associated with the former Sultanate and traditional Arab upper class in general.

Masheitani ya habeshia are found exclusively in urban areas and mostly choose as their human hosts women of Arabic origin belonging to the upper strata of society, although people from other tribes and occupying less prestigious positions may also become inhabited by spirits of this tribe. With its imagined divisions into queens, kings and slaves, the social organisation of these spirits bears clear resemblances to that of the former royal court, although this milieu also consisted of military personnel and other kinds of employees which are not included in the spirit world. These spirits represent a society consisting of a small Arab dynasty and a great majority of slaves and, like this dynasty, the spirits remain distant to most Zanzibari women and men. In a contemporary context, these spirits are explicitly associated with what is today referred to as the royal family in Zanzibar, that is, the descendants of the late president Karume, the first president following the 1964 revolution.

Spirits, humans and negotiations of identity

Masheitani ya ruhani and *Masheitani ya rubamba* seem to conform more easily than the other categories of spirits to general values and social hierarchies based on notions of religious piety, knowledge, morality and ethnic identity. However, *Masheitani ya ruhani* are associated with Arabic and Muslim ideals and respectability, while *Masheitani ya rubamba* are linked to non-Arabic features, representing Bantuness and what is considered an original African way of life. Although perceived as less civilised than truly Arabic conduct, this way of life is not necessarily perceived as immoral or un-Islamic. By contrast, *Masheitani ya kibuki* and *Masheitani ya habeshia* appear to represent smaller urban groups, whose ideals and ways of life remain foreign to most Zanzibaris, and which refer directly to social stratification and rank rooted in ethnic identity and associated with the institution of slavery. While *Masheitani ya ruhani* and *Masheitani ya rubamba* are equally present both in urban and rural areas, *Masheitani ya kibuki* and *Masheitani ya habeshia* appear only in urban areas. Despite this difference, the various tribes of spirits attach themselves to people of all different ethnic groups recognised in Zanzibar. However, only *Masheitani ya kibuki* are closely associated with people of Comoran origin.

Zanzibari women and men do adhere to what they perceive to be strict categories of spirits. Distinctions between what is perceived as various tribes of spirit are as distinctions between different tribes of humans embedded in and expressed through aesthetics and sensory devices. However, while the identity of spirits is seen as univocal, the identity of human beings is multifaceted. It is humans, not spirits, that manipulate and manoeuvre across what are defined as ethnic boundaries. It is the identity of humans, not of spirits, that can be linked to several places of origin simultaneously. Important markers of distinction are, as described, food, dress and knowledge. Food was also a central marker of identity during British colonial rule when people defined as Arabs, Asians or Africans had access to different kinds of food. Thus, food was already then established as a marker of ethnic identity. The preference of humans and spirits for certain dishes is one way of inscribing localities onto human bodies and, hence, of localising spirits socially and spatially. The importance attached to dress as a marker of identity is also linked to the body as a means of moulding identity and belonging, and to the significance of sensory experience in marking similarities and differences between humans and spirits. Yet, while spirits keep strictly to the kind of dress associated with their tribe, humans use this as a means to manipulate and reform their identity. Knowledge is another ethnic marker in the sense that *Masheitani ya ruhani* and *Masheitani ya rubamba* are associated with different kinds of knowledge, and women and men gain access to extensive knowledge about Islam, healing or sorcery through the intermediary of spirits, thus enabling them to alter their position in society and become, for example, medical experts of renown. In addition, since *Masheitani ya kibuki* and *Masheitani ya habeshia* are hierarchically ranked, people who become inhabited by spirits of high rank are able to achieve elevated positions in their ritual group through the mediating power of their spirits.

Differences in the definition of ethnic belonging at a societal level are directly rooted in perceptions of self-identity. In the human world several places of origin may be evoked at the same time, in a discursive process where belonging is continuously modified, and ethnicity redefined, across existing boundaries. In the process of negotiating identity and belonging, various tribes of spirits also come to dramatise historical periods and social hierarchies as markers of identity, embedded in differences between free-born and slave, urban and rural, and Arabness and Bantuness.

These aspects of social life are, by and large, muted in everyday negotiations of social relationships but are often manifested in ritual contexts where, through the classification of spirits, historical narratives are enacted and represented without explicit reference to politically and ideologically charged events. The presence of spirits contributes to the creation of circumstances which enable people to contest their given identity and negotiate new ones through spiritual embodiment. In this context, spirit possession serves as a vehicle for the expression of the ethnic identities of humans and spirits which can be fundamentally different in nature. Difference is thus presented as a fundamental part of everyday life and is expressed in aesthetic form, so as to encompass the complexities of Zanzibari history and ethnic diversity. Spirits enable the social embodiment of identities as diverse as the Arab, African, Ethiopian, Malagasy, Muslim, Christian and pagan, all constitutive parts of contemporary Zanzibar.

I now turn to the case study of Fatma Abdirahman to illustrate how these connections between spirits and humans operate, and to highlight the instrumentality of these relationships in the shaping of social memory. This case exemplifies how people, through ritual participation, continuously constitute themselves as particular Zanzibaris, in the process creating Zanzibar as a place opposed to other localities.

Embodying localities, localising bodies

Fatma belongs to a milieu of relatively affluent Zanzibaris, who are well-travelled in Europe and Arabia. She sometimes drinks alcohol, occasionally frequents the bars in Zanzibar Town, and smokes cigarettes in public settings, a practice which few Zanzibari women engage in. Having been married and now divorced, she has more possibilities than many other women to move about freely. Some say that Fatma is a loose woman (*muhuni*). Her relationships with *sheitani ya kibuki*, her Christian spirit of high military rank from Madagascar, reflects her life history and position in society. Her spirit's name is Ndamarufali, and is said to assist her in situations of need:

> I was very ill before I found out that I had a *sheitani ya kibuki*. I became very thin. First, I did not believe in spirits, and I knew nothing about them. At home nobody spoke about these things. In my family there are many that are *mashehe*,[23] and they did not want to believe in the spirits. Later, I came to know that almost every-body on my father's side has *masheitani ya kibuki*, so it is no wonder that I have one as well. It runs in the family (*ya asili*).

Fatma, who is Muslim, has a Christian spirit and voices critical opin-ions about her relatives whom she perceives as 'too pious' (Islamic). Her relationship with her Christian spirit expresses an openness towards reli-gious forms other than Islam, and a muted protest against what she perceives as too narrow a definition of what it means to be a 'good Muslim', rather than an open resistance to Islam itself or Zanzibari ideals and values. She can thereby be seen to comment on her own social conditions and history. Like most people, Fatma only partially complies to Zanzibari ideals and moral values, without coming into conflict with what is considered acceptable. Her relationship with her spirit enables her to negotiate her own endorsement and rejection of moral expectations while avoiding open confrontation, since the spirit provides the ideal guise for requesting what she defines as a Western life-style, symbolised by cigarettes, alcohol and a wish for worldly success. He also allows her criticisms to go unpunished. Finally, spirits in general enable the expression of various human ethnic identities by revealing their own local origins. Like many others, Fatma can define her past history through selective remembering, in the process constructing her future identity (see Bloch 1996).

The case of Fatma Abdirahman highlights the distinctions which underpin a Zanzibari discourse on the Other by focusing on differences in tribal affiliation. Fatma's father and mother belong to different tribes, the former stemming from the Comoro Islands and the latter from the African mainland. Fatma considers herself of Comoran origin (*Mgasija*), an opinion shared by most people in her surroundings. Nevertheless, when introducing herself as *Mgasija*, or when introduced by others as such, it will also immediately be stressed that her mother is of African origin. In addition, her spirit originates in Madagascar, adding to the complexity of Fatma's identity since she too becomes associated with this locality.

Fatma's relationship with a spirit from Madagascar can also be understood to strengthen her links to her patrilineal relatives, and to (re-)vitalise her ties to her Comoran background since close social links are believed to exist between the Comoros and Madagascar. In this light, Fatma's relationship with a *sheitani ya kibuki* may be viewed as an attempt to (re-)negotiate her own identity and ethnic affiliation, thereby reconstructing her identity as *Mgasija* (Comoran) rather than African, strengthening her ties to urban rather than rural areas. Being inhabited by *sheitani ya kibuki* Fatma is also associated with what is perceived as a European way of life involving, among other things, attending bars, smoking cigarettes and drinking alcohol. Her relationship with her spirit allows for the expression of other moral standards and is used to explain her behaviour, deemed inappropriate according to more strictly defined Zanzibari Muslim morality. Being associated with a foreign spirit whose habits (*tabia*), customs (*desturi*) and social power (*uwezo*) are seen as different from Zanzibari ideals, Fatma's position in the social hierarchy can be re-narrated and, to some extent, enhanced.

Spirit possession as historical narrative

Differences between various ethnic categories, enacted through spirits and in rituals performed on their behalf, highlight ways of belonging in Zanzibari society with respect to social milieux and historical periods. A focus on differences associated with locality emphasises affiliations to various tribes, and is actively used to conceptualise identities. The case presented above illustrates the extent to which people negotiate current relationships with reference to tribe and notions of belonging, and how ethnic differences, as identity markers, draw upon the past in order to negotiate the present. By means of this negotiation, women and men shape their history in everyday, contemporary situations. Historical narratives are thereby created in practice through spirit possession. Zanzibaris negotiate their social relations in terms of historical processes, their own life histories and their way of classifying spirits, although these links are seldom made explicit. Spirit possession, as a process shaping identity, can be interpreted as the crossroads where several narratives meet, encompassing the selective remembering of historical events and contemporary experiences, and subjecting these events to routinised forgetting. The various narratives become associated with particular localities which Zanzibaris use to produce, reproduce and acknowledge stereotypes of difference which are then easily transformed into alliances based on notions of 'us and them'. Also at stake, as is illustrated in Fatma's life history, are notions of dignity, self-identification and the desire to command respect from people in one's surroundings. The narratives dramatised and expressed through the spirit classifications are, to a large extent, silenced in public debates, yet remain highly present in the lives of Zanzibaris. Zanzibari spirit classification also confirms that rituals serve to suppress controversial discourses, yet it may, paradoxically, also expose them. Memories expressed through spirit possession bridge public and private representations. In everyday life, important notions relating to the construction of identity include, for instance, perceptions of Arabness/Bantuness, urban/rural, rich/poor, more or less civilised, of free-born or slave origin, and whether one holds a socially prestigious position or not. Being Muslim, as such, is not at all brought up in public discourse since almost the entire population is, in effect, defined as Muslim. By focusing on localities beyond Zanzibar and on discourses about style, Zanzibar as a place and, by the same token, Zanzibariness as a way of life emerge as identities to be negotiated. Zanzibariness itself is associated with multifaceted identities, with an origin in multiple localities. What it means to be Zanzibari – what it takes to become a moral human being, to be civilised according to Zanzibari standards – remains a pivotal question to which, it seems, Zanzibaris accept no simple answer. Persistent spirits whose habits, customs and ethnic identity are perceived as fixed enable Zanzibari women and men to transgress the very same distinctions the spirits maintain.

Acknowledgement

* This article is based on fieldwork conducted in Zanzibar from 1984 to the present. I would like to thank several colleagues for valuable comments on the content of earlier drafts. In particular, I wish to thank Nadia Lovell, Ingjerd Höem, Sidsel Roalkvam, Jo Helle-Valle, Eduardo Archetti, Marianne Lien, Frank Brun and Anders Jahnsen.

Notes

1 Only Zanzibaris of Indian origin who are Hindus (*wabanyani*), Bohoras (*wabohora*) or Catholics (*wagoa*) have other languages than Swahili as their first language.
2 97 per cent of the population is Muslim. The remaining 3 per cent are either Christian or Hindu.
3 The term 'tribe' is widely criticised for its inaccuracy and ethnocentric assumptions. In this chapter I have chosen to use ' tribe' as a direct transla-tion of the Swahili/Zanzibari term *kabila*, as the English term covers the meanings inherent in the term *kabila* .
4 More correctly, the term *Wagasija* probably refers to people from the Comoran island called *Ngasija*. Zanzibaris, however, translate *Ngazija* as Comoro Islands.
5 *Waarabu* is again divided into *Wamanga*, people from Oman, and *Washihiri*, people from Hadharamout.
6 Laura Fair (1994) writes that, following the first two decades after the aboli-tion of slavery, the majority of former slaves redefined themselves as Swahili, an ethnic identity which then implied free-born heritage. As the same men and women gained access to urban and rural property, they once again initi-ated the process of redefining their ethnic identities. Between 1924–31 the number of people on Unguja who identified themselves as Swahili declined by 86 per cent; yet the overall population on the island increased by only 5.6 per cent during the same period.
7 These groups were, in turn, divided into twenty-three ethnic or communal associations. There were also Zanzibaris who found themselves on the fringes of this system, and who had never been slaves. Among these were the *Washirazi*, who were descendants of early immigrants from Persia, the *Wahadimu*, who are said to be the indigenous Zanzibaris, and the *Watumbatu* from the island of Tumbatu.
8 Omanis were land and plantation owners, and held elevated positions within the state bureaucracy, dominating the political arena. There were also the

Washihiri, immigrants from Hadhramout in Yemen who were peasants, fishermen and petty traders, rather than landowners or members of the political elite as was the case for the Arabs from Oman.

9 For example, between 1924–31 the number of people on the island Unguja who identified themselves as Swahili declined by 86.6 per cent while the overall population increased by only 5.6 per cent during the same period (Fair 1994).

10 During the recent multi-party election, a law was again introduced disallowing political parties to be formed on the basis of ethnic identity.

11 This characterisation of the recent political debate in Zanzibar is, of course, very simplified. However, my contention is that, although a rough simplification, it denotes central lines of ideological and political identification.

12 During the Omani period, the term for civilised, *uungwana*, was replaced by *ustaraabu*, meaning 'being like an Arab' (Allen 1974: 1; Pouwels 1987: 72; Fuglesang 1994: 48).

13 Swahili coastal culture is a dynamic synthesis of African, Arabian and even Indian ideas within an African historical and cultural context which is distinctively Swahili (see also Giles 1987; Swartz 1991; Yusuf 1992). It is only recently that scholars have begun to stress the indigenous bases of 'Swahiliness', noting that what appears as alien and as an Arabic veneer must be seen as an illusion based on ideological and relatively recent historical trends (Abdulaziz 1979; Strobel 1979; Nurse and Spear 1985).

14 Unguja is the island on which Zanzibar Town is situated.

15 The food (*chano*) served to *masheitani ya ruhani* consists of honey, *halua* (a kind of Turkish delight), small, sweet bananas, boiled eggs, dates, raisins, sugar-cane cut in small pieces and asimini flowers, *hal-ud* (alcohol-free perfume), rose-water, *sharbat* (a kind of grape juice) and coffee. The dish on which their food is served is covered with a white cloth.

16 Sometimes, *rubamba* spirits are categorised as *masheitani ya kichawi*, although this classification is subject to several exceptions. In addition, *rumbamba*, *umundi*, *kumbaya*, *punbwa*, *mchanja*, and *mchakavi* are all categorised as *masheitani ya kiswahili*. I shall not elaborate further on these sub-divisions, as they fall outside the scope of this paper.

17 The food of *masheitani ya rubamba* is, in many ways, similar to that of *masheitani ya ruhani*, but is served differently. Their dish consists of dried rather than fried octopus, sugar-cane which is not peeled nor cut into small pieces, large bananas (*ndizi ya mkono~*), a mixture of coconut meat and sugar, raw eggs, a bread called manda, cassava, popcorn, *halua*, coffee and honey.

18 *Masheitani ya kibuki* are associated with people from Comoro, but people from other tribes may also be possessed by *masheitani ya kibuki*.

19 Only female members of ritual groups participate in rituals for these spirits, although homosexuals possessed by *masheitani ya kibuki* may be part of the audience. Other men may watch from a distance. Men can also become possessed by *masheitani ya kibuki*, but prefer to arrange for their *masheitani ya kibuki* to possess them in the home of the ritual leader, with no one else present.

20 As their *chano* (meal), *masheitani ya kibuki* want honey, imported brandy, *sharbat*, tobacco and *tambuu* (leaf of the betel plant, betel nut and clove),

silver bracelets and, especially, 'silver coins'. Rupia and Maria Theresa coins are preferred, although ordinary Tanzanian shillings are also accepted.

21 As their *chano*, *masheitani ya habeshia* demand *halua*, which they themselves mix with popcorn on mats laid out on the floor before inviting people present to eat with them. The food preferred by *masheitani ya habeshia*, such as *halua*, popcorn, coffee and ginger tea, is considered clean, in that it is also served during religious ceremonies.

22 Zanzibaris explicitly link these spirits to the Zanzibari royal court. They hold that these spirits have been brought to Zanzibar by an Ethiopian concubine, i.e. an Abyssinian from the harems of the Zanzibar Omani sultan. Linda Giles writes that *masheitani ya habeshia* usually come in pairs of contrasting status, for instance royalty/servant (Giles 1995: 100).

23 *Mashehe* refers to the religiously pious and learned in religion. Fatma Abdirahman defines her relatives as *mashehe*, thus stressing what she perceives as their exaggerated piety.

References

Abdulaziz, M.H. (1979) *Muyaka: Nineteenth-Century Swahili Popular Poetry*, Nairobi: Kenya Literature Bureau.

Allen, J. de V. (1974) *The Desturi za Waswahili of Mtoro bin Mwinyi Bakari*, Berkeley, CA: University of California Press.

Appadurai, A. (1995) 'The Production of Locality', in R. Fardon (ed.), *Counterworks: Managing the Diversity of Knowledge*, London: Routledge.

Biersack, A. (1991) *Clio in Oceania. Towards a Historical Anthropology*, Washington, DC: Smithsonian Institution Press.

Bloch, M. (1996) 'Internal and External Memory: Different Ways of Being in History', in P. Antze and M. Lambek (eds), *Tense Past: Cultural Essays in Trauma and Memory*, London: Routledge.

Boddy, J. (1989) *Wombs and Alien Spirits: Women, Men and the Zar Cult in Northern Sudan*, Milwaukee, WI: University of Wisconsin Press.

Carrier, J.G. (1992) *History and Tradition in Melanesian Anthropology*, Berkeley, CA: University of California Press.

Connerton, P. (1989) *How Societies Remember*, Cambridge: Cambridge University Press.

Csordas, T.J. (1990) 'Embodiment as a Paradigm for Anthropology', *Ethos* 18: 5–47.

—— (ed.) (1994) *Embodiment and Experience: The Existential Ground of Culture and Self*, Cambridge: Cambridge University Press.

Fair, L. (1994) 'Pastimes and Politics: A Social History of Zanzibar's Ng'ambo Community 1890–1950', unpublished doctoral thesis, University of Minnesota.

—— (1997) 'Kickin' it: Leisure, Politics and Football in Colonial Zanzibar, 1890s–1950s', *Africa* 67 (2).

Fuglesang, M. (1994) *Veils and Videos*, Stockholm Studies in Social Anthropology 32, Stockholm: University of Stockholm.

Giles, L. (1987) 'Possession Cults on the Swahili Coast: A Re-Examination of Theories of Marginality', *Africa* 57 (2): 234–57.

—— (1995) 'Sociocultural Change and Spirit Possession on the Swahili Coast of East Africa', *Anthropological Quarterly* 68(2): 89–106.

Howes, D. (1991) 'To Summon All the Senses', in D. Howes (ed.), *The Varieties of Sensory Experience*, Toronto: University of Toronto Press.

Jackson, M. (1983) 'Thinking Through the Body: An Essay on Understanding Metaphor', *Social Analysis* 14: 127–48.

—— (1989) *Paths Toward a Clearing: Radical Empiricism and Ethnographic Inquiry*, Bloomington, IN: Indiana University Press.

Lambek, M. (1996) 'The Past Imperfect: Remembering As Moral Practice', in P. Antze and M. Lambek (eds), *Tense Past: Cultural Essays in Trauma and Memory*, London: Routledge.

Larsen, K. (1989) *Unyago – Fra Jente til Kvinne*, Oslo: Oslo Occasional Papers, University of Oslo.

—— (1995) 'Where Humans and Spirits Meet: Incorporating Difference and Experiencing Otherness in Zanzibar Town', unpublished Ph.D thesis, University of Oslo.

—— (forthcoming) 'Morality and the Rejection of Spirits', *Social Anthropology*.

Lofchie, M. (1965) *Zanzibar: Background to Revolution,* Princeton, NJ: Princeton University Press.

Makris, G.P. (1996) 'Slavery, Possession and History: The Construction of the Self among Slave Descendants in the Sudan', *Africa* 66(2).

Meyers, A.G. (1993) *Reconstructing Ng'ambo: Town Planning on the Other Side of Zanzibar*, unpublished Ph.D thesis, University of California.

—— (1997) 'Sticks and Stones: Colonialism and Zanzibari Housing', *Africa* 67(2).

Middleton, J. (1992) *The World of the Swahili: An African Mercantile Civilization*, New Haven, CT: Yale University Press.

Nurse, D. and Spear, T. (1985) *The Swahili: Reconstructing the History and Language of an African Society, 800–1500*, Philadelphia: University of Pennsylvania Press.

Parkin, D. (1995) 'Blank Banners and Islamic Consciousness in Zanzibar', in A.P. Cohen and N. Rapport (eds), *Questions of Consciousness*, London and New York: Routledge.

Pouwels, R.L. (1987) *Horn and Crescent: Cultural Change and Traditional Islam on the East African Coast, 800–1900*, Cambridge: Cambridge University Press.

Sheriff, A. (1987) *Slaves, Spices and Ivory in Zanzibar: Integration of an East African Commercial Empire into the World Economy, 1770–1873*, Portsmouth, NH: Heinemann.

Sheriff, A. and Ferguson, E. (eds) (1991) *Zanzibar under Colonial Rule*, London: James Currey Ltd.

Strobel, M. (1979) *Muslim Women in Mombasa 1890–1975*, New Haven, CT: Yale University Press.

Swartz, M.J. (1991) *The Way the World Is: Cultural Process and Social Relations Among the Mombasa Swahili*, Berkeley, CA: University of California Press.

Yusuf, I. (1992) 'An Analysis of Swahili Exegesis of Sûrat Al-Shams in Shaykh Abdullah Saleh Al-Farsy's Qurani Takatifu', *Journal of Religion in Africa* 22(4): 350–66.

Chapter 6

The need for a 'bit of history'

Place and past in English identity*

Jeanette Edwards

Much has been written in recent years about the burgeoning heritage industry said to have taken hold in Britain since the mid-1970s. Robert Hewison has argued that, at the end of the twentieth century, there is 'an unhealthy dependency on the past'. He suggests this is due to a crisis in confidence: 'Had we more faith in ourselves and were we more sure of our values, we would have less need to rely on the images of the past' (Hewison 1987: 138). Patrick Wright had previously extended a similar argument to Western Europe as a whole. Focusing on Britain and on the formation of 'national pasts' as political ideology, he writes:

> the national past is formed within the historical experience of its particular nation state. Among the factors which have influenced the definition of Britain's national past, therefore, are the recent experience of economic and imperial decline, the persistence of imperialist forms of self-understanding, early depopulation of the countryside . . . the extensive and 'planned' demolition and redevelopment of settled communities which has occurred since the Second World War. . . . Similarly, while an anxious readiness-to-receive the past exists as something of a generality in modern everyday life, closer historical attention will also reveal that very different versions and appropriations of the past continue to emerge from different classes and groups – even if these sometimes seem to compete with a shared romantic orientation.
>
> (Wright 1985: 25)

Hewison and Wright agree that present-day versions of the past are riddled with romanticism, and that nostalgia is the dominant emotion in this harking after it – a nostalgia that filters out unpleasant items, and reveals only a sanitised version of history. In a recent defence of his earlier thesis,[1] Wright poses the question of how to reconcile the way in which the past is used as part of a political agenda[2] with all the ways in which people, in their daily lives, appear to be attached to, intrigued by and fascinated with it.[3]

This chapter is concerned with the latter. Instead of posing the problem, as Wright does, in terms of 'why are people attached to the past?', my interest lies in the way in which the past is mobilised in the formulation and composition of local identities and senses of belonging. Which elements of the past are selected as relevant in belonging (or not) to a place and, in turn, how are places themselves constituted by the different ways in which people belong to them? This chapter looks at some of the ways in which local identity and notions of belonging are formulated and put to work by residents of an English town at the end of the twentieth century. It is clear that local identities are more than individual affairs created from just 'thin air'. They comprise a selection from myriad elements in social lives, congealed as 'identity' for specific purposes. Belonging, like identity, is neither monolithic nor all-encompassing, and belonging to a locality or place is not always relevant. This chapter explores the way in which belonging is forged through a variety of connections and a diversity of attachments, which include links to pasts and persons, as well as to places. Belonging to locality is comparable to belonging, for instance, to a particular family or a particular past. It is through the expression of an inclination either to belong or not that pasts, places and significant social relationships are conceptualised.

A post-industrial setting?

Let us call the place to which my ethnography refers Alltown.[4] With a population of 15,000 people, it is one of many towns across the northwest of England which grew with the textile industry, and shrank with its decline. Although mixed in terms of social class, its residents are predominantly white. As in other localities in Britain, they make finely tuned distinctions between each other (Ennew 1980; Strathern 1981; Wallman 1984; Frankenberg 1990; Rapport 1993; Macdonald 1997). One way in which differentiation is made explicit is through place of origin. Hence one broad distinction made in Alltown is between 'Alltown born and bred' and 'incomer' (Edwards 1993, forthcoming). In the late 1980s many residents defined themselves, and were defined by others, as 'Alltown born and bred'. They trace their ancestors to labouring families who came to the town in search of work, at a time when the region was known as the 'Golden Valley' and when, it is said, mills and houses were springing up 'almost overnight'. Between 1861 and 1881 the population of the town more than doubled, reaching 25,034 inhabitants. 'Incomers', then, are not a new phenomenon. Throughout the nineteenth century, with the development of the cotton industry, there was an influx of labouring families in search of work. The Alltown *Times* of 10 June 1876 noted: 'There is quite a colony in Rossendale of what are termed "foreigners" – people from the Midland counties, in particular Cambridgeshire' (cited in Aspin 1983).

There has been a steady out-migration since 1881. Shoe factories and small, often temporary, manufacturing units replaced the cotton mills as places of employment and, by the mid-1970s, middle-class immigrants in search of 'the country'[5] had replaced working-class immigrants in search of work. These recent 'incomers' tend to come from the nearby conurbation, and either retire to Alltown or commute out of town to work, while residents who identify themselves as 'Alltown born and bred' trace their ancestors to rural counties of England or to Ireland, and emphasise working-class backgrounds and employment histories in textile and construction industries. Both Alltown people and recent 'incomers' dwell on the enormous social changes they perceive to have occurred in their lifetime. The past features large in their narratives about the town, and themselves.

Given the political and economic changes that have occurred in this region since the development and collapse of the textile industries, and the readiness of residents to evoke the past, it could be argued that Alltown is a good example with which to explore the assertion that a contemporary British preoccupation with the past is driven by nostalgia in the face of economic and social decline in a fragmented and post-industrial world. Indeed, elderly residents recall an Alltown which used to be a thriving, busy milltown where, on a Saturday evening, recalls one woman, you could 'hardly fit on the pavement' because there were so many people taking a stroll. Parading themselves and their families (if single, looking for romantic liaisons and, if married, for affirmation), Alltown people appropriated public spaces. Elderly residents, as well as the not-so-elderly, tell me that although 'people used to be poor', they looked after each other. Doors were left unlocked without fear, and 'neighbouring' (described as a constructive and intentional activity) was more prevalent than today. Such narratives do indeed portray nostalgia. But the same people also talk of how dirty and polluted the town was: factory chimneys bellowed out smoke and soot, houses were dark and overcrowded, health was poor and life and living difficult. The majority of Alltown people, they remind you, had to work long hours, in poor conditions, for little reward, and women recall the injustices perpetrated by men as bosses, husbands and fathers. There is no evidence of nostalgia in these narratives, and no sentimental longing for an expurgated past.

The remainder of this chapter aims to portray some of the ways in which the past is constantly excavated, re-presented and reformulated, with elements of it put together in novel ways. It argues that nostalgia is inadequate to explain the quotidian ways in which the past is put to work in affirming or denying local identity. The past presents people with a problem: what to select and what to ignore; what to emphasise and what to screen out. Stories about the past do not merely render visible a person's connections to persons and places, they make and break those connections. They constitute local identities and include elements of, amongst other things, class, gender and ethnicity. All memory is selective, and belonging requires a selection of which elements to pick out, which social relationships to mark (people belong to persons as much as they do to places) and which identities to promote. Stories about the past, or that feature the past, are as much to do with forging local identities and senses of belonging, as they are with history.

From natural to local history

When I went to live in Alltown I was not looking for the past, but was told of it daily, partly because people defined it as an appropriate and relevant topic of study for a student of anthropology who wanted to 'find out about Alltown' and, partly, because residents, like anthropologists, indicate the authority with which they speak by placing themselves in the locality by (amongst other things) revealing the event of their arrival and their origins (see Pratt 1986; Moore 1994). At the same time, the telling of narratives about the past – such as selected and selective elements comprising histories of the town, or stories about, for example, 'th'owd characters',[6] or accounts of the antics of friends, family, acquaintances and strangers (no less about the past for occurring last week as opposed to last century) – is, for the most part, a pleasurable activity. It exercises the skills of the raconteur, establishes rapport in the composition of shared memories, and makes explicit a commonality of past experiences. The performance of the past, in the present, composes and shapes specific pasts.

The Alltown Natural History Society, known locally as The Nat, is run by local historians who meet socially at least one evening a week. Members are predominantly men over fifty years of age, who would for the most part define themselves as 'Alltown born and bred'. Two female committee members have recently been appointed, one of them younger than average for The Nat (a fact often commented upon). In 1987 and 1988 many Nat members expressed the need for the society to attract younger members, but at that time it seemed to be relatively unsuccessful in doing so. The museum opened in 1873 with a natural history collection (including, among other things, blown bird eggs, stuffed small mammals, pinned butterflies, and glass-encased birds, insects and reptiles). By 1987, this collection had been relegated to the margins of the museum, and the paraphernalia from a more recent industrial and post-industrial era had taken pride of place. Today, the museum is filled to bursting point with artefacts. Machine parts, gadgets, items of clothing and jewellery, household furniture and fittings, kitchen utensils, gas masks, wooden toys, pharmaceutical, dental and medical instruments, postcards, cigarette cards and letters, slippers, shoes and clogs manufactured in Alltown factories, models, ornaments and embroidered samplers made in Alltown homes, are just some of the things that jostle for space in drawers and in cases, hanging from the ceiling and on every available surface. The museum is open to the public one evening a week and, in addition, the curator arranges for individuals and groups from, for example, schools, churches and informal organisations to visit the museum at other times. He gives an amusing, informative and ever-changing guided tour, studded with examples and demonstrations which animate these objects that are a long way from their original places, in time more than space.

At Nat meetings, members regaled me with anecdotes and legends, with poetry and dialect that displayed, publicly, an insider knowledge based on experience. They evoked past and present connections to the town. Henry Frazer, a long-standing member of The Nat, director of a local shoe factory, the donor of many an unusual artefact and a skilled raconteur, was invited, then persuaded, to tell me the story of 'The newcomer and his cottage'. I present it here for three reasons. First, it shows the way in which distinctions between Alltown people and 'incomers' are made and sustained. Second, it highlights the common recognition among Alltownians that the pursuit of a 'bit of history' is an understandable and worthwhile activity. Finally, it illustrates how a distinctive, and distinguished, history is required: not 'any old history' will do.

Henry tells us that one Sunday afternoon he went for a drink with George, his friend and fellow Nat member, to the Deerplay Inn. The Deerplay, he tells me while assuming that everybody else knows, is 'up on the moors', on the town's northern boundary. When George and

Henry arrived in the pub, they spotted and greeted 'a local lad' they knew. The 'local lad' was chatting to a man who, according to Henry, 'was obviously an outsider'. This outsider, Henry told us, was 'dying for a bit of history for his new cottage', and had been asking 'everybody' he met whether they knew anything about the house he had recently purchased. Upon seeing Henry and George across the room, 'the local lad' advised 'the newcomer' to go over and speak to them. He told him that Henry and George were experts and, if there was 'owt to know, then they'll know it'.

Henry had already heard of this newcomer, and was already aware that he was 'dying for a bit of history', so he 'guessed what was going on' when he saw him coming in their direction. The stranger introduced himself and, after some preliminary 'chit-chat', asked them if 'by chance' they knew anything about the row of cottages 'over there', waving his hand vaguely in the direction of 'over there'. Henry and George looked pensive. They shook their heads, slowly. 'No, can't say I have', offered Henry. The man looked disappointed and, according to Henry, 'his shoulders slumped'. Henry and George continued to look thoughtful; their brows furrowed: 'Just a minute. Come to think of it', Henry conceded he had heard something about '*one* of them cottages. In fact, it was the second one from the top'. The man perked up. Henry continued. There were two brothers who lived up there, 'That's right, now I remember, they were hung up there!'. With George's help, Henry provided some convincing biographical detail of 'Francis and Virgil Pugh'. They had been executed, sent to the gallows, in fact. The man was excited: 'What did they do?' he asked. 'It is said', replied Henry weighing up his words carefully 'that they rode with Dick Turpin!'.[7] The man was suitably impressed. He eagerly asked more questions and Henry and George answered to the best of their ability. Finally he took his leave and, according to Henry, was 'happy to have a bit of history for his cottage'.

Henry then confided in us he had been aware all along that the house he mentioned was the same as the one purchased by the newcomer. In addition, he admitted, the inspiration for the name 'Pugh' had come from the John Pugh who, alive and well, was sitting directly in front of them 'minding his own business and quietly supping his pint'.[8] We laughed. Henry and George had a joke at the expense of the newcomer who, in this story, is portrayed as the unworldly one, in spite of his supposedly worldly credentials. There is also, however, a proud acknowledgement, in Henry's narrative, that the pursuit of a 'bit of history' is an understandable activity, and that Henry and George, as local people and members of the Natural History Society, are well placed to provide this history.

When Henry related this tale, and after he had finished, another member of The Nat and of the audience, told us that the following week a local newspaper had published an item about Dick Turpin. It reported that Dick Turpin used to drink in the Deerplay Inn. This provoked further laughter. Not only had Henry and George duped the newcomer, but the story had gained in conviction and had been picked up by the newspaper. At the time, it was not clear to me whether the joke was on the newspaper also or whether it had colluded in the joke. Surely, I thought, Dick Turpin is older than The Deerplay Inn. But this, of course, is not the point. I was being provided with further evidence of the connectedness of Henry and George: a local journalist, having heard the story either directly or as it was told and embellished in the pubs and clubs of Alltown, took it up. Once the connection had been made (in writing, and in the newspaper) between Dick Turpin and The Deerplay Inn, the association between Dick Turpin and the newcomer's cottage was confirmed. The appendix to the story not only renders visible the connectedness of Henry and George, and the unconnectedness of the newcomer, but itself does the work of connecting and disconnecting.

Henry and George were both well aware that not 'any old history' would do'. Rather, an idiosyncratic and colourful history was required. Other stories were told to me, which portrayed the flamboyant and idiosyncratic nature of 'th'owd characters', of life in the mills and of the antics of friends, family and neighbours. Such narratives feature 'back-to-back' houses,[9] pubs, clubs and churches, connecting them and drawing them together as all belonging to Alltown. On more than one occasion, I was presented with rich and evocative accounts of the etymology of the place name. On one occasion, I betrayed some scepticism, and was assured 'that was *really* where it came from'. The point is that Alltown, and those who tell of its past, do have a history, but not 'any old history'. In the words of one woman, 'we have a nice history'.

Origins and original Alltown families

Certain patronyms are said to belong to what are considered 'original' Alltown families. Names such as Whittacker, Hargreaves and Howarth are identified as 'original' Alltown names.[10] They are associated with rural counties of England, for instance Norfolk, Cambridgeshire and Leicestershire, and often with Protestant but non-conformist religion, mainly Baptist and Methodist. Other patronyms such as Murphy,

Connolly and Daley are said to designate Irish families, often characterised as 'big' and Catholic. Although both those who trace their
ancestors to England and those who trace them to Ireland define themselves as 'Alltown born and bred' and could, theoretically, pinpoint the
arrival of their ancestors in the town to the same decades of the nineteenth century, the identification of an 'original' Alltown family involves
privileging links with rural counties of England and Protestantism,
rather than Ireland and Catholicism. It also includes a Lancashire, rather
than Irish, dialect and an occupational history of mill work.

Is this ethnicity at play? Since Frederick Barth's (1969) salient injunc-
tion prompted anthropologists to look at the boundaries between
'ethnic groups', rather than focus on what defines a group as such, there
has been a call to return once again to the content of those boundaries,
what Barth referred to as the 'stuff of culture' (see also Jenkins 1997).
Boundaries (albeit permeable) and their maintenance are not suitable
metaphors for what I wish to portray in Alltown. A configuration, such
as the one prevalent in Alltown, of particular social aspects of identity
including patronyms, origins, language, occupation and religion does
not, in this case, create a 'group', but rather a perspective. Any of these
aspects of identity can be screened out, or brought to the fore, to afford
a shift in perspective. So, for instance, when discussing what they
perceive to be a deterioration in council services, Alltown people might
suspend the distinctions they make between themselves in terms of place
of origin, patronyms or religion, since what is relevant in this context is
the difference between Alltown people in general, who have a claim on
the town's resources by virtue of belonging, and administrators and
service providers who, as incomers or outsiders, are perceived not to
belong to the town. Hence its resources should not belong to them.[11]
Similarly they cannot lay claim to the town's past.

However, a close identification with Alltown is not always relevant,
since it does not inevitably connote status, a position of authority or privileges. It may at times be in one's interest to play down connections to a
locality where access to facilities associated with prestige, such as jobs
and houses, are limited. Just as Alltown people locate themselves in an
Alltown that they themselves formulate, they also position themselves in
a wider, cosmopolitan world which they also compose in the process by
demoting, albeit temporarily, Alltown connections and by bringing into
focus extra-town links, such as with kin in Ireland and work that takes
them around and out of the country. Global connections are thus
created in terms of 'the environment', shopping or travel, and in the
rhetoric of nationalism expressed in contexts such as Europe or sport.

People connect themselves to the town by enlisting persons and 'things', concrete and abstract (factories, houses, dialects and kinsfolk). They screen out such connections when they enlist a different, albeit partially overlapping, set of persons and 'things'. Making connections always entails breaking connections.

There are particular characteristics associated with 'proper' or 'real' Alltown,[12] and they hold both positive and negative connotations. An association with 'real' Alltown conveys stability, strength and authenticity, but also fixity, stubbornness and parochialism. Status is made manifest through evidence of belonging or, alternatively, not belonging to the locality. Which of these two is mobilised depends on context and social relationships. To me, middle-class Alltowners might stress their out-of-town connections in order to reiterate what they perceive to be our shared social position (including perceived shared interests and concerns), and to mark the distinction between ourselves and, for example, 'troublesome Alltown folk'. Similarly, working-class Alltowners may, for instance, stress origins in Ireland and their connections with family there, in an attempt to mitigate belonging to a locality where they perceive their access to resources, such as employment or new housing, to be limited.

Those who define themselves self-consciously as 'Alltown born and bred' may also identify 'typical Alltown people' as 'the big Irish families'. These are not endogamous groups nor are they, in a Barthian model of ethnicity, 'biologically self-perpetuating' (Barth 1969: 10). However, they are stereotyped as if they were. Hence I was told that amongst 'the big Irish families', 'cousins marry cousins'. The same idioms of endogamy and closure are used to describe Alltown as a whole, as seen from non-Alltown perspectives. An often heard refrain is that Alltown people intermarry (again 'cousins marry cousins') and that Alltown is consequently cliquish, even parochial. Despite the difficulty from an analytical perspective of discerning bounded social groups that act with a common identity within Alltown and which might be defined in terms of ethnicity, Alltown people themselves constantly categorise each other in exclusive and inclusive ways. Further, while the distinction between families of Irish and English origins does not map onto discrete social groups, this distinction amongst others is nevertheless mobilised as a conceptual means of differentiation. Hence when 'trouble' is attributed to the named families said to be big, Irish and Catholic, and 'original Alltown people' are characterised as parochial and backward, speakers are excluding themselves from those they thus categorise. Every expression of exclusion, however, is also an act of inclusion. As the man quoted below suggests, differentiations based on places of origin are irrelevant in other contexts:

> There used to be a lot of Irish that spoke Irish, but now their children's children are coming up, they speak just like us . . . now they're Alltown people.

Another category of Alltown person, defined by some residents as 'th'ippies'[13] and who sometimes refer to themselves as 'freaks', emphasise belonging to 'a community' of like-minded travellers. 'Freaks' born in the town do not necessarily, or always, dwell on a 'born and bred' status and, in conversations with me, tended to screen out their connections to Alltown, emphasising instead their links to other 'freaks' in different parts of the country. Here, differences are writ large in terms of such features as 'lifestyle', and particular emphasis and value are placed on the impermanency of residential arrangements and employment. 'Freaks' shun what they perceive to be the household trappings and traps of urban and suburban life and their upkeep. While 'housework' is a deprecated activity, much thought, time and effort are given to childrearing, and 'freaks' place a positive value on allowing children freedom of movement and expression, and on a hospitality which offers shelter and sustenance to fellow travellers.

This process of bringing particular kinds of identity and belonging in and out of focus is not confined to those who define themselves as 'Alltown born and bred', or 'freaks'. Recent 'incomers' do the same. I refer here to those mentioned earlier, who started arriving in Alltown in the mid-1970s, leaving behind the larger conurbation and what many of them refer to as 'the rat race'. They point out that it is the rural charm and 'sense of community' which attracted them to Alltown: those things, they argue, which have been lost in the places they left behind. Hence neighbourhoods in the city of Manchester are cited as examples of the deterioration in community spirit, neighbourliness and safety. Paradoxically, Alltown people use exactly the same idioms in describing changes that have occurred in Alltown. They too point to the disappearing sense of community due, in their view, to the recent influx of strangers who do not share the same values of neighbourliness and friendliness. As one young man put it:

> The people who are now moving into the area do not speak to their neighbours – they're from Cheshire and Stockport and Bury – and they do not speak to each other like we do.

A different Alltown perspective, however, portrays these same recent 'incomers' as 'becoming just like us' and, in the words of one woman: 'they are learning our ways and have begun to smile and let on[14] when they walk past'. Just like 'the Irish' described in a previous quote, people migrating from Manchester, for example, can also be assimilated to Alltown provided they exhibit those characteristics deemed a prerequisite for 'belonging'. 'Incomers' can and do, however, exploit the ambiguity of both belonging and not belonging. 'Incomers' of fifty years standing, who may have raised their children in Alltown and who have every intention of spending the rest of their lives there, will ironically refer to themselves as 'furriners'.[15] They may go to great lengths in making explicit their non-Alltown origins; and while they may at times depict themselves as, for example, 'almost Alltownian' or 'Alltown more or less', they also dissociate themselves from the place and its people by emphasising their own origins, and by reflecting on Alltown as a closed, parochial community, full of unsophisticated and unworldly folk. Recent and established 'incomers', Alltown people (of all kinds of different origins) and 'freaks' mobilise similar idioms of belonging and community, in describing Alltown and their place in it. They value different forms of sociability, display different modes of attachment to 'the community' and differentiate themselves from each other, but the raw materials of belonging and not belonging, and the process of constructing them, are similar.

Shifting perspectives

Identity and belonging, then, are not simple matters. If these are referred to here as ambiguous or fragmentary, this is not to suggest that they are wanting in patterns or regularities (see Comaroff and Comaroff's (1992) discussion of Leach). Unlike a Whalsay identity which, in Anthony Cohen's (1982, 1987) evocative accounts, becomes meaningful at the boundaries of locality, Alltown identity shifts internally and, while strong, fades in and out of significance. Stories are constantly told in Alltown of past events and characters, just as they are in Whalsay, and they also act as a 'mnemonic of collectivity' (Cohen 1987: 195). Yet the boundaries between belonging, and not belonging do not appear to be as clearly drawn and preserved in Alltown as they are in Whalsay. It would be wrong to see this, however, as some kind of loss or lack, or as disintegration from a prior, more stable sense of identity.[16] Rather than talk of boundaries, it is more useful to talk of constantly shifting perspectives. Alltown people do not 'belong' categorically, even when they define themselves as 'Alltown born and bred'. This aspect of belonging and identity, uttered with pride on the understanding that it accrues status,[17] fades into the background when status inheres in other aspects of social identity, such as class or gender.

During the winter of 1987–8 an acrimonious debate took place between some Alltown residents and some members of the local council over changes that had been made to the layout of the town centre. There had been, the year before I lived in Alltown, a garden containing flower beds and benches and enclosed by a hedgerow in the middle of the town and in front of the Conservative Club. A decision was made by local government officials, including the town planner, to 'open up' the town centre and 'landscape' the area. This involved removing the plants and the hedgerow, covering the area with stone flagging, and replacing the old benches and bus stop with new ones.

Members of the local council were proud of the fact that the area had been paved with Yorkshire stone (a valuable material, judging from stories told of the spectacular thefts of large and very heavy paving stones, dug up in the middle of the night and, it is said, taken by van to London), but many residents were not impressed by this prestigious substance. Several half-jokingly raised the issue of long-standing antipathy between Yorkshire and Lancashire.[18] Why indeed, they pointed out, would they want *Yorkshire* stone in Alltown? Residents complained that the stone was cold, a condition exacerbated by the fact that the River Irwell runs underneath the town centre. This comment implicitly suggests that any 'sensible' person who knew the town could have predicted this state of affairs. I was told on numerous occasions that the stone paving freezes over in winter and, consequently, becomes slippery and unsafe: 'like a skating rink', remarked one woman, 'especially when it's wet which, let's face it, is a lot of the time'.[19] The stone, according to the town planner, was 'in keeping' with the materials used in the surrounding civic buildings, such as the library and the bank (now the Job Club) and the Conservative Club. These, he went on, had been built by 'the Victorians'. Hence the new benches, installed in a row along the main road, the railings separating them from the road, and the bus shelter are decorated with what he called 'Victorian detail'.

It seems that members of local government, supported by some residents and opposed by others, wished to promote an image of 'olde worlde charm'. Conflict centred partly on whether the gardens had been 'a mess' or 'a haven' prior to their refurbishment, and it generated unpredictable allies and foes, cross-cutting the distinction between local and incomer. Two of the most vociferous opponents of the decision were a couple, Jean and Malcolm Griffiths, who had moved to Alltown five years previously. They initiated a petition and directly challenged the council, both face-to-face and through the media. Jean was incensed by the lack of consultation, and saw what she called 'the demolition of the gardens' as senseless and wanton destruction. She argued that the council had destroyed a place where young and old could mix, and had thus quickened the demise of 'the community'. The gardens were peaceful, she argued, 'they fulfilled a need' and, now they were gone, there was nowhere for people to sit, meet and 'have a chat'. Jean noted that their demolition had happened just after Chernobyl and the bombing of Libya. She suggested that all three were the arrogant actions of patriarchal and imperialist regimes, out of touch with the needs of 'ordinary people'.

The objections raised by Alltown people echoed some of those aired by Jean. They added, however, that the council were wasteful and fickle (digging up hundreds of pounds worth of flower bulbs that they had not long ago planted). They also attributed the lack of consultation to a desire on the part of council officials to be punitive. They believed the council viewed Alltown as a 'troublesome place' (filled with 'troublesome people') and, therefore, undeserving of proper consultation. Alltown was being punished, amongst other things, they said, for past acts of vandalism: it was being punished for the behaviour of a minority of 'troublemakers'. It was also generally thought, and often mentioned, that since the local government reorganisation in 1974 (when a neighbouring town had become the seat of local government), Alltown had been 'left out'. Alltown people readily associated the 'demolition of the gardens' with other examples of the way in which their town had been marginalised in favour of other localities in the borough, perceived to have been prioritised and obtaining preferential treatment. One Alltown man pointed out that, while it was true that the gardens were 'always being vandalised', had they been anywhere other than Alltown the council would have looked after them better.

Pragmatic objections were also raised: 'we want it looking nice but we also want it sensible and practical'. I have already noted that criticisms of the 'landscaping' project were often couched in terms of 'safety', for instance, in emphasising the danger posed by the paving stones freezing over. Such a criticism is of the same order as objections raised about the removal of cobblestones from a street which runs steeply uphill towards the primary school. It was said to be much more hazardous now that the cobblestones had been removed, as the previously uneven surface had automatically slowed down traffic. Another example of pragmatic reasoning emerges when people talk about the preservation of mills. A conservation society, based in a nearby town, had fought long and hard to preserve a particular mill as part of the region's 'heritage'. Alltown people often questioned the reasons for such an activity, wondering why it was important to spend money preserving derelict mills which are 'of no use to anybody'. One woman emphatically pointed out that they had been dirty, dark and dangerous places to work, and she could not understand the reason for keeping them. Another woman argued that pressure groups 'go blindly down the path of preserving but they have no experience of working in "satanic mills"'. These comments do not reflect a nostalgia for a past way of life. They are realistic appraisals of the difficult and dangerous living and working conditions which faced working-class people during the height of the textile industry in the region. They also reflect a general concern that mills do not constitute an appropriate 'heritage'. The most popular etymology of Alltown reflects a 'nice history', and tells of frolicking deer on hillsides. Symbols of tradition should reflect appropriately positive qualities. Mills and working in them, like "back-to-backs" and living in them, are not always appropriate elements of the past with which to identify.

There was a general, sometimes grudging agreement among Alltown people that the town centre was much 'tidier' now, but there were caveats, and tidiness was obviously not 'the end all and be all'. Apart from the issue of safety, particularly for the elderly, there was an issue of aesthetics. People remarked that they missed the flowers: 'the splash of colour', as one woman put it. Those who believed the town centre had been 'spoiled' pointed out that it now looked cold and empty. It was, in other words, uninviting. There were others who thought the gardens had been an 'eyesore'. One man, who had moved to Alltown twelve years previously, worked as a volunteer in the Citizen's Advice Bureau and professed to know Alltown like the back of his hand, thought that the gardens had been 'a disgusting mess', and it was clearly much better now. As if providing evidence of the folly of their ways, he remarked disdainfully that 'old Alltownians thought they were historic!' I recall a colleague, visiting me in Alltown, commenting that the town centre was 'pleasing to a middle-class eye'.

I have mentioned that one of the town planners, a graduate of Liverpool University, born in Manchester and resident in a nearby town, was keen to 'restore' what he identified as 'the Victorian detail' which, he said, was in keeping with the surrounding architecture. Both opponents and supporters of the landscaping of the gardens couched their arguments in terms of 'preserving tradition'. Local government officials wanted to preserve a particular image of Victorian England which had never previously existed, at least in its present form, while those who desired the gardens returned to their previous state wished to preserve 'a tradition of community' and face-to-face interaction. Many agreed that the council had behaved badly in neither discussing nor publicising the proposed alterations. To belong to a locality implies that you belong along with all kinds of other things such as houses, factories, services and pasts. Belonging entails a claim on, and a connection to, these things and, therefore, a say in any changes to them, especially changes engineered from the outside (by those who do not belong). The town itself, its artefacts, its buildings and its 'landscape', are seen to belong to Alltown people, in the same way that they themselves belong to the locality.[20] From this perspective, the gardens were altered by people who did not belong to Alltown, and with no reference to those who did.

Belonging and ethnicity

Do these kinds of local identities bear any relationship to ethnic identity (Barth 1969; Cohen 1982, 1987; Comaroff and Comaroff 1992; Amit-Talai 1996; Banks 1996; Jenkins 1997)? Identity and ethnicity are both problematic terms, yet they remain overdetermined and overused as if they were unambiguous. It is crucial to tease out whether these identities are, in fact, part of the social world to be explained by the anthropologist, or whether they are useful analytical concepts to be deployed in order to shed light on particular aspects of social life (Cohen 1974; Comaroff and Comaroff 1992), or both.[21] How are populations who do not think of themselves as sharing an 'ethnic' identity to be perceived? Can they be said to belong to 'an ethnic group'?

Some anthropological perspectives treat 'identity' as a substitute and replacement for 'ethnicity' in analysing the particular ways in which people classify and order their immediate social world (see, for example, Ardener 1989). All too often, however, both ethnicity and identity are equated with minority status (Macdonald 1993; Tonkin et al. 1989) or peripheries (Cohen 1982, 1987). But, as Sharon Macdonald cogently reminds us, 'Majorities may have identities too – though perhaps they are less likely to be expressed in a form which is regarded as "an identity". We should not assume either that majority identities are necessarily secure, unambiguous or morally dominant' (Macdonald 1993: 8).

If ethnicity is sometimes conflated with identity it is also at times conflated with place of birth, nationality or culture. For example, in a study of household resources in one neighbourhood of inner London,

Sandra Wallman (1984) uses place of birth as a criterion for ethnic status, and identifies those born in south London to south London parents as being of 'south London ethnic origin'. Similarly, Rosemary McKechnie (1993) discusses her Scottishness in terms of both ethnic status and nationality. She provides an account of how (during fieldwork in Corsica) islanders with whom she worked interpreted her Scottishness through the similarities they perceived to exist between Scotland and Corsica, despite there being no word for 'Scottish' in the Corsican language. For some Corsicans, it was clear that since England imposed its will and hegemony over Scotland as France did on Corsica, McKechnie was bound to empathise with their cause. For other Corsicans, this same Scottishness was a reason for suspicion, for it was thought that she was bound to empathise with nationalist causes. Her reflections on her own 'ethnic status' led to insights into the way in which Corsican identity shifts according to the context in which it is relevant: 'Reflecting on what was read into my own ethnic status uncovered an *ad hoc* bricolage of ideas about identities in Western Europe that allowed considerable latitude for interpretation of my presence in both positive and negative terms' (McKechnie 1993: 119).

If Scottishness is defined as an ethnic identity through its opposition to English dominance and hegemony, then how is Englishness itself to be defined? Is it only ever made manifest at its boundaries with non-Englishness?

> It has been cogently argued that it is at the boundaries of ethnic groups that ethnicity becomes meaningful; that is, groups become aware of their ethnic identity when they engage with others. . . . The same is true of localities too, and not surprisingly, for ethnicity and locality are both expressions of culture. Thus one can state a more general principle: that people become aware of their culture when they stand at its boundaries.
>
> (Cohen 1982: 3)

Cohen equates locality with ethnicity: each comes into being at boundaries and each expresses cultural identity. It is clear that ethnic identities are emphasised in times of conflict, and this decade has thus far witnessed too many inhumane examples of this. Without denying this, I wish to avoid conflating ethnicity with nationality, with locality or with 'culture' Rather, I have been interested in the way in which residents of an English town, towards the end of the twentieth century, bring histories and origins, and other features analysed by some scholars as integral to ethnic identity, in and out of focus without claiming ethnic identity for themselves. They do so by making explicit their belonging, or not, to a locality which itself is conceptualised in the process.

Pasts as futures

The excavation and 'preservation' of 'the history' of Alltown by members of The Nat, for instance, cumulatively furthers an understanding of locality (the greater the amount of information the more that is known about the place). It also guarantees a future. To lose the past would be to lose a present identity which could not, in turn, be projected ahead. The indigenous exercise of writing history and formulating pasts becomes more than a reflection on present preoccupations: 'knowing' Alltown entails knowing its past. A unique past has moulded a distinctive Alltown character, but different elements of that past, and different features of that character, are selected according to the question being addressed. An idyllic, romantic past may be evoked. For example, beautiful moors and frolicking deer are seen to inhabit a pre-industrial landscape, while sociability and mutual support dominate the industrial one. By contrast, a harsh and inhospitable land marred by violence, pollution and ill health may dominate the past. Ultimately, however, honest, resilient, clean and humorous characters emerge from an unhealthy, unfriendly and inhospitable environment.

The weather, mills, back to back houses and dialect are all markers of the historic landscape which evoke a distinctive and idiosyncratic Alltown. Religion, material culture, history and language are some of the elements central to anthropological notions of ethnicity. Yet, the problem with ethnicity as a theoretical concept, as many scholars have noted, is that it assumes a rigidity not apparent in the ethnographic detail. Ethnicity is like kinship: it appears and disappears, is both central and marginal in English social life (Strathern 1992, 1993). It emerges when links are made between people based on common places of origin, or particular patronyms, only to be screened out when an alternative (albeit sometimes overlapping) set of connections is mobilised in terms, for instance, of occupational histories or individual mobility.

An apparent preoccupation with the past addresses distinctions between 'then' and 'now', as it addresses distinctions between categories of person, both past and present. Importantly, it projects a future. It is much more than an effect of nostalgia which prompts Alltown people to dwell on the past, but an active fabrication of the links and connections which endure over time and override the present.

Acknowledgements

* My thanks go to participants in the workshop 'Locality and Belonging', convened by Nadia Lovell and chaired by Richard Werbner at the 1996 EASA conference in Barcelona; and to Nadia Lovell for helpful editorial comments. Fieldwork, on which this chapter draws, was supported by the Economic and Social Science Research Council. I am also grateful for support received since fieldwork from the Esperanza Trust and Manchester University.

Notes

1 At a symposium 'Heritage on the margins' convened by John Urry, Lancaster University, June 1996.
2 Wright argues that, between 1975 and 1995, the British government was particularly successful in promoting specific and selected images of the past.
3 This question is raised partly in response to criticisms of writings on the 'invention of tradition' (see Hobsbawm and Ranger 1983). Michael Herzfeld (1991: 12), for example, notes that while providing a useful critique of the way in which political elites manipulate history, this kind of analysis ignores both the fact that all history is selective and partial, and denies the participation of 'ordinary people' in 'real history'.
4 Places and persons are disguised in this account. I remain indebted and more than grateful to friends and acquaintances in Alltown.
5 Countryside.
6 The old characters, with names like Mad Ab, Ailse O'Fusser and Robert the Devil.
7 Dick Turpin was a 'highwayman', reported to have been the leader of a gang of thieves which terrorised travellers during the early part of the eighteenth century. He was arrested and executed in 1739 at the age of thirty-four. The image of the highwayman, in the popular imagination, is of a masked and cloaked figure, wearing a tricorn, riding a horse, pointing a pistol at his victims and shouting: 'Stand and deliver. Your money or your life'.
8 Drinking his pint of beer.
9 High-density Victorian housing characteristic of northern England.
10 See also Strathern (1981) for an example from a different part of England.
11 By the town's resources, I refer to features such as housing, factories, pubs, public spaces, schools and clinics, all of which can be classified together as belonging to the place, alongside the speaker. Of course, history and sentiments, values and characteristics, might also be thought of as resources which belong to people by virtue of belonging to the place (see Edwards and Strathern 1998).
12 'Proper' in the sense of authentic, rather than decorous.
13 The hippies.
14 To 'let on' means to greet.
15 *furriners* means foreigners. A well-known cliché about English villages is that you can live in one for a lifetime and still not 'belong'.

16 See also Gledhill (1994) for discussion of this on a larger scale.
17 Especially when talking to a social anthroplogist whose stated aim is to 'find out about Alltown'. A born and bred status, in this context, relays an expertise based on an experience of the town over time. To belong to Alltown is 'to know' it.
18 Alltown is just inside the county of Lancashire, near its border with Yorkshire. Rivalry between the two counties is expressed today in, for example, cricket. Reference is made, in this context, to the Wars of the Roses. This conflict, English schoolchildren are taught, lasted twenty-five years between 1460 and 1485. It was primarily a battle between various 'noblemen' for control of England, rather than a conflict between Lancashire and Yorkshire *per se*. The aristocratic families rallied around either the House of Lancaster or the House of York, and it was dubbed the Wars of the Roses in the nineteenth century by Sir Walter Scott, because the emblem of the Lancastrians was a red rose and that of the Yorkists a white rose. These emblems are still used today and the border between Lancashire and Yorkshire provides a means of imaging differentiation. Alltown people jokingly commiserate with residents of the neighbourhood directly on the border with Yorkshire, with statements like: 'We all have our cross to bear'.
19 Much is made of what is said to be the harsh climate of Alltown, and the weather is often unfavourably compared with that of surrounding places. It is often evoked as further evidence of the hardiness and resilience of Alltown folk, compared to the softer and more feeble city dwellers.
21 One Alltown man made explicit what he perceived to be wider political repercussions of the 'destruction of the gardens': in the subsequent local election, he told me, 'people voted Labour because the Tories knocked down the gardens'.
22 Genocide of the 1990s, labelled as 'ethnic cleansing', means we need to study ethnicity as particular kinds of identities and sets of relations, which inform *actual* processes of inclusion and exclusion.

References

Amit-Talai, V. (1996) 'The Minority Circuit: Identity Politics and the Professionalisation of Ethnic Activism', in V. Amit-Talai, V. Knowles and C. Knowles (eds), *Re-Situating Identities: The Politics of Race, Ethnicity and Culture*, Toronto: Broadview Press.

Ardener, E. (ed.) (1989) *The Voice of Prophecy and Other Essays*, Oxford: Basil Blackwell.

Aspin, C. (1983) *Mr Pilling's Short Cut to China*, Helmshore Local History Society.

Banks, M. (1996) *Ethnicity: Anthropological Constructions*, London: Routledge.

Barth, F. (1969) 'Introduction', in F. Barth (ed.), *Ethnic Groups and Boundaries: The Social Organisation of Cultural Difference*, London: George Allen & Unwin.

Cohen, Abner (1974) *Urban Ethnicity*, London: Tavistock.

Cohen A. (ed.) (1982) *Belonging: Identity and Social Organisation in British Rural Cultures*, Manchester: Manchester University Press.

—— (1987) *Whalsay: Symbol, Segment and Boundary in a Shetland Island Community*, Manchester: Manchester University Press.

Comaroff, J. and Comaroff, J. (1992) *Ethnography and the Historical Imagination*, Boulder, CO: Westview.

Edwards, J. (1993) 'Explicit Connections: Ethnographic Enquiry in North-west England', in J. Edwards, E. Hirsch, S. Franklin, F. Price and M. Strathern (eds), *Technologies of Procreation: Kinship in the Age of Assisted Conception*, Manchester: Manchester University Press; 2nd edn with additional material, London: Routledge, 1998.

—— (forthcoming) *Born and Bred: Kinship and New Reproductive Technologies in Britain*, Oxford: Oxford University Press.

Edwards, J. and Strathern, M. (forthcoming) 'Including Our Own', in J. Carsten (ed.), *Cultures of Relatedness: New Approaches to the Study of Kinship*.

Ennew, J. (1980) *The Western Isles Today*, Cambridge: Cambridge University Press.

Frankenberg, R. (1990 [1957]) *Village on the Border: A Social Study of Religion, Politics and Football in a North Wales Community*, Prospect Heights: Waveland Press.

Gledhill, J. (1994) *Power and its Disguises: Anthropological Perspectives on Politics*, London: Pluto Press.

Herzfeld, M. (1991) *A Place in History: Social and Monumental Time in a Cretan Town*, Princeton, NJ: Princeton University Press.

Hewison, R. (1987) *The Heritage Industry: Britain in a Climate of Decline*, London: Methuen.

Hobsbawm, E. and Ranger, T. (eds) (1983) *The Invention of Tradition*, Cambridge: Cambridge University Press.

Jenkins, R. (1997) *Rethinking Ethnicity: Arguments and Explorations*, London: Sage.

Macdonald, S. (ed.) (1993) *Inside European Identities*, Oxford: Berg.

—— (1997) *Reimagining Culture: Histories, Identities and the Gallic Renaissance*, Oxford: Berg.

Moore, H. (1994) *A Passion for Difference*, Cambridge: Polity Press.

McKechnie, R. (1993) 'Becoming Celtic in Corsica', in S. Macdonald (ed.), *Inside European Identities*, Oxford: Berg.

Pratt, M. (1986) 'Fieldwork in Common Places', in J. Clifford and G. Marcus (eds), *Writing Culture: The Poetics and Politics of Ethnography*, Berkeley, CA: University California Press.

Rapport, N. (1993) *Diverse World-Views in an English Village*, Edinburgh: Edinburgh University Press.

Strathern, M. (1981) *Kinship at the Core: An Anthropology of Elmdon, Essex*, Cambridge: Cambridge University Press.

—— (1992) *After Nature: English Kinship in the Late Twentieth Century*, Cambridge: Cambridge University Press.

—— (1993) 'A Relational View', in J. Edwards, E. Hirsch, S. Franklin, F. Price and M. Strathern (eds), *Technologies of Procreation: Kinship in the Age of Assisted Conception*, Manchester: Manchester University Press.

Tonkin, E., McDonald, M. and Chapman, M. (eds) (1989) *History and Ethnicity*, London: Routledge.

Wallman, S. (1984) *Eight London Households*, London: Tavistock.

Wright, P. (1985) *On Living in an Old Country*, London: Verso.

Chapter 7

The politics of locality

Memories of District Six in Cape Town[*]

Anna Bohlin

Introduction

While shared conceptions of locality play an important role in the creation of 'imagined communities' (Anderson 1983), recent studies show how political contestation lies at the heart of the construction of notions of belonging (Bourquet *et al.* 1990; Bender 1993; Johnson 1995; Hirsch and O'Hanlon 1995). The physical landscape can be employed as a symbolic resource in the fashioning of a homogenising, nationalist culture, but it may as well be used in the construction of more restricted, and partial, social, ethnic or gendered identities (Bodnar 1994: 75–6; Johnson 1995: 51–3). In discourses about power and its legitimacy, social change and political strategies, the historical meanings ascribed to places are often challenged, negotiated and rejected according to the perceived needs and interests of social groups in the present. The criteria for belonging to territorialised groups tend to change over time, in a process which creates complex and partly overlapping identities.

In contemporary South Africa, issues concerning place and placelessness have assumed a special significance. Due to the policies of segregation most effectively enforced during the era of apartheid, but present also in earlier periods in the history of the nation, the lives of a majority of South Africans have been shaped by troubled and ambiguous experiences of localities. These have come to be experienced, for instance, as places to which one has belonged, from which one has been excluded, or to which one has been forced to belong. Millions of people have been compelled to leave their neighbourhoods and forced to set up new lives in unfamiliar surroundings in townships, homelands or abroad, whereas others have had to defend their houses, homes and territories through the use of weapons.

Today, intense efforts are directed at redressing the experienced inequalities resulting from this former segregation policy. A significant contribution made by the new government has been the introduction of the Land Restitution Act in 1994. Under this law, which has become a political symbol of tremendous importance, those who lost land or homes under the previous constitution can apply to the newly established Land Claims Court to have their land returned or, where this is not possible, to receive economic compensation for their losses years ago. In post-apartheid South Africa, therefore, issues concerning local identity, the morals of locality and the question of rightful belonging are of immediate importance to a large part of the population.

The demolition of District Six

Until the 1970s, District Six was a crowded, busy residential part of Cape Town. Situated on the edge of the central business district, with a view over the Atlantic Ocean on one side and the slopes of Table Mountain on the other, it was considered 'one of the most cosmopolitan areas in the Cape, if not the whole of sub-Saharan Africa' according to the historian Bickford-Smith (1995: 43). Since the turn of the nineteenth century, District Six attracted a mixed group of inhabitants: sailors, newly arrived immigrants, labourers, merchants, artists, musicians and writers, as well as gamblers and prostitutes. It became a lively, vibrant locality with a rough and colourful street life.[1] By 1900 the population consisted of what the government referred to as Malay (i.e. Muslims) or 'coloured' people, descendants of slaves from southeast Asia or the outcome of marriages between European settlers and Khoi, San and other Africans, as well as Indians, Chinese, Australians and Jews from Tsarist Russia (Bickford-Smith 1995: 37). During apartheid, the residents of District Six were referred to simply as 'coloured', a broad category including those who, according to the authorities, were neither 'black' nor 'white'. However, there is (and has been in the past) little consensus as to the legitimacy of the term 'coloured'. It is often rejected due to its perceived misleading and derogatory connotations. In other circumstances, however, it might be seen as an adequate 'ethnic' label.[2]

Because of its diverse cultural and ethnic population, District Six became known as one of the areas in the otherwise segregated South Africa where citizens of various ethnic backgrounds could mix with relative ease. Sophiatown, outside Johannesburg, offers another similar example (see Hart and Pirie 1984; Hannerz 1996). Commonly referred to as a 'grey zone', it provided an alternative to the racially ordered society prescribed by apartheid. Like Sophiatown, District Six was destroyed. In 1966, a decision was taken by the municipal authorities of Cape Town that the area should be reserved for white residents. The decision, made possible by the Group Areas Act of 1950, resulted in the forced removal of between 55,000 and 65,000 residents, who were transferred to designated areas in townships outside Cape Town.[3] The remaining buildings were demolished, with the exception of a few rows of houses and some mosques and churches such as the Moravian church, St Mark's Church, the Aspeling Al Hazar Mosque and the Muir Street Zainatul Islam Mosque.

The decision to erase District Six was met with an overwhelmingly negative response, and provoked an unprecedented level of protests, both among those who were immediately affected by the expulsion and among opponents of apartheid in general. As the forced removal plan was set into motion, activities to halt white developments in the area intensified.[4] One important strategy of protest against the demolition was the continued use of the remaining churches and mosques in District Six by those who had been evicted. Despite living in the remote Cape Flats, many of the former residents travelled the long distance from the townships to District Six in order to attend services in their former places of worship. This quiet but persistent form of resistance has continued to the present day.

The protests did not put a halt to the removal policy, nor to the demolition of the district, yet had a decisive impact on the future of the evacuated land. Details of the protest movement itself, and its effects, have been discussed in depth by Hart (1990: 124–37) and lie outside the scope of this chapter. Suffice it to say in this context that the land became nearly impossible to sell: 'the ground was to be treated as salted earth', as one journalist expressed it (*Weekly Mail and Guardian*, 24 November 1995).

Today, fifteen years after the last family was evicted in 1982, most of the area is still empty. It contains a few residential buildings, one technical college, the Cape Technikon, and some rows of renovated Victorian houses towards the upper end of the slope. The rest of District Six, approximately forty hectares of land, remains in the same condition as when the demolition vehicles left it. The area is covered with rough grass, scattered with kitchen utensils, pieces of vinyl floor covering and other evidence of previous inhabitants. What is possibly most striking is the presence of the few remaining churches and mosques, standing alone in the middle of the deserted fields.

Meanings and memories of District Six

The conspicuous absence of new developments on the land is what makes District Six so different from other cases of forced removals in South Africa. All over the country, a large number of people have been shifted about and forcibly removed in accordance with the apartheid goal of racial segregation. In the Cape area alone, some forty communities have been displaced in this manner. In most of these cases, however, new buildings have replaced old ones and new communities have settled where old ones used to live. With the exception of District Six, it is difficult today to find concrete evidence of the large-scale social engineering carried out in South Africa twenty or thirty years ago.

That landscapes have a symbolic, commemorative dimension, conveying culturally constructed meanings and messages, is one of the central points presented in the work of Halbwachs (1992). This has also been acknowledged and discussed by social anthropologists and cultural geographers in more recent studies (Cosgrove 1989; Fentress 1992; Middleton and Edwards 1994; Hirsch and O'Hanlon 1995). As a physical landscape, District Six can be understood to serve as an aide-mémoire. It presents an external, relatively durable structure, which invites people to engage in the discourses and practices of remembering. The solemnity of the empty space communicates a powerful message about the events which have taken place there, and its mere existence serves as an invitation to comment and ask about what caused this peculiar scenery. In Koonz's words, it embodies 'a reality beyond words' (1994: 259).

The deserted land, therefore, which contrasts with the image of the previously lively community, acts as a powerful icon, symbolising the pain and humiliation suffered during apartheid. It has been referred to as 'an open wound', 'a gigantic urban desert' and as 'South Africa's Hiroshima' (*Weekly Mail and Guardian*, 2 September 1994). However, the empty land also has positive connotations. Since the land was never redeveloped according to the apartheid plans of racial segregation, it signifies the ultimate failure of the authorities to obliterate the district. In this way it serves as a tangible symbol of the inefficiency and futility of apartheid: forty hectares of prime business land in central Cape Town have remained in disuse for fifteen years. The land, in this mode of perception, is associated with hope and confidence in the future:

> Marked as it is by its bitter past, and standing as a daily reminder to
> the world of apartheid's most heinous face, few places have better

credentials as a healing symbol for a new and reconciled South
Africa.

(Jeppie and Soudien 1990: 13)

Not surprisingly, District Six has been the focus of much public attention in the twenty years since the area was declared (in official intention
at least) 'white'. Poetry collections, newspaper articles, novels, two
musicals, a few documentaries and even a television soap opera about life
in District Six have been produced. In the 1960s some residents began
to extensively photograph the area which they knew was soon to be
destroyed, and cultural activities aimed at raising awareness of the demolition, as well as preserving the memory of District Six, continued
throughout the following two decades. With the changing political
circumstances in the late 1980s, the interest in District Six intensified; on
his release from prison, District Six was one of the first places that Nelson
Mandela visited. The interest culminated in the establishing of the
District Six Museum in the early 1990s. In between passing the City Hall
and Parliament, the guided bus tours in Cape Town now drive through
the deserted land and, in the last two or three years, foreign dignitaries
such as the Dutch and Swedish royal families, the president of Ireland
and the vice-president of the United States have been taken to view the
museum during their state visits.

District Six seems to be undergoing what Kopytoff (1986) refers to as
a process of singularisation whereby an object or, as in this case, a particular landscape is singled out and removed from the sphere of everyday
exchange and commerce, acquiring a status as unique and non-
exchangeable icon. There is a strong opinion among former residents
against treating the district as any ordinary piece of land, simply to be
sold or redeveloped according to the conventional considerations of city
planners. Instead the historical uniqueness of District Six is emphasised,
and it is now described as a neighbourhood which had a particularly
strong sense of community spirit, an exceptionally rich street life and an
unusually high level of racial tolerance among its members.

In addition to the symbolic healing power ascribed to the area,
District Six is also associated with more immediate political and
economic interests. With the change of government in 1994, new hopes
have been raised relating to the issue of land redistribution. The new
Land Restitution Act, intended to rectify the injustices of the former
system by giving land back to its former owners, has opened up possibilities for ex-residents to be compensated for their losses. Nevertheless, it
is far from clear how and in whose name such claims should be made,

and the question as to what should be done with the empty area is hotly controversial. There are at present intense debates concerning the future of District Six. While around 900 people have submitted individual claims for compensation for losses of land, others would prefer to see the issue handled as a collective claim in order to ensure the largest number of beneficiaries. Yet others would prefer to leave the land untouched, and turn it into a memorial park.

Recently the Land Commissioner granted authority to a group of former residents, the District Six Beneficiary Trust, to provide suggestions on how to redevelop the area and compensate the displaced community. The decision was taken in August 1997, when the District Six Museum was temporarily transformed into a court room. In December 1997 the museum once more became the stage for a historic event, when the trust launched its new constitution inside the exhibition hall. The capacity of the museum for re-appropriating the land of District Six, and reconnecting it with its former residents, thereby transcends the symbolic level. The exhibition is transformed into an event with far-reaching pragmatic and judicial consequences.

Retracing the streets of District Six

The District Six Museum is the result of a private initiative undertaken by former residents of District Six wishing to create an interactive public space where the former residential area could be remembered. The intention is to transform the museum into a permanent place of commemoration. It is situated in a former Methodist church in Buitenkant Street, at the edge of the central business district. This church has an eventful history. Used originally by freed slaves, it became a meeting place for banned anti-apartheid organisations during the apartheid years. Political prisoners used to hide behind the many-sided doors in the building after escaping from the nearby police station. The church has played an important role in the movement of resistance to apartheid, and its history is understood to have made it well suited to house the current exhibition. Staff members at the museum told me that the locale is geographically highly appropriate, since Buitenkant Street constitutes an interface between the grounds of District Six and the city core. Located right on the edge of District Six, the street is the geographical beginning and end of the area, just as the temporal beginning and end of the era of apartheid constitute the theme of the exhibition.

The museum concentrates on two dimensions of District Six. The first deals with the abrupt destruction of the former residential area, when thousands of peoples' homes were demolished and disappeared. The second focuses on the new, dynamic process of commemoration and symbolic recreation taking place inside the exhibition hall. One of the most striking features of the exhibition is a mobile made of street signs, suspended from the ceiling inside the church. The street signs are originals from District Six, in slightly rusty, blue and white enamel, bearing the names of streets which no longer exist. The circumstances of how they were saved and later brought to the exhibition hall are well-known to Cape Tonians. A request was published in the press, asking former residents to donate photos or artefacts from District Six in order to found a museum. As people began to respond, one of the organisers found through a newspaper cutting that a private collector still owned street signs from District Six. The man, who had been in charge of the original demolition, had been ordered to dump whatever remained of the buildings in Table Bay in order to reclaim land from the sea. However, having read about how British people rescued street signs from being destroyed during the Nazi bomb raids during the Second World War, he decided to follow their example. Despite his fear of reprimand, he saved some seventy street signs from the rubble and hid them in his cellar for about twenty years, until he heard of the request for artefacts.[5] After many attempts to persuade him – he still feared repercussions for 'stealing' the street signs – these were finally returned to the ex-residents in late 1994 and became a core feature of the present exhibition.

This story is told to everyone visiting the exhibition, and is widespread in the media. It suggests an equation between what happened to District Six and the atrocities committed by the Nazis during the Second World War. The demolition is likened to the terrifying and morally condemnable German bombing raids. Moreover, the immorality of the act of demolition is emphasised by the way the signs were rescued: even the person in charge of the demolition reacted against the brutality of the task set before him, and subverted orders he had received. The story thereby anchors the interpretation of the event within a broader, more general moral universe, establishing a framework for what is considered good and evil. Regardless of its historical truth, it provides a 'myth of origin' for the museum, conveying important information about the fundamental values and moral principles that underpin its own foundation.

The mobile made of street signs constitutes the core of the exhibition. The central position of the mobile, and the reactions and comments of visitors, suggest this. What seems particularly significant is its capacity to symbolically link the exhibition hall with the actual District Six. Each sign, displaying the name of a street in the former district, serves to establish a mnemonic and metonymic link connecting the present in the exhibition and the past in the district. A name like 'Hanover Street' evokes associations to the entire row of houses, homes, shops, meeting points, traffic and pedestrians that constituted that particular street as a social environment. In its entirety, the mobile of streets signs captures and signifies the memory of the whole area, with its conglomerate of streets and buildings. According to one review of the exhibition, 'the street signs have become signifiers of extraordinary power . . . layer after layer of meaning sediments around them' (*Weekly Mail and Guardian*, 3 February 1995).[6]

When asked what he experiences when watching the signs, one former resident told me:

> Oh, I see too many memories . . . because I walked most of those roads, you see. I was there. I played there, and I kissed for the first time in one of those roads, so for me it's there. I can touch it, it comes real like a little video recorder playing it over in my head. It's great, because people come here and they can touch it.

In the rest of the hall, artefacts, photos, letters, newspaper cuttings and extracts from street directories, testimony to different periods in the history of District Six, are displayed in glass cases, on cardboard screens and on the walls. One glass cabinet, supplied with a sign reading 'Archaeology Department of the University of Cape Town', displays a plastic hair clip, a plastic doll's head, a spoon and some pieces of china. The setting resembles an excavation site, with the objects lying directly on a layer of earth, some still partly covered in soil, conveying associations to an archaeological documentation of some long-gone ancient civilisation. Yet most artefacts are not old but modern, contemporary ones.

Portraits, displaying former residents of the area, are mounted on large, semi-transparent sheets suspended from the side balconies. Unknown, 'ordinary' residents are included as well as a selection of well-known politicians, activists and artists from District Six, such as Eddie Daniels, Cissy Gool, Benny Kies and Johaar Mosaval. On the floor are two stone sculptures in the shape of lions, which used to guard the entrance to District Six, as can be seen on a large painting behind them. There is also a slab of stone, one of what were originally seven steps,

which used to be a well-known meeting point and hang-out for the
young and, later, for gangs: the territory of the Seven Steps, for example,
was controlled by the Globe Gang. Towards the 1960s, the Seven Steps
became infamous for being a centre for violence and criminality, and
became a highly mythologised place. During the demolition the Seven
Steps were among the last features of District Six to be removed, and
were left standing alone for some time after the surrounding buildings
had been demolished. They were subsequently taken to a nearby church
and later to the museum. One visitor commented on the presence of the
stone in the following way:

> I don't think people actually believe it, they kill themselves thinking
> 'Oh, one of the original stones is still here'. We don't know what
> happened to these landmarks . . . all the guys would drive up there
> with their cars, it was almost like a historical monument. Everybody
> used to associate with it, somebody could come and pick you up at
> the Seven Steps, go to the movies . . .

The capacity of objects to function as memory aides has received
increasing recognition (Yates 1974; Boholm 1983; Kopytoff 1986;
Radley 1990; Rowlands 1993; Johnson 1995; Swiderski 1995). In the
case of the exhibition, the collected objects convey a metonymic presence, where the perceived real, genuine landscape of District Six is
symbolically exhibited inside the exhibition hall.[7] Judging from visitors'
reactions, a striking feature appears to be the authenticity ascribed to the
objects. Since the street signs are all original ones, rescued from being
sunk into the depth of Table Bay, they possess a significant 'cultural
biography' (Kopytoff 1986), imbuing them with a special kind of value
and instilling in observers a sense of awe and reverence.

As Radley (1990: 52) points out, the way objects evoke memories
cannot be separated from how they have been displaced over time. In
this case, the objects displayed have been transformed by their survival of
the demolition and are imbued with the symbolism attached to the
destruction of the district. Parts of the landscape can again be inspected
and experienced in real life, after years of being accessible only in the
form of mental or photographic representations. Touching the surfaces
of the stone lions and the street signs, one can remember the details of
their original setting and the meetings taking place there. By virtue of
being displayed in the museum-like setting, the objects are designated
the role of memorabilia, evoking the full social and cultural setting of
which they used to be a part. In this way, the objects can be regarded as

material aspects of a 'myth', evoking the narrative of District Six which, to some extent, imbues them with pre-defined meanings. What will be remembered is partly given, inherent in the way the objects have been selected and placed in the museum.[8]

This process of commemoration can also be understood in the light of Swiderski's account of how certain objects acquire the capacity to conjure up a 'memory room', an imagined room, containing emotionally significant objects and people (1995: 96). In the case of the District Six Museum, the memory rooms created by the objects are both personal and collective. While stimulating individuals to reflect on their personal perceptions of the past, the objects simultaneously allow for the comparison and mirroring of personal memories with those of a larger group. A link is established between an individual's personal, biographic experiences and experiences common to the neighbourhood as a whole. In this way an 'imagined community' of former District Six residents can be created in both past and present.

The selectivity involved in the choice of objects conveys information about the nature of the community imagined in this way. First of all, the objects in the exhibition are ordinary: a hair clip, a spoon, some pieces of china and the like. The everyday characteristics of the artefacts become significant when viewed against the background of the extreme economic and social differences which characterise South Africa, and the importance generally attached to notions of social and economic status, differentiation and hierarchy. By contrast to this discourse of categorisation and stratification, the objects, alongside the portraits of former residents, present an image of the former inhabitants as 'ordinary' people, belonging neither to a certain ethnic group nor to a particular social stratum. During the apartheid era District Six was often described, in the discourse of politicians, civil servants and city planners, as a working-class area or as a quaint but neglected 'slum of slums' (*Cape Times* in Hart 1990: 127). In the exhibition, however, the area is described as inhabited by all kinds of people: 'There were professional people, highly educated people, ordinary people. That is what District Six was made of, all kinds of people, Christians, Jews, Hindus, Muslims, we all lived together' (conversation with a former resident and organiser of the exhibition).

This emphasis on the social heterogeneity of the area and its inhabitants serves to overcome social distance: the victims of the removal policy were not 'other' people, but resembled anyone visiting the exhibition today. The design of the exhibition serves to destabilise and challenge externally imposed categorisations of the district or its inhabitants. The identity of the community, and its position within the wider South African society, is redefined and re-established through the objects on display. In this way the exhibition can be compared to the 'vernacular' cultural expressions described by Bodnar (1994: 75). 'Official' cultural manifestations, originating from leaders and authorities at all levels of society, tend to have in common an interest in social unity, the continuity of existing institutions and loyalty to the status quo. While official culture 'desires to present the past on an abstract basis of timelessness and sacredness' (Bodnar 1994: 75), vernacular culture tends to articulate partial interests focusing on a restatement of reality which is based on first-hand experience in local communities. This is precisely what the District Six Museum achieves: it provides an insight into a certain historical period as having been lived and situated, with a defined beginning and end. The museum is a political and moral manifestation in which people appropriate for themselves the right to define and express the events they have personally experienced, thereby contesting the official version of history to which they have been subjected.

Another item in the exhibition is a large-scale map that outlines the street grid of District Six as it appeared at the time of its destruction. It covers most of the floor beneath the street sign mobile, and is painted in the same blue colour. The map is covered with thick, transparent plastic and supplied with a felt tip pen. Former residents are invited to kneel down and mark out the sites where their homes used to be located. Any other places they consider relevant might also be scribbled down: corner shops, post offices, cinemas, restaurants or meeting points. In this way the surface of the map has gradually changed in appearance, and been transformed into a dense scribble of names and addresses.

Apart from being encouraged to sign the map and the scroll, former District Six residents are also invited to actively participate in the exhibition by bringing personal photos, letters or artefacts from District Six to the museum. Visitors' new addresses and other, more spontaneous pieces of information such as personal reactions to the exhibition can be written on a large roll of calico standing to the side of the map. Through these interactive aspects of the exhibition, a kind of 'virtual reality' is created. The imagined past and present communities of District Six are not merely mentally recollected or verbalised, but are given a visible, tangible and accessible form of existence on the map and the scroll.

Like the other objects in the museum, the physical appearance of the map conveys information about how District Six should be remembered according to the organisers of the exhibition. Its design is egalitarian. No distinction is made between landowners and tenants, and the common denominator is belonging to District Six in the sense of previously having had an address in the area.[9] The map emphasises the communal aspect of life, subsuming individual differences under the synthesising formal structure of the map. Above all there is a conspicuous absence of any references to ethnic, cultural or religious groupings and affiliations in the exhibition. Although, as is shown throughout the exhibition, there were different kinds of people living in District Six, these individual differences are presented as containable within, and as contributing to, the social whole rather than as challenging its homogeneity. The social heterogeneity of the area is thereby reconstructed in a non-threatening way.

The act of signing the map and the scroll of calico provides an example of Radley's 'social practices' (1990: 47) in which people objectify memory through their engagement with the material world. The importance attached to writing one's personal signature can be understood as part of a more general tradition in modern society in which texts and scripts are viewed as authoritative. According to such a tradition, signatures can be seen as ultimate manifestations of authenticity, commitment and truth. Signing the map carries two significant implications. First, the power of the written word is used to establish the authenticity of the exhibition as a whole. The signatures on the map can be understood as a collective stamp of approval for the exhibition and its layout. By signing, visitors actively take part in the exhibition and dissolve the formal distinction between organisers and visitors. This helps to underline the claimed grassroots character of the exhibition. One visitor told me that 'this museum was really put together by the people for the people'.

Second, by signing the map and the calico, former residents are able to verify the authenticity, and indeed the existence itself, of their particular history and the events referred to in the exhibition. As one former resident explained:

> People put down their name and their District Six address, and sometimes they put a little message on the map. It is so important for them, because District Six was totally destroyed, and now, at least, there is a little report where people can put their names down.

Similar to inscriptions and engravings on tombs, grave stones and monuments, conveying information about events in the past to future generations, the map and the scroll come to serve as a collective 'symbolic document', bearing witness to the experience of the dispersed community. Significantly, the map combines elements from both 'inscribing' and 'incorporating' practices which, according to Connerton (1989), are two distinct modes of cultural transmission of memory (see also Rowlands 1993: 142). The act of signing the map is clearly an inscribing process, borrowing elements from a Western, monumental tradition in which a message is transmitted by being inscribed on some durable, physical object. Yet, the map also has a transient and dynamic quality more reminiscent of incorporating traditions, which generally depend on iconic symbolism.[10] Like District Six itself until its destruction, the map is dynamic and changing, and it unfolds with the passing of time. In contrast to other official monuments or memorials, the map is not commemorated or celebrated on certain set dates or at regular intervals. Rather, it is continuously transformed and attributed with meanings by the informal and emotionally loaded commemorative activities of visitors.

Signing the map also has other practical and symbolic implications, in some cases helping to restore broken social links. Signatures of old friends and relatives might be unexpectedly encountered and remembered, and old friends or neighbours might meet each other at the museum, as indicated by the following comment by a visitor, writing his name on the map:

> It's good to know where our family was. People will remember my family, other people will come by and remember where my grandfather or my auntie stayed. People will remember each other. If I saw some names now that I would remember I would go and see them, like for example this chap I'm seeing this afternoon. Yes, seriously, [laughing] I'm going to see him this afternoon.

Territoriality and the question of belonging

Notions of inclusion and exclusion are at play in the exhibition, shaping the self-identities of visitors. The exhibition is partly exclusive, defining a category of people who used to live in the area and to whom the imagined community of District Six primarily pertains, as expressed by a staff member at the museum:

> This museum has become a symbol for the people to come to, where they know that they had a history, they had a past, they had a culture, they had traditions. Even though we were all separated and

sent to different parts of the Cape Flats and so on, this museum is really a link to the past. It is for the people of District Six; to know that there is a place that they can come to.

The objects in the museum, the layout of the exhibition, the explanatory leaflets and the newspaper cuttings all signal to visitors a clear distinction between those supposed to be subjective participants in the commemoration, and those supposed to be counted as more detached observers. It is, for example, unlikely that visitors who never lived in District Six would sign the map. The moral 'right' to sign is reserved for an authorised 'we', a category consisting of former residents or relatives of former residents, whose memories are considered authentic. The criteria of belonging to this group are grounded in territoriality and memories of belonging, and the borders of this category are well defined and inflexible. While this group of people have the right to participate in the making of the history of District Six, others remain outside of this process and can merely watch it unfold before their eyes.

There is, however, another, more inclusive notion of territoriality in the exhibition, in which the category of 'we' is broadened to encompass all those who suffered under apartheid. With time, the District Six Museum has become a 'forum for healing, celebration and information',[11] not only for those directly affected by the demolition but for anyone who wishes to learn about South Africa's past. The museum has become a meeting point for a broad audience interested in questioning, confirming or reshaping its particular knowledge or experience of apartheid.

One of the organisers told me how, on one occasion, a young woman whose parents had taken their family into exile in New York for eight years, had visited the museum. She was now back to see her country for the first time since they had left:

> she stood there and she just wept and wept and I went up to her and asked her what is the matter, and she said: 'I didn't live here in District Six, but here I feel I'm back home. I was out of South Africa for eight years, and now I'm back. I can't help thinking that I lost so much of my country in those eight years, and yet I'm very happy to be back home.' She was so emotional that it took her a while to recover.

It was obvious, from the way this story was told, that the woman's emotional response to the commemoration of a place which she had never lived in, and her experience of a sense of longing and belonging, were very much appreciated by the organiser. On several occasions, staff members at the museum explicitly stated that 'the museum belongs to everyone' and is a place where the image of the new, reconciled, non-racist South Africa can take shape. The audience – whether wishing to mourn a lost past, or to make amends for one's own (sometimes tacit) contribution to apartheid – is invited to share in the experiences of District Six and in the forced removals and, in a sense, to adopt these memories.[12] The memories of the demolition of District Six thereby become 'vicarious' (Climo 1995). In other words they are perceived as personally significant also for those who never directly experienced these events, and are regarded as forming part of a common stock of collective remembering. As Climo points out, vicarious memories play a crucial role in the transmission of feelings of belonging, providing individuals with a powerful means of identification with a certain group, a past or a territory. The key to understanding such vicarious memories lies, according to Climo:

> in the realm of emotions; such memories evoke powerful feelings in individuals, which link them to important group events they did not experience directly in their individual lives – but which impact them greatly on their identities and connect them profoundly to their heritage and culture.
>
> (Climo 1995:174)

The vicarious aspect of memories related to the destruction of District Six is also present in the official discourses about, and responses to, the museum. As previously mentioned, foreign state visits to South Africa as a nation have on several occasions included a trip to the museum. One of the main reasons for treating it as a national monument is its easy incorporation into the ideal of the inclusive and multi-cultural 'Rainbow Nation', a slogan popularised and promoted through the South African media. It refers to the present government's goal of creating a pluralistic society, free from racial or cultural hierarchies, in which all ethnic groups can coexist on an egalitarian basis. Rather than celebrating the idea of 'coloured' identity, the museum emphasises the heterogeneous population of the area, and its purported liberal and unprejudiced attitude towards matters of ethnicity or race. The exhibition, therefore, is a celebration and icon of a 'pastness' which can be described, to borrow Bodnar's words, as 'cleansed of any ideals that could in the least way be construed as politically oppositional' (Bodnar 1994: 81) by the present official cultural leaders.

The sense of locality thus expressed in the exhibition refers to a geographical entity – the land of District Six – while simultaneously becoming the epitome of a vision of equality, justice and non-racialism for a larger territorial unit, the entire new nation of South Africa. The nature of District Six, its celebrated multi-culturalism and alleged tolerance, help explain why it serves as a perfect representation of how South Africa should ideally be shaped in the future.

Memories of District Six are construed as vicarious for the new nation as much within South Africa itself as within a wider international context. The District Six Museum has attracted a great deal of attention abroad, and it has recently been decided that the Swedish International Development Co-operation Agency (SIDA) would fund the museum for at least two years in the future – 'a proportionately large contribution for being to a single project', according to the official in charge of the matter.[13] The financial support will be used mainly to set up a sound archive in which music and oral culture pertaining to District Six will be recorded and documented. This project is also part of a cooperation scheme with Malmö Stadsmuseum in Sweden.

In the SIDA reports, the District Six Museum is described in the following ways:

> The project will serve as a model for other initiatives to preserve specifically South African cultural manifestations before and during apartheid for coming generations. As a multi-cultural project it can serve as an important source of inspiration for other multi-cultural initiatives in the country.
>
> (promemoria from SIDA, May 1997, my translation)

> The District Six Museum . . . fulfils an important function, serving as a guide to the future, with a given role in the great task of truth and reconciliation.
>
> (application to SIDA by Malmö Stadsmuseum, February 1997, my translation)

The Swedish government endorses the view that District Six and the ideals it conveys are representative of South Africa, being 'specifically South African'. It seems that it is both the multi-cultural composition of the district itself, and the manner in which the community and the forced removals are now commemorated, which are regarded as being intrinsically South African. This 'essence' is regarded as very much worth preserving, and is seen as a useful resource in the building of the future nation. In this discourse District Six, rather than being portrayed as unique and contained within a specific 'ethnic' territory, is construed as belonging to everyone in the new nation. In as far as there is an international interest in preserving this 'specifically South African' essence, the memories of District Six also belong to the international community, in much the same way as there exists a shared sense of property of the memories of the two world wars and the Holocaust.

To conclude, the museum effectively uses a landscape as a symbolic resource for the construction of collective identities. The exhibition is a concrete, tangible and, importantly, social, manifestation of the notion of local identity. It serves as a symbolic re-appropriation of land which was destroyed, providing former residents with an imagined community with clear boundaries, to be contrasted with the way in which the former residential community was shattered and dispersed during the forced removals. In addition, the exhibition has also become an open forum, belonging to anyone wishing to be engaged in the process of shaping the new South African nation. In this discourse, the memories of the events in District Six are construed as belonging collectively to all South Africans, regardless of race, economic status and political affiliation.

This is an example of how collective memories, rather than being the memories of an undifferentiated whole, are subjected to contestation by different groups, each with their own, partly overlapping, criteria for inclusion. As Tonkin argues (1992: 105), Halbwachs's account of collective memory is insufficient in that it lacks an appreciation of the divided and discontinuous nature of society. While memory for Halbwachs is 'like an album of photographs', we need instead to look at its creative and structuring aspects, realising that 'cognitively, the recognition of dislocation and difference is built into us all, and we are all creatures of choice' (Tonkin 1992: 106). In South Africa today, local identity is as much an outcome of processes of exclusion and the reification of difference, as it is the result of collective identification and the creation of a common past.

Acknowledgements

* Preliminary fieldwork, made possible by a grant from the Institute for Advanced Studies in Social Anthropology, Göteborg University, was carried out in Cape Town in 1995. Subsequent work was supported by

grants from the Royal Swedish Academy of Sciences and the Swedish Council for Research in Humanities and Social Sciences. I am grateful to the staff at the District Six Museum in Cape Town for their generous assistance, and to the former and current residents of District Six. I would also like to thank Mikael Tykesson, Per Binde, Åsa Boholm and the editor of this volume, Nadia Lovell, for their valuable comments on this paper.

Notes

1 The anthology by Jeppie and Soudien (1990) is a good source for material on the rich social and cultural life of District Six, not forgetting its poverty and problems with overcrowded housing, lack of sanitation facilities and criminality.
2 In the social sciences, definitions of race based on categories of skin colour are regarded as being analytically inadequate, and ethically and politically unacceptable. Nevertheless, any of the race categories created during apartheid continue to play a significant, albeit problematic, role in South Africa. Such terms, used in the context of this paper, should be understood as discursively construed, and remain contested categories with no correspondence to any culturally or biologically given essentials.
3 The Group Areas Act of 1950 was one of the central pillars in the apartheid grand plan of racial segregation. Until the dismantling of apartheid in the 1980s, it remained a much-hated symbol of racial discrimination.
4 Two organisations that played a central role in this campaign were the District Six Residents' Association and the Friends of District Six committee. In 1983, about 20 per cent of the land was renamed a 'coloured' area. A housing project was started, and a number of houses completed, before the project was abandoned. As many former residents regarded this as a mere token gesture, it never received much popular support, and was boycotted by a majority of former District Six residents.
5 I was told two other versions of this story, one suggesting that the signs were hidden in the foreman's garage, and another that they were hidden under his bed.
6 The old, tarnished street signs, displaying street names which by now have an almost mythical quality, can be compared with the anonymous 'names' given by the authorities during apartheid to the streets in one of the townships outside the city core, Guguletu, formerly known as Nyanga West. There, around one hundred and sixty streets are named Ny 1, Ny 2, Ny 3 and so on, ending with Ny 160 (Ny is an abbreviation for Nyanga).
7 The symbolism ascribed to the material aspects of the landscape is also reflected in the way District Six is associated with another part of the cityscape, the Victoria and Albert Waterfront. When District Six was demolished, the rubble and remains of the area were dumped in Table Bay in order to reclaim land. According to former residents, the gravel was dumped on the spot where the Waterfront, an area for commerce and recreation, was built and created through the conservation and restoration of the neglected

maritime environment of Table Harbour. Since the Waterfront has been predominantly used by white people, the reaction of many of the former residents of District Six has been antagonistic. The Waterfront is informally known as 'the new District Six', an ironic epithet evoking the contrasts between what is regarded as the authentic community spirit of District Six, and the modern, commercial and artificial atmosphere of the Waterfront. When used as the fundament for the new development, the rubble becomes imbued with a symbolism that extends far beyond its ordinary referential meaning. It is then seen to embody District Six itself, albeit in an inverse, negative way.

8　This can be compared with Hawes's (cited in Radley 1990: 52) experiment, in which people produced the narrative of the American pioneer myth when presented with selected objects from a folk museum, such as a candlestick, an axe and a cooking pot.

9　Of the total of some 6,122 properties, 1,094 were owned by coloured people and 655 by Indians, while the rest belonged to white owners (Hart 1990: 126). A large percentage of the forcibly removed residents were tenants.

10　It also resembles the counter-monuments described by Gillis (1994: 17), which are intended to de-sacralise remembering and make it a part of everyday life.

11　Quote from a project proposal by the District Six Museum to the Swedish International Development Co-operation Agency (SIDA).

12　For example, when the Swedish writer Per Wästberg visited the exhibition, he noticed how people of 'Boer' origin 'come to the museum, look for the altar and ask for forgiveness' (*Dagens Nyheter*, 29 February 1996).

13　Personal communication in July 1997.

References

Anderson, B. (1983) *Imagined Communities*, London: Verso.

Banks, M. (1996) 'Ethnicity and Nationalism', in M. Banks (ed.), *Ethnicity: Anthropological Constructions*, London: Routledge.

Bender, B. (ed.) (1993) *Landscape: Politics and Perspectives*, Oxford: Berg.

Bickford-Smith, V. (1995) 'The Origins and Early History of District Six to 1910', in S. Jeppie and C. Soudien (eds), *The Struggle for District Six: Past and Present*, Cape Town: Blackshaws.

Bodnar, J. (1994) 'Public Memory in an American City: Commemoration in Cleveland', in J.R. Gillis (ed.), *Commemorations: The Politics of National Identity*, Princeton, NJ: Princeton University Press.

Boholm, Å. (1983) 'Memorialism', in *Swedish Kinship: An Exploration into Cultural Processes of Belonging and Continuity*, Göteborg: Acta Universitatis Gothoburgensis.

Bourquet, M.N., Valensi, L. and Wachtel, N. (eds) (1990) *Between Memory and History*, London: Harwood.

Cape Argus (1997) 'Call to Consult Past Residents of District Six', 13 June.

Climo, J.J. (1995) 'Prisoners of Silence: A Vicarious Holocaust Memory', in M.C. Teski and J.J. Climo (eds), *The Labyrinth of Memory: Ethnographic Journeys*, Westport, CT: Bergin & Garvey.

Connerton, P. (1989) *How Societies Remember*, Cambridge: Cambridge University Press.

Cosgrove, D. (1989) 'Geography is Everywhere: Culture and Symbolism in Human Landscapes', in D. Gregory and R. Walford (eds), *Horizons in Human Geography*, London: Macmillan.

Dagens Nyhetes (1996) 'Luften Full av Idéer', 29 February.

Fentress, J. (1992) 'Remembering', in J. Fentress and C. Wickham, *Social Memory*, Oxford: Blackwell.

Gillis, J.R. (1994) 'Introduction', in J.R. Gillis (ed.), *Commemorations: The Politics of National Identity*, Princeton, NJ: Princeton University Press.

Halbwachs, M. (1992 [1950]) *On Collective Memory*, Chicago: Chicago University Press.

Hannerz, U. (1996) 'Sophiatown: The View from Afar', in U. Hannerz (ed.) *Transnational Connections: Culture, People, Places*, London: Routledge.

Hart, D.M. (1990) 'Political Manipulation of Urban Space: The Razing of District Six, Cape Town', in S. Jeppie and C. Soudien (eds), *The Struggle for District Six: Past and Present*, Cape Town: Blackshaws.

Hart, D.M. and Pirie, G.H. (1984) 'The Sight and Soul of Sophiatown', *Geographical Review* 74: 38–47.

Hirsch, E. and O'Hanlon, M. (eds) (1995) *The Anthropology of Landscape: Perspectives on Place and Space*, Oxford: Clarendon Press.

Jeppie, S. and Soudien, C. (eds) (1990) *The Struggle for District Six: Past and Present*, Cape Town: Blackshaws.

Johnson, N. (1995) 'Cast in Stone: Monuments, Geography and Nationalism', *Environment and Planning: Society and Space* 13: 52–65.

Koonz, C. (1994) 'Between Memory and Oblivion: Concentration Camps in German Memory', in J.R. Gillis (ed.), *Commemorations: The Politics of National Identity*, Princeton, NJ: Princeton University Press.

Kopytoff, I. (1986) 'The Cultural Biography of Things: Commoditization as Process', in A. Appadurai (ed.), *The Social Life of Things: Commodities in Cultural Perspective*, Cambridge: Cambridge University Press.

Middleton, D. and Edwards, D. (eds) (1994) *Collective Remembering*, London: Sage.

Radley, A. (1990) 'Artefacts, Memory and a Sense of the Past', in D. Middleton and D. Edwards (eds), *Collective Remembering*, London: Sage.

Rive, R. (1990) 'District Six: Fact and Fiction', in S. Jeppie and C. Soudien (eds), *The Struggle for District Six: Past and Present*, Cape Town: Blackshaws.

Rowlands, M. (1993) 'The Role of Memory in the Transmission of Culture', *World Archaeology* 25(2): 142–51.

Swedish International Development Co-operation Agency (SIDA) (1997) Promemoria 21 May: *Stöd till District Six-Museet i Kapstaden genom Malmö*

Stadsmuseum, Application 12 February: Ansökan om stöd till musikarkiv vid District Six Museum, Kapstaden, Sydafrika 1997–8.

Swiderski, R. (1995) 'Mau Mau and Memory Rooms: Placing a Social Emotion', in M.C. Teski and J.J. Climo (eds), *The Labyrinth of Memory: Ethnographic Journeys*, Westport, CT: Bergin & Garvey.

Tonkin, E. (1992) *Narrating our Pasts: The Social Construction of Oral History*, Cambridge: Cambridge University Press.

Weekly Mail and Guardian (1994a) 'To Cap it All, a Real Community Project', 2 September.

—— (1994b) 'Editorial: New Symbols or Bust', 16 September.

—— (1995a) 'An Archaeology of Memory', 3 February.

—— (1995b) 'New Struggle for Coloureds', 24 March.

—— (1995c) 'District with a View of the Bay', 24 November.

Yates, F. (1974) *The Art of Memory*, Oxford: Oxford University Press.

Chapter 8

The *potrero* and the *pibe*

Territory and belonging in the mythical account of Argentinean football*

Eduardo P. Archetti

Introduction

National identity would probably lose much of its enchantment without the appeal and the mystique of a particular territory. National symbols often serve to reflect and strengthen the historical continuity associated with a particular landscape: its natural contour is explored, mapped, lived and transformed into a homeland. Schama (1995) has convincingly argued that inherited landscape myths and memories share two common characteristics: their surprising endurance through time, and their power to shape contemporary meanings and institutions (Schama 1995: 15). According to his interpretation, national landscapes are imagined as unique, and the notions of belonging and identity perceived as internal and exclusive. A nation is a territory which is not shared with others (the non-national) and, in principle, not shaped by external forces. Moreover, landscape imagery is powerful because of its tendency to combine a geographical belonging with complex narratives of human exploits, extraordinary characters and cultural-historical heroes. Thus, important cultural and social practices will be linked to the idea that territories empower those who belong to them (Morphy 1995; Toren 1995).

This chapter explores how, in the context of Argentinean football, such imagery and myths appear in areas other than the rural, thus encompassing also urban territories. It will postulate that powerful national representations and key symbols work at different levels, and that reflections on national identity, or nationhood, are not only related to the realm of the state and its dominant institutions: schools, police, bureaucracy, postal systems and military barracks. In Argentina, football is an eminently masculine social arena, also strongly associated histori-cally with the construction of national identity through the international successes of the national team and the 'export' of great players to Europe since the 1920s. The sense of belonging to a place is built around such moments of recognition as when a social practice like football, introduced to the country by the thousands of British immigrants and workers in the 1880s, suddenly exposes its connections to a peculiar vision of territory. The memory of football, its mythical foundation, will thus be influenced by the imagery of the territories of the *pampa*, the *potrero* and the *baldio*. The idea of a given immutable territory, populated by mythical figures, as something typically national needs to be qualified. One of the main arguments here is that dominant national imageries work primarily through the transformation of meanings, semantic extensions and analogical uses (and abuses). Consequently, national narratives are constructed and reconstructed in different fields of activities, and in the interplay between internal and external forces. Notions of Argentinean identity are not exclusively constructed internally, within given boundaries. They can also be conceptualised in contraposition to other identities, recognised or not by the natives themselves. The ideas and images of the 'national' are quite often a mirror in which the glance of others is as crucial as the glance of the natives themselves.

In Argentina, football is a privileged arena for the analysis of the formation of national identity and the construction of masculinities (Archetti 1994). At the beginning of the twentieth century, football was seen as an imported British sport, which became national and internal to Argentina at a moment when the global network of exchanges and sports competitions was developing. Football made it possible for Argentinean men to compete, and become visible, on the world scene (the Olympic Games, South American tournaments and, since 1930, the World Cup). Ideas of territory and belonging are asserted and redefined through the imagery of football where, for instance, the importance of external forces is recognised in the contrasts created between the various playing styles of national elites and outsiders. Notions of territory and belonging are also expressed through the contrasts and inversions established between rural and urban images, reflected onto the identities and bodies of particular football players.

Historical narratives

In some dominant historical narratives the *pampa*, the extensive wild treeless humid plains of Argentina, was perceived as a rich ecosystem that could sustain life almost independently of human agency.[1] This wilderness was out there, in the heart of the country, awaiting discovery, and would provide the antidote for the poisons of modernity, capitalism and industrialism. Although portrayed as virgin territory, the *pampa* was during the Spanish colonial period a territory populated by Indians, wild livestock, horses and the *gauchos*, the free *mestizo* horse riders of mixed blood who later became the symbol of the nation. Such mythology therefore betrays an inherent contradiction: namely that this territory, pictured as the epitome of freedom was, nevertheless, the product of culture, namely that of the original *criollos* (creoles), the *gauchos*. In this imagery, the mythologised and idealised instinct of survival of the local Indian population merges with its increased marginalisation, related to a continuous process of creolisation. Indians are portrayed as an immobile, doomed race, unable to accept mixing (*mestizaje*), stuck in the compulsion to repeat the same ineffective campaigns of resistance until, at last, they perish along with their names and their history. In the dominant ideology of *mestizaje*, both the Indians and the Spaniards are portrayed as the opposite of the *gauchos*. The *gaucho* becomes the typical hybrid, which mixes Indian and Spanish blood and presupposes the creation of a new identity.

The post-colonial period is defined by a process of transformation initiated in the second half of the nineteenth century. This was characterised by the conquest of the Indian territories, occupation and privatisation of the *pampa*, a rapid technological change in agriculture and livestock, a massive British investment in railways and an unprecedented immigration of European farmers and rural labourers. However, this domestication was not total, and spaces without agriculture and pastures were kept free of pesticides and industrial machinery. One of these spaces was the *potrero*, a portion of a given estate owned privately, where livestock and horses could peacefully graze under the protection of the *gauchos* and their horses, now transformed into paid labourers. The process of domestication of the *pampas* left the *potreros* as a relatively free territory, neither entirely wild, as it had been in colonial times, nor colonised by modern agriculture.

The *pampa* and the *potrero* are powerful metaphors for imagining an original Argentinean landscape not totally metamorphosed by the rapid transformations in agriculture and livestock production. The *pampa* is seen as the original, wild and extremely fertile prairie while the *potrero* is, in many ways, what has been left over after the massive technological changes brought by the introduction of modern agriculture. The wild *pampa* metaphorically lives on in the *potreros*, the exclusive domain of the *gauchos*. The analogies between the *potrero* as semi-wild landscape, the relatively free grazing animals which inhabit this territory, and the *gauchos*, as hybrids combining original belonging with modern colonial identities, mirror cultural and social developments in the history of Argentina. Territorial liminality is central to the constitution of a nation. The *pampa* is a portion of the Argentinean territory defined as unique. It is literally on the border of other territorial units similar to adjacent nations, and the *potrero* can be conceived as a liminal territory in relation to the totally cultivated land. The *gaucho* was historically located on the border of Indian land, the territory that was not controlled by the expanding nation-state in the nineteenth century.[2] The *gaucho* was a frontiersman like a Bedouin, an American cowboy, a Basque, a Mexican rancher or an Australian frontiersman. All frontiersmen are usually represented in national mythologies as rebellious, resistant to authority and are, paradoxically, simultaneously transformed into national symbols. As Norton writes:

> The territorially liminal become signs of the nation because they are, territorially, not unambiguously national. They become signs of the capacity for conquest, incorporation, and production because they are constantly in danger of being themselves conquered and incorporated into a foreign body, with their nature consequently altered. They signify what they lack. The ambivalence of liminality extends not only to the traits and the ascriptive character of liminars, but to the function of liminality in the political culture as well.
>
> (Norton 1993: 61)

The *gauchos*, as all territorially liminal people, can be invested with several of the traits attributed by Turner to liminality: suspension of kinship ties and obligations, reference to mystical powers, madness, equality, inversion of authority, creativity and solidarity (1969: 106–8). The liminality of those on the frontier enhances the importance of metaphors of incorporation and exclusion. The image of the foreign can be seen in the mirror of the liminal. I argue, as a typical case of semantic extension, that the liminality of the *gaucho* as a free, rebellious and uncontrolled rider is transferred to the imagery of the *pibe* (a young boy), the mythical figure of Argentinean football. For Argentineans, the *pibe* belongs to the *potrero* as the *gaucho* belongs to the *pampa*. In contrast to the *pibe*, the foreigner is represented in local discourse by the player of British origin.

The analysis begins with an examination of written material taken from the weekly magazine *El Gráfico*. Founded in May 1919 in Buenos

Aires, *El Gráfico* was in the beginning, literally, a graphic magazine 'for men', being produced by the Atlántida publishing house, which also brought out very successful magazines for children and women. *El Gráfico* included, in different measures, political articles, sports, photographs of news and artists, and reports on leisure activities. After 1921, *El Gráfico* gradually became a sports magazine, although photographs of women artists and even daring nude pictures of unknown and allegedly foreign dancers would be published until the end of the 1920s. The circulation of *El Gráfico* increased, levelling out at 200,000 in the 1930s. Its authority and influence derived from the capacity of its journalists to create a mythical and ahistorical account of Argentinean football. Some of these journalists were excellent writers, and provided a model for successive generations of aspiring sports correspondents in Argentina. *El Gráfico* was, and still is, the most authoritative sports magazine in the country.

The written accounts available in *El Gráfico*, now part of the Argentinean mythology of football, will be contrasted with the opinions of informants, specifically on the meaning of Diego Maradona, the most successful football player produced by the Argentinean *potrero*.[3] This analysis sets out to examine the complex and interwoven paths leading to the production, by intellectuals in the past (sports journalists), contemporary informants, and anthropologists (my interpretation), of local categories of players and territories. I hope in this way to trace some of the transformations of mythical images in Argentinean football which have occurred between then and now, and to show that the *pibes* and the *potreros* of the past live in the present through the performances of Maradona while, at the same time, Maradona today lives in a past shaped by mythical accounts. From there, I postulate that an analysis of territory and belonging in Argentinean football must be historically located, since mythical accounts of territory are related to categories of place and actors, both of which are historically defined.

The imaginary of freedom: the *pibe* and the *potrero* as symbols of a style

No identity can ever exist by itself and without an array of opposites, negatives and contradictions. In the colonial context, the *creoles* opposed the Spaniards while, in the post-colonial period after independence, the British became a relevant Other in the process of imagining cultural and social differences. The emergence of contrasting styles in sport, particularly in football, is intimately related to a search for national identity. To encounter national styles in sport as they are created (and experienced) displays a temporality of culture and social consciousness in tune with the idea that national identity is much more than simply political, or articulated only at the level of the state.

As we have seen, football was introduced by British immigrants in the 1880s, and this initial period of amateur football in Buenos Aires was dominated by British clubs. The importance of the British colony transformed the city into a privileged place to be visited by famous English first division teams. From 1904, English professional teams of great prestige, such as Southampton, Nottingham Forest, Everton and Tottenham, visited Buenos Aires. They played several matches against the British local teams and, in all cases, returned to England undefeated. These visits coincided with the era of British dominance. From 1887 to 1911 (the date when the hegemony of the Alumni, known to locals as the 'glorious British club', was broken) players of British origin predominated:

> The English who came to the River Plate were the first to play the sport and their sons continued to do so in English schools, where other sports like cricket were also played. Thus River Plate football had English origins in its first stages and the first lesson in advanced technique came from Southampton, and then Nottingham Forest, Everton, Tottenham Hotspur, etc. All completely English, as can be seen and appreciated in the famous stars of our football beginnings who were called Brown, Weiss, Lett, Ratcliff, Buchanan, Moore, Mack, Watson, Hutton and so many others whose names are indistinguishable from football players in the Fair Albion.
> (*El Gráfico* 1928, 470: 15, my translation)

The emergence of a truly *criolla* (creole) foundation began in 1913 when Racing Club, a football association started in 1903 by Argentinean natives and Italian immigrants, without a single player of British origin, won the first division championship for the first time. From that moment the British clubs declined in importance and their players disappeared from the Argentinean national teams. According to *El Gráfico*, this change became possible because 'when football began to spread, the stars with British names gave way to those with purely Latin, especially Italian and Spanish surnames like García, Martínez, Ohaco, Olazar, Chiappe, Calomino, Laforia, Isola, etc.' (*El Gráfico* 1928, 470: 15, my translation).

In the 1920s, *El Gráfico* developed a theory relating the emergence of Argentinean football to two fundamentally different influences, or foundations (*fundaciones*): the first was British (*fundación británica*), and the second was *criolla* (hybrid, *fundación criolla*). These denominations refer to the ethnic origins of the players in the most famous club teams, and of those playing for the Argentinean national team. *Los criollos* are identified primarily with Spanish and Italian surnames. *Lo criollo*, as a club, was founded through the sons of Latin immigrants. The sons of 'English' or 'British' immigrants were never conceived of as *criollos* and could not become *criollo* by playing football. This notion of difference in origin between *los criollos* and English football players extended to include perceived differences in the style of football played. *El Gráfico* explains:

> it is logical that as the years have gone by all Anglo-Saxon influence in football has been disappearing, giving way to the less phlegmatic and more restless spirit of the Latin. . . . Inspired by the same school as the British, the Latins soon began modifying the science of the game, and fashioning one of their own, which is now widely recognised . . . it is different from the British in that it is less monochrome, less disciplined and methodical, because it does not sacrifice individualism out of respect for collective values. In English football everything tends towards destroying personal action in order to form a solid whole, so that a team is not important because of its separate members but because of the uniform action of the whole group. For this reason, British football is really powerful and has the regular and driving force of a machine, but it is monotonous because it is always uniformly the same. River Plate football, by contrast, does not sacrifice personal action entirely and makes more use of dribbling and generous personal effort, both in attack and defence, and for that reason is a more agile and attractive football.
>
> (*El Gráfico* 1928, 470: 15, my translation)

In the texts of *El Gráfico*, 'Britishness' is identified with being phlegmatic, disciplined, methodical, and concentrated around elements of the collective, of force and of physical power. These virtues help to create a repetitive style, similar to that of a 'machine'. The author recognises that this style allows one to conceptualise British football as 'perfect', that is, industrially perfect. The *criollo*, due to the Latin influence, is exactly the opposite: restless, individualistic, undisciplined, based on personal effort, agile and skilful.

The conceptual oppositions between British and *criollo* physical virtues have become encrusted in common perceptions of football. The British (English) physical virtues are still associated with 'force and physical power', while the virtues of the *criollos* are those of agility and virtuoso movement. The metaphor of the 'machine', as opposed to individual creativity, is constant in contemporary Argentinean football imagery.[4] 'Britishness' is still associated with the industrial, and the *criollo* with the pre-industrial social system. During a game, when faced with the British machine or repetitive play, the typical *criollo* response would be the 'dribble', later to be called the *gambeta* (a word derived from *gaucho* or gauchoesque literature which describes the running motion of an ostrich). This manifestation of style is eminently individual and cannot be programmed. It is the opposite of the industrial, collective game of the machine.

In the context of these developments in the conceptualisation of national identity and otherness, and their respective associations with particular styles of play, Borocotó (a star journalist of *El Gráfico*) developed his theory of *criollo* dribbling in 1928.[5] Borocotó believed that the personal qualities of the *pibes criollos* (young boys of hybrid origin) derived from their relationship to the social and spatial contexts which allowed them to develop these qualities (*El Gráfico* 1928, 480). Unlike in England where, according to Borocotó, football was integral to the school system, the *pibes* played football spontaneously in the *potreros*, without any teachers. In addition, in Borocotó's view, the *pibe criollo* realised, when he saw the English teams play, that this style had no room for improvisation or imagination. With so many other players in such a confined space, the only way for the *pibe* in the *potrero* to keep control of the ball for some time was to become an inveterate dribbler. Borocotó also identified dribbling as the distinguishing feature which enabled Argentinean football to become known throughout the world. At the time, the players leaving Argentina to play in Europe were the best dribblers. Borocotó emphatically argued that until the late 1920s, Argentina had been known throughout the world mostly for exporting its valuable frozen beef and its quality cereals, 'non-popular products' in the sense that they came from the large estates of the *pampa*-based landowning classes. Therefore, it was important that Argentina should become known for its more popular product: the exquisite technical quality of Argentinean football players.

The creative power of the *pibe*

In this mythical account, clearly, the *pibe* (the young boy), without any form of teaching, becomes the inventor of the *criollo* style in the *potrero*. The *pibe* is placed in a mythical territory that inherently empowers those who belong to it. This image, developed by Borocotó, partly emphasises the infantile beginning of Argentinean football (as is manifest perhaps in any game), but also points to the importance of freshness, spontaneity and freedom during play. These values are commonly associated with childhood, and are usually lost with the advent of maturity and resulting adult responsibilities. In the canonical narratives of *El Gráfico*, the privileged image of the ideal player is the *pibe*. The authentic Argentinean player will never stop being a child. Football allows a man to go on playing and remain a *pibe*. One could say that the imaginary world of football reflects the power of freedom and creativity in the face of discipline, order and hierarchy.

We have already seen how the idea of the *potrero* was associated with a rural landscape in the *pampa*. This notion of the *potrero* subsequently (through increased industrialisation and modernisation) came to be transferred to an empty space in the city, the *baldío*. Borocotó would explicitly come to associate the wilderness of the *potrero* with the urban *baldío*, a much more limited space or small patch of irregular ground in the city which has not yet been cemented over. More precisely, a *baldío* is an empty space between two buildings. Borocotó argued that the Argentinean players came either from the *potrero* or the *baldío*. They did not come from the playgrounds of primary or secondary schools or from the clubs, the spaces controlled by teachers and trainers. The *potrero* and the *baldío* were portrayed as exclusively open, free, male spaces, with no women and no teachers. Consequently, the great players were considered the pure products of this freedom, which allowed them to be creative and improvise without the constraints and rules imposed by experts or pedagogues. *Pibes* came to be seen as liminal figures in the construction of Argentinean masculinities, and *potreros* became territories associated with the experience of freedom and creativity. The foreign British and English styles offered an image very much opposed to that of the liminal figures of the *pibes*.

Borocotó suggested that Argentina should raise a monument in 'any walkway' to the inventor of dribbling, which became the symbol of Argentinean national, post-colonial football. This monument would have to represent:

a *pibe* with a dirty face, a mane of hair rebelling against the comb; with intelligent, roving, persuasive trickster eyes, and a sparkling gaze that seems to hint at a picaresque laugh, but which does not quite manage to form on a mouth full of small teeth perhaps worn down through eating yesterday's bread. His trousers are made of a few roughly sewn patches. A vest with Argentinean stripes, with a very low neck and with many holes eaten out by the invisible mice of use. A strip of material tied to the waist and crossing over the chest like a sash serves as braces. . . . His knees covered with the scabs of wounds disinfected by fate; barefoot or with shoes whose holes in the toes suggest that they have been made through so much shooting. His stance must be characteristic, it must seem as if he is dribbling with a rag ball. This is important: the ball cannot be any other. A rag ball and preferably bound by an old sock. If this monument is raised one day, there will be many who will take off our hat to it, as we do in church.

(*El Gráfico* 1928, 480: 11, my translation)

As part of the reflection on *criollo* style, portraits of players were presented as archetypes of these values. For Borocotó, Carlos Peucelle, a legendary player from the World Cup team of 1930, was a paradigm of these values. Borocotó entitles his article, 'Carlos Peucelle, citizen of the *baldío*', and writes:

he is the personification of the *potrero*, the citizen of the *baldío*, he is the wasteground in motion . . . look at him in his stride, out there in the game, his freckled, smiling face, like a naughty child, and you will agree that he is harnessed to the *potrero*. . . . He has the *baldío* in his heart. Observe him. Look at him as he stops in the centre of the field, with his stooping gait, whirling his arms and shaking his wavy locks that are at war with hair cream. See how he seems to be telling the boys in their striped jumpers pressed against the wire fencing: Wait for this to finish and we will go off to the *potrero*.

(*El Gráfico* 1933, 716: 4, my translation)

To be a citizen of the *baldío* is to be a 'free man' in a world of equals. The *baldío* is presented as the democratic truth: after the game, Peucelle can go off to the *potrero* with the spectators for a kickabout. Peucelle has the *baldío* in his heart and his body movements reveal it. The unity of heart and soul is celebrated.

Peucelle also looks like a *pibe*, he seems like a 'naughty child' and for that reason, he retains his freshness. This is a salient paradox: an important masculine virtue is to preserve, as far as possible, this pure, childlike style. Through his style, Peucelle transmits the idea that football is a game and, as such, can only be fully enjoyed when one has pure freedom. In the democratic world of football, players are all *pibes*, they are all children, they are not tied to the authority of their parents and have escaped from schools and clubs, from power and hierarchies. The *baldío* is not a world of mature hard men, of duellists, it is not peopled by the *compadritos* (brave and courageous men) of the tango lyrics, prepared to fight and, if necessary, to kill to defend their stained honour. The *baldío* is a world of naughty, wilful and crafty boys.

The *potrero* and the *baldío* are systematically opposed to the blackboard and the school. Borocotó comments on a photograph depicting a 'football teacher', an English international player, with a ball in one hand and a pointer in the other, in front of a blackboard containing a clear outline of a football field:

> Yes sir, yes sir; English football is more technical, more effective, whatever you like, it is all the same to me. Goals are the mark of a victory, but there are victories that are ordinary and there are defeats which are clear triumphs. I recognise that discipline is very important, but please old man, don't come to me with a blackboard. Only the English could think of football in terms of a blackboard. We have to make a fuss . . . there they have to go to school to learn football, here you have to play truant from school. There we have an international with a ball in one hand and rules in the other, in front of a blackboard; here we have a leather ball and lots of boys mucking in. There we find a honed, severe, conscious technique; here we have the *gambeta*, grace and improvisation. On the one hand the coldness of numbers and hypotenuses; on the other, the joy and emotion of the spectacle. . . . Between the blackboard and the *baldío*, between those over there and those over here, I prefer our game a thousand times over, even if we lose, because in every melée there is a touch of grace, in every conquest there is a tiny grain of emotion.
>
> (*El Gráfico* 1931, 614: 6, my translation).[6]

This opposition is epitomised in the style of one of the great defenders of the time: Fernando 'El Marquéz' Paternoster. This Racing Club player was in the national team for the World Cup in 1930, then triumphed in Brazil before starting a successful career as a trainer in Colombia. *El Gráfico*, in one of its many unsigned articles, describes him in the following way:

> There is something English about his impeccable positional play, but he becomes South Americanised in the elasticity of his swerves, the lack of urgency in beating off the attack and above all, in his elegant indolence. . . . It is enough to say that he is an Argentine to know that he has not studied theory, or learned from a blackboard. . . . He was one of the *pibes* from the *potrero*; his lack of physical size showed him that he would have to get on through cunning; and effective cunning is nothing less than a sign of intelligence . . . he has a magician's art and speed which comes from both agility and an instant reading of the game.
>
> (*El Gráfico* 1931, 633: 16, my translation)

This description of Paternoster makes explicit reference to his small physical size. In this relationship between physique and style, Paternoster makes up for his size through ability and technique, like a *pibe* in any *potrero*. The author of this article is merely confirming with this particular example the theory developed some years previously by Chantecler, another star journalist of *El Gráfico*, about the necessary relationship between physique and style. According to Chantecler, since the English style is stolid, strong, disciplined and harmonious in its collective play, it needs 'big and strong men'. *Criollo* style, which is light, quick, delicate, with more individual skill and less collective play, needs 'small and weak' men (*El Gráfico* 1928, 467: 21). We will now explore the persistence of these ideas in contemporary Argentina.

Maradona: the *pibe* and the *potrero*

Maradona is, without any doubt, the most famous contemporary Argentinean football star. He has been world champion twice, once with the junior Argentinean national team, and he has for several years played for the best sides in Europe. Maradona is still called *el pibe de oro* (the golden young boy), hence the other great *pibes* of the history of Argentinean football are, metaphorically, made only of silver or bronze, less prestigious metals. Moreover, Maradona was discovered as a prodigious player at the age of ten and, when he was twelve, the media declared that Argentinean football had never seen such a talent. At fifteen he played his first league match for Argentinos Juniors in the first division. At sixteen he was admired by the people as a precious gift to the nation. At seventeen he played his first international match with the Argentinean national team. At eighteen, as captain, he won the first gold medal for Argentina in the Junior World Cup in Tokyo. At twenty-six, as captain, he won the second gold medal for Argentina in the World Cup in Mexico City. His precocity and, of course, his ability was a confirmation of his quality as a *pibe*.

For many years, and without any doubt for most of my informants, Maradona looked like a *pibe*. They would say that he really looked like a happy *pibe* when he received the World Cup trophy in Mexico City in 1986. This image is perhaps the most perfect symbol of his achievements and global fame. Moreover, he seemed like a 'naughty child', and for that reason, he retained his freshness. This paradox, a mature young man at the top of his career being defined as a *pibe*, is significant: an important virtue for the best Argentinean players is to preserve, for as long as possible, this pure, childlike style. To be, and remain, a *pibe* is a powerful image because in football, the most creative period for some players is associated with immaturity. My informants do not deny the role of experience and the passing of the years (*el paso de los años*), in the development of physical automatisation and tactical sense. These qualities are also considered important for expected performances. But a *pibe* is, by definition, an unpredictable player finding unexpected solutions in the most difficult moments of a game. The magic of Maradona is always understood as a performing skill, for it produces inexplicable effects and illusions paralysing opposing players and charming his audience. This is defined as a powerful, bewitching quality. This image of the childish, unruly *pibe* serves to portray football as a game to be fully enjoyed only when total freedom is granted, and achieved. Conversely, football is ideally perceived as a perfect game for children.

Maradona has the benefit of the shape of his body. It is easy to associate his status of *pibe* with his height, his roundness, his tendency to be fat, his sudden acceleration, his theatrical exaggeration, his way of walking with short movements, and his constant struggle against rude and aggressive defenders. Maradona has looked casual, unkempt, unfit and, in many ways, inelegant for long periods of his career. My informants compared Maradona's body with the bodies of other great international heroes of Argentinean football: Di Stéfano, the legendary player of Real Madrid in the 1950s, and Sívori, the skilful 'angel with a dirty face' (then a *pibe*) who captivated the supporters of Juventus in the 1960s. Both were forwards, and Sívori was, like Maradona, a typical inside-left. In the comparison, Sívori comes close due to his dribbling style and ability, but he is said to have been a more disciplined player. Di Stéfano was blond, almost of Scandinavian type, his figure was stylised and he experienced premature baldness. Energetic, a real leader, a fighter and very elegant, Di Stéfano was defined as a mature, hard man. In our conversations we identified, of course, several players who could be described as *pibes*, such as René Houseman, the right winger of the Argentinean team which won the 1978 World Cup. Houseman was perceived as a 'brother', as the cultural and almost genetical kin of Maradona, but with an opposing body image. Houseman was short, nonchalant, bony, nonconformist and daring. We agreed that there are different bodies, or figures, that can represent the ideal image of the *pibe*. The imagery of the *pibe* is thus also plural and full of ambiguities.

Thus the meaning of *pibe* is multifaceted, relating to a cluster of features that promote, yet also limit, the social construction of the stereotype. One such feature is the small body, particularly in terms of height. In addition to body shape, the content of bodily performances seems to be another important feature. The image of a typical *pibe* player is based on an exuberance of skill, cunning, individual creativity, artistic feeling, vulnerability and improvisation. In this sense it is easy to understand that the image of a powerful, disciplined and perfect athletic body is absent. A third related feature is the kind of daily life *pibes* lead. In the case of a *pibe*, a considerable amount of disorder is expected, and tolerated. Chaotic behaviour is the norm. There is a tendency to disregard boundaries, to play games even in private life (life is experienced as a permanent game or gamble if needed). There is a capacity to recompense, penalise or forgive others in an exaggerated way, to convey arbitrary judgements and choices, to display stupid and irrational heroism, a capacity to 'die', metaphorically (by being imprisoned, becoming a drug addict or an alcoholic) and be resurrected, and a special talent in critical games to make the unexpected move, ensuring victory for the team. Thus, a *pibe* is creative, free of strong feelings of guilt, self-destructive and, eventually, a bad moral example to other players. In the global moral evaluation of this kind of player the ultimate criterion is the creativity of their bodies. My informants, and I imagine supporters in general, tend to forgive the lack of moral and social responsibility of the *pibes*. In this sense, Maradona is not alone. The amount of joy provided by the *pibes* is more important to the public than any consistent moral statement they might make. Tomás, one of my informants, explained to me that:

to be a *pibe* is not only to be liberated from several responsibilities. To be a *pibe* means that one does not feel the pressures from the authority of family, parents, and school . . . but also to be a *pibe* implies that it is easier for others to see only the positive aspects and to forgive the imperfections. It is common to say here, in Argentina, and perhaps in a lot of other places too, 'but he is a *pibe*, just a *pibe*, let him be a *pibe*'. Maradona is a *pibe* and will remain a *pibe*. He represents this state of perfection and freedom, when we disregard the most negative traits of an individual. This spontaneity, to be fresh and to do things just right without thought of negative consequences, are qualities that we appreciate. A great football player must have these qualities.

In many ways, Tomás is less idealistic than Borocotó. To be a *pibe* also implies an awareness of the pressures from family and society, while remaining imperfect and impervious to their expectations. The imperfections, in Tomás' interpretation, are contrasted to what is expected of a mature person. Yet for him, Maradona, a real *pibe*, is not perfect as a man, but he is perfect as a player. His perfection is attained, and maintained, because he is still a *pibe*. He, like Peucelle, has the *potrero* in his heart.

Liminality and nationhood

As has already been pointed out, we can classify the *pibes* as liminars, as being on a threshold, in a state 'betwixt and between', a kind of transformative period. My informants, however, put the stress on the fact that in football 'once a *pibe*, always a *pibe*'. The category of *pibe* is marked by ambiguity, ambivalence and contradictions because the model of interpretation is based on potential disorder: *pibes* will not become mature men. The recognition of liminal marks makes possible the differentiation of players and of particular bodies and performances. The image of the *pibe*'s body is the image of imperfection. Liminal individuals provide an object of identification which evokes, for others, the condition of being an 'eternal *pibe*' through an identification with players like Maradona. This process involves the differentiation of qualities proper to an established dominant ideal of masculinity, based on reason and responsibility, from those alien to it. The *pibes* thus serve as mirrors and, at the same time, operate as models defining a style, a way of playing. The image of Maradona contains both these aspects.

Appadurai has argued that what have been termed 'rites de passage' are concerned with the production of local subjects (natives) in a particular locality, actors who belong to a spatially defined community of kin, neighbours and compatriots. Therefore, certain rituals become techniques for the inscription of locality onto bodies (1995: 205). Parkin has also shown the importance of redefining ritual in terms of spatial direction and bodily division. He argues that, through ritual, people reach 'tangled states', spatial and bodily states of confusion, admixture and complexity which the ritual serves to untangle by exposing them to view. These tangled states are rarely calculated in advance, but tend to arise when participants disagree with each other's interpretations of events and experiences (Parkin 1992: 23–4).

My analysis has shown that there is a powerful bodily and social symbolism in the meaning of football, the imagery of the *potrero* and the role of the *pibes*. Against the political ideology of a nation-state where rituals such as obligatory schooling, compulsory military service, marriage and the constitution of a family are all meant to produce an 'ordered' identity, football appears as a realm of freedom and latent disorder. The *potrero* is closely associated with the wilderness, and the *pibe* will never transform himself into a mature man. Football clearly evokes an alternative masculinity and, by extension, a different kind of nationhood. Nations, like narratives, lose their origins in a mythical belonging which, in most cases, precedes the emergence of a state. The ritual of football reproduces the idea of the nation as liminal. Thus Argentina, as nation-state, is 'new' and 'historical' while the national imagery of football tends to manifest an immemorial past that slowly glides into an unending future. Maradona merges identities as national, historical agent with those of the *pibe* as an ahistorical, mythical figure. Cities have dates of birth, while the *potrero* is eternal.

These arguments, triggered by a rich imagery, were forcefully presented by my informants. Sergio, a man in his late twenties and a devoted follower of Maradona's exploits, remembered well a 'historical television program with Maradona, a real *pibe* at that time.' He told me that when Maradona was twelve years old, Pipo Mancera, at that time a famous television entertainer, showed Maradona juggling with a ball, doing incredible things that even a worshipped professional player would have enormous difficulty imitating. After a minute of juggling, 'a minute that was eternal' according to Sergio, Mancera asked Maradona what his dreams were, as a football player and, without hesitation, he answered that he had three dreams: to play in the first division league, to wear the shirt of the Argentinean national team in a World Cup, and to win it. Sergio explained to me:

> It was like in the famous tango *El sueño del pibe* (The *pibe*'s dream), do you remember? But Maradona was more aspiring and conscious of his capacity. Well, the lyrics narrate the story of a talented *pibe* who, while crying with joy, shows his mother a letter from his club telling him that he has been accepted as a player in the junior team. That night, he dreams that, like so many crack Argentinean players, he will reach the First Division and that in his debut he will score the winning goal. Look, in this tango the *pibe* is a forward, and he scores after dribbling past all the defenders of the opposing team.

This image has been used on countless occasions in Argentina and international television programmes devoted to the life of Maradona. The perfect synchronicity of the performance, the age of the performer and his future career parallel real life with the flavour and melodrama of a soap opera. Nothing is better for committed football supporters than when fiction is transformed into reality, as in this case. In the dramatic theatre of football, mirrors and models are created and reproduced. In this process, social and personal identifications fuse in a pervasive and, perhaps, perverse way. Maradona is himself a concrete individual, and, at the same time, a kind of archetypal person representing a style and a mythical condition. Tomás clearly expressed this idea:

> You imagine the *pibes* as the best players, as being a part of our style, our way of playing, and then, suddenly, the most perfect one appears. It is perfect. You have been dreaming along with thousands and thousands of football fanatics, and one day your dream is transformed into a reality.

The assurance of Tomás and other informants, without one single exception, made me feel that an entire nation had been waiting for this occasion to materialise. The figure and the performance of Maradona can be seen as the continuation of *el mito del pibe* (the myth of the *pibe*), and also as its most perfect mythical realisation.[7]

The imagery of Maradona is even more complete because he is the product of one of the poorest neighbourhoods of Buenos Aires, where *potreros* still exist. He was born in Villa Fiorito in 1960 and one could write that 'everything started in Villa Fiorito, a forever forgotten neighbourhood where prosperity never arrived, in a remote day . . . in a humble house . . . ' (Casas and Chacón 1996: 5). It is easy to presume that in Villa Fiorito the streets were without asphalt and there was a plethora of *potreros*. The most original Argentinean player comes from the *potrero* of Fiorito which is now used as a mythical name, as the essence of *potrero* (see Fontanarrosa and Sanz 1994: 53–4). We are not told to which school Maradona went (this is not important), and we are told that when he joined his first serious club he was already a crack player (Gilbert 1996: 17). What has not been learnt in the *potrero* cannot be taught elsewhere. Carlos explained to me:

> Maradona is pure *potrero* even when he is not playing football. Well, I can put it this way: he still lacks civilised manners, and he has obvious problems in accepting boundaries and control. In the *potrero*, you learn how to be free and to improvise. Later in life you realise that this situation is temporary, then you change and adapt to society. This happens even in a football club, and is the task of managers and trainers. In addition, trainers will try hard to teach players new tricks, to make them improve technically and think in tactical terms. You will hear some players saying that they are thankful to a given coach because he taught them many things, or because they became accomplished players due to his knowledge and advice. Well, you never heard Maradona say that anyone taught him anything. I believe that is true. His knowledge and skills were developed in the freedom of the *potrero*. His ability and capacity for inventing new tricks is something that is impossible to learn from a coach. On the contrary, I will postulate that his creativity is a victory against discipline and training. You can write, if you want, that his accomplishment is the victory of the *potrero*. I assure you that I am not exaggerating.

In several discussions my informants insisted on the importance of situating Carlos' arguments historically. They emphasised that Maradona appeared as a player at a moment when national and international football was dominated by ideas of the superiority of elaborate tactical systems, based on an integrated, machine-like team. The international dominance of Dutch and German football in the 1970s was related to these aspects. Franz Beckenbauer and Johan Cruyff were perceived as emblematic players, but they were also considered exceptional because they possessed the ability to intensify the performance of their team-mates. In other words, their influence upon the teams they played for surpassed their own ability. They were the main component in a complex and well-lubricated engine. Maradona, however, will always impregnate the teams for which he plays with his solitary and unique style. One of my informants used the metaphor of the aroma of the *potrero*:

> The teams which Diego the *pibe* played for were transformed by his aroma. His aroma was in a way the aroma of the *potrero* of Villa Fiorito. I mean, an aroma that you cannot resist and that will follow him all his life. I do not like it when people say that he has the *potrero* in his blood. Well, this is perhaps true but what I prefer to imagine is the *potrero* and its aroma.

Conclusion

My informants did not read Borocotó and some of them could hardly place him. They were not really astonished when I presented, in great detail, Borocotó's ideas on the role of *pibes* and *potreros* in the creation of a football mythology. They perceived themselves as part of a 'national narrative', as Carlos said, and they remembered articles in *El Gráfico*, in other magazines, in *Clarín*, the largest Argentinean newspaper, and discussions on television where the importance of belonging to a territory (the *potrero*) was crucial in the definition of a football style. We agreed that Maradona had transformed a myth into reality, and automatically reproduced it. This illustrates the power of mythical accounts. We concluded in agreement that new Maradonas would appear only in the worlds of *pibes* and *potreros*.

In a global scene where the production of local territories and identities is supposedly difficult to sustain because of the dispersed nature of globalism and nationhood, and where the life-worlds of local subjects tend to become deterritorialised, diasporic and transnational, Argentinean football supporters and sports writers tend in the opposite direction. The modes of belonging to the *potrero* and the *pibe* in no way contradict a simultaneous sense of belonging to the imaginary territory of a nation. The two become intrinsically connected on the playing fields of football. It should by now be clear that the *potrero* and the *pibe*, as represented through this game, pertain to a mythical account reproducing a tradition of belonging in past and present, and which mediates a transition from colonial to post-colonial experience and the rise of national identity. The post-colonial logic of the *pampa* and the *gaucho* emerges in new clothing and with renewed vigour in the contemporary arenas of football, *potrero*, and *pibe*.

Acknowledgements

* I thank Nadia Lovell for her instructive comments and critical suggestions. Kristi Anne Stølen also read the last draft and made helpful
observations.

Notes

1   See Borges (1993: 21–5), Martínez Estrada (1986: 40–69) and Giberti
    (1974).

2   During the post-colonial period in Argentina, initiated in 1810, the unity,
    expansion and consolidation of a powerful state was threatened by a long-
    lasting civil war which ended in 1853. The free *gauchos* were integrated into
    the different provincial armies as soldiers, a role they also played during the
    liberation war against the Spanish colonial power. The different Indian
    groups, occupying a vast part of the *pampa* area, remained outside of what
    was considered 'national population' and of course the embryo of the future
    Argentinean national state. They were the internal others, defined as wild
    and a threat to civilisation. Once the civil wars ended the expansion of the
    'civilised world' began. This epoch was defined as the 'expansion of the fron-
    tier' which meant the expulsion and extermination of the Indians from the
    fertile *pampa*.

3   Informants' accounts were collected during conventional fieldwork carried
    out amongst football supporters living in Buenos Aires. The choice of the
    capital city of Argentina was not accidental: Buenos Aires is also the capital
    city of football. Periodic exchanges on the meaning of football in
    Argentinean masculine culture have been conducted with these informants
    since 1984 (see Archetti 1994, 1995, 1996a, 1996b). These accounts consti-
    tute the 'hard core' of the oral memory component of my research. The
    majority of my informants belong to the well educated Argentinean middle
    class, but some are from the lower class, service workers and unskilled state
    employees.

4   Kanitkar argues that the imperial British created the image of the sporting
    boy (1994: 186). The games recommended were team sports which
    required qualities of leadership, working together and loyalty. To be part of a
    team was conceived of as being part of a perfect machine (1994: 187).

5   Borocotó became one of the most influential sports journalists in Argentina.
    Born in 1902 in Montevideo, Uruguay, he joined *El Gráfico* in 1927 and
    retired, as managing editor, in 1955. From 1927, he was active as a radio
    journalist. He was author of many best-sellers and was also successful in the
    film world. He wrote the script for one of the classics of Argentinean cinema,
    Pelota de Trapo (Rag Ball), made in 1948. The film describes with 'spon-
    taneity and lyricism the world of children and their passion for football'
    (Maranghello 1984: 102).

6   This is a clear example of the way in which *El Gráfico* deals with the 'British'
    and the 'English'. The 'British tradition' is generic but the players, albeit
    representatives of this tradition, have different nationalities. In this case, the
    international player in the photo is English.

7   Maradona has refused to be identified with a national tradition. His talent is
    an individual and 'divine gift'. He has often declared that he is touched by
    the magic of God and not by the power of his Argentinean football ancestors
    (see *Corriere della Sera*, 11 November 1985: 1). However, he usually accepts
    that he learned everything as a *pibe* in the Argentinean *potreros*. In his lecture
    at the Oxford Union Debating Chamber, 6 November 1995, he clearly
    stated that he is a *pibe*, a pure product of *potreros* (John King, personal
    communication). Maradona's account, at this level, is empirical and entirely
    related to his lived experience. My Argentinean informants move further,
    making the connection between individual cases and a football tradition.
    They take part in the production (and reproduction) of an ideological
    account.

References

Appadurai, A. (1995) 'The Production of Locality', in R. Fardon (ed.), *Counter-works: Managing the Diversity of Knowledge*, London: Routledge.

Archetti, E.P. (1994) 'Masculinity and Football: The Formation of National Identity in Argentina', in R. Giulianotti and J. Williams (eds), *Game without Frontiers: Football, Identity and Modernity*, Aldershot: Arena.

—— (1995) 'Estilos y Virtudes Masculinas en *El Gráfico*: La Creación del Imaginario del Fútbol Argentino', *Desarrollo Económico* 35: 419–42.

—— (1996a) 'Playing Styles and Masculine Virtues in Argentine Football', in M. Melhuus and K.A. Stølen (eds), *Machos, Madonnas, Mistresses: Contesting the Power of Gender Imagery in Latin America*, London: Verso.

—— (1996b) 'The Moralities of Argentinean Football', in S. Howell (ed.), *The Ethnography of Moralities*, London: Routledge.

Borges, J.L. (1993 [1926]) *El Tamaño de mi Esperanza*, Buenos Aires: Seix Barral.

Bourdieu, P. (1991) *Language and Symbolic Power*, Cambridge: Polity Press.

Casas, F. and Chacón, P. (1996) 'San Dieguito. La Novela de Maradona. La Película de Maradona', *Página 30* 5(69): 6–11.

Fontanarossa, A. and Sanz, A. (1994) *El pequeno diccionario ilustrado: el fútbol Argentino*, Buenos Aires: Clarin-Aguilar.

Giberti, H.C.E. (1974 [1954]) *Historia Económica de la Ganadería Argentina*, Buenos Aires: Solar/Hachette.

Gilbert, A. (1996) 'Cebolla de Fiorito. Maradona Jurásico', *Página 30* 5(69): 16–21.

Kanitkar, H. (1994) '"Real True Boys": Moulding the Cadets of Imperialism', in A. Cornwall and N. Lindisfarne (eds), *Dislocating Masculinities*, London: Routledge.

Maranghello, C. (1984) 'La Pantalla y el Estado', in *Historia del Cine Argentino*, Buenos Aires: Centro Editor de América Latina.

Martínez Estrada, E. (1986) *Radiografía de la Pampa*, Buenos Aires: Hyspamerica.

Morphy, H. (1995) 'Landscape and the Reproduction of the Ancestral Past', in
    E. Hirsch and M. O'Hanlon (eds), *The Anthropology of Landscape: Perspectives
    on Place and Space*, Oxford: Clarendon Press.
Norton, A. (1993) *Reflections on Political Identity*, Baltimore: The Johns
    Hopkins University Press.
Parkin, D. (1992) 'Ritual as Spatial Direction and Bodily Division', in D. de
    Coppet (ed.), *Understanding Rituals*, London: Routledge.
Schama, S. (1995) *Landscape and Memory*, London: Harper Collins.
Toren, C. (1995) 'Seeing the Ancestral Sites: Transformations in Fijian Notions
    of the Land', in E. Hirsch and M. O'Hanlon (eds), *The Anthropology of Land-
    scape: Perspectives on Place and Space*, Oxford: Clarendon Press.
Turner, V. (1969) *The Ritual Process*, Ithaca, NY: Cornell University Press.

Index